Getting Started with LLVM Core Libraries

Get to grips with LLVM essentials and use the core libraries to build advanced tools

Bruno Cardoso Lopes

Rafael Auler

[PACKT] open source ✲

PUBLISHING   community experience distilled

BIRMINGHAM - MUMBAI

Getting Started with LLVM Core Libraries

First published: August 2014

Production reference: 1200814

Published by Packt Publishing Ltd.
Livery Place
35 Livery Street
Birmingham B3 2PB, UK.

ISBN 978-1-78216-692-4

www.packtpub.com

Cover image by Aniket Sawant (aniket_sawant_photography@hotmail.com)

Credits

Authors

Bruno Cardoso Lopes

Rafael Auler

Reviewers

Eli Bendersky

Logan Chien

Jia Liu

John Szakmeister

Commissioning Editor

Mary Jasmine Nadar

Acquisition Editor

Kevin Colaco

Content Development Editor

Arun Nadar

Technical Editors

Pramod Kumavat

Pratik More

Copy Editors

Dipti Kapadia

Insiya Morbiwala

Aditya Nair

Alfida Paiva

Stuti Srivastava

Project Coordinator

Priyanka Goel

Proofreaders

Simran Bhogal

Mario Cecere

Jonathan Todd

Indexers

Hemangini Bari

Mariammal Chettiyar

Tejal Soni

Graphics

Ronak Dhruv

Abhinash Sahu

Production Coordinators

Saiprasad Kadam

Conidon Miranda

Cover Work

Manu Joseph

Saiprasad Kadam

About the Authors

Bruno Cardoso Lopes received a PhD in Computer Science from University of Campinas, Brazil. He's been an LLVM contributor since 2007 and implemented the MIPS backend from scratch, which he has been maintaining for several years. Among his other contributions, he has written the x86 AVX support and improved the ARM assembler. His research interests include code compression techniques and reduced bit width ISAs. In the past, he has also developed drivers for Linux and FreeBSD operating systems.

Rafael Auler is a PhD candidate at University of Campinas, Brazil. He holds a Master's degree in Computer Science and a Bachelor's degree in Computer Engineering from the same university. For his Master's work, he wrote a proof-of-concept tool that automatically generates LLVM backends based on architecture description files. Currently, his PhD research topics include dynamic binary translation, Just-in-Time compilers, and computer architecture. Rafael was also a recipient of the Microsoft Research 2013 Graduate Research Fellowship Award.

About the Reviewers

Eli Bendersky has been a professional programmer for 15 years, with extensive experience in systems programming, including compilers, linkers, and debuggers. He's been a core contributor to the LLVM project since early 2012.

Logan Chien received his Master's degree in Computer Science from National Taiwan University. His research interests include compiler design, compiler optimization, and virtual machines. He is a software developer and has been working on several open source projects, including LLVM, Android, and so on. He has written several patches to fix the ARM zero-cost exception handling mechanism and enhanced the LLVM ARM integrated assembler. He was also a Software Engineer Intern at Google in 2012. At Google, he integrated the LLVM toolchain with the Android NDK.

Jia Liu started GNU/Linux-related development in his college days and has been engaged in open-source-related development jobs after graduation. He is now responsible for all software-related work at China-DSP.

He is interested in compiler technology and has been working on it for years. In his spare time, he also works on a few open source projects such as LLVM, QEMU, and GCC/Binutils.

He is employed by a Chinese processor vendor, Glarun Technology — you can just call it China-DSP. China-DSP is a high-performance DSP vendor; the core business of the company is processor design, system software, and an embedded parallel processing platform that provides independent knowledge of electricity, telecommunications, automotive, manufacturing equipment, instrumentation, and consumer electronics.

> I want to thank my father and my mother; they raised me. Thanks to my girlfriend; in fact, I think she is my life's mentor. Thanks to my colleagues; we happily work with one another.

John Szakmeister holds a Master of Science in Electrical Engineering from Johns Hopkins University and is a co-founder of Intelesys Corporation (www.intelesyscorp.com). John has been writing software professionally for more than 15 years and enjoys working on compilers, operating systems, sophisticated algorithms, and anything embedded. He's an avid supporter of Open Source and contributes to many projects in his free time. When he is not hacking, John works toward his black belt in Ninjutsu and enjoys reading technical books.

> I would like to thank my wife, Ann, and our two boys, Matthew and Andrew, for being so patient and understanding while I was reviewing this book.

www.PacktPub.com

Support files, eBooks, discount offers, and more

You might want to visit www.PacktPub.com for support files and downloads related to your book.

Did you know that Packt offers eBook versions of every book published, with PDF and ePub files available? You can upgrade to the eBook version at www.PacktPub.com and as a print book customer, you are entitled to a discount on the eBook copy. Get in touch with us at service@packtpub.com for more details.

At www.PacktPub.com, you can also read a collection of free technical articles, sign up for a range of free newsletters, and receive exclusive discounts and offers on Packt books and eBooks.

http://PacktLib.PacktPub.com

Do you need instant solutions to your IT questions? PacktLib is Packt's online digital book library. Here, you can access, read, and search across Packt's entire library of books.

Why subscribe?

- Fully searchable across every book published by Packt
- Copy and paste, print, and bookmark content
- On demand and accessible via web browser

Free access for Packt account holders

If you have an account with Packt at www.PacktPub.com, you can use this to access PacktLib today and view nine entirely free books. Simply use your login credentials for immediate access.

Table of Contents

Preface

LLVM is an inspiring software project that started with the passion for compilers of a single person, Chris Lattner. The events that followed the first versions of LLVM and how it became widely adopted later reveal a pattern that may be observed across the history of other successful open source projects: they did not start within a company, but instead they are the product of simple human curiosity with respect to a given subject. For example, the first Linux kernel was the result of a Finnish student being intrigued by the area of operating systems and being motivated to understand and see in practice how a real operating system should work.

For Linux or LLVM, the contribution of many other programmers matured and leveraged the project to a first-class software that rivals, in quality, any other established competitor. It is unfair, therefore, to attribute the success of any big project to a single person. However, in the open source community, the leap from a student's project to an incredibly complex yet robust software depends on a key factor: attracting contributors and programmers who enjoy spending their time on the project.

Schools create a fascinating atmosphere because education involves the art of teaching people how things work. For these people, the feeling of unraveling how intricate mechanisms work and surpassing the state of being puzzled to finally mastering them is full of victory and overcoming. In this environment, at the University of Illinois at Urbana-Champaign (UIUC), the LLVM project grew by being used both as a research prototype and as a teaching framework for compiler classes lectured by Vikram Adve, Lattner's Master's advisor. Students contributed to the first bug reports, setting in motion the LLVM trajectory as a well-designed and easy-to-study piece of software.

The blatant disparity between software theory and practice befuddles many Computer Science students. A clean and simple concept in computing theory may involve so many levels of implementation details such that they disguise real-life software projects to become simply too complex for the human mind to grasp, especially all of its nuances. A clever design with powerful abstractions is the key to aid the human brain to navigate all the levels of a project: from the high-level view, which implements how the program works in a broader sense, to the lowest level of detail.

This is particularly true for compilers. Students who have a great passion to learn how compilers work often face a tough challenge when it comes to understanding the factual compiler implementation. Before LLVM, GCC was one of the few open source options for hackers and curious students to learn how a real compiler is implemented, despite the theory taught in schools.

However, a software project reflects, in its purest sense, the view of the programmers who created it. This happens through the abstractions employed to distinguish modules and data representation across several components. Programmers may have different views about the same topic. In this way, old and large software bases such as GCC, which is almost 30 years old, frequently embody a collection of different views of different generation of programmers, which makes the software increasingly difficult for newer programmers and curious observers to understand.

The LLVM project not only attracted experienced compiler programmers, but also a lot of young and curious minds that saw in it a much cleaner and simpler hackable piece of software, which represented a compiler with a lot of potential. This was clearly observed by the incredible number of scientific papers that chose LLVM as a prototype to do research. The reason is simple; in academia, students are frequently in charge of the practical aspects of the implementation, and thus, it is of paramount importance for research projects that the student be able to master its experimental framework code base. Seduced by its newer design using the C++ language (instead of C used in GCC), modularity (instead of the monolithic structure of GCC), and concepts that map more easily to the theory being taught in modern compiler courses, many researchers found it easy to hack LLVM in order to implement their ideas, and they were successful. The success of LLVM in academia, therefore, was a consequence of this reduced gap between theory and practice.

Beyond an experimental framework for scientific research, the LLVM project also attracted industry interest due to its considerably more liberal license in comparison with the GPL license of GCC. As a project that grew in academia, a big frustration for researchers who write code is the fear that it will only be used for a single experiment and be immediately discarded afterwards. To fight this fate, Chris Lattner, in his Master's project at UIUC that gave birth to LLVM, decided to license the project under the University of Illinois/NCSA Open Source License, allowing its use, commercial or not, as long as the copyright notice is maintained. The goal was to maximize LLVM adoption, and this goal was fulfilled with honor. In 2012, LLVM was awarded the ACM Software System Award, a highly distinguished recognition of notable software that contributed to science.

Many companies embraced the LLVM project with different necessities and performed different contributions, widening the range of languages that an LLVM-based compiler can operate with as well as the range of machines for which the compiler is able to generate code. This new phase of the project provided an unprecedented level of maturity to the library and tools, allowing it to permanently leave the state of experimental academia software to enter the status of a robust framework used in commercial products. With this, the name of the project also changed from Low Level Virtual Machine to the acronym LLVM.

The decision to retire the name Low Level Virtual Machine in favor of just LLVM reflects the change of goals of the project across its history. As a Master's project, LLVM was created as a framework to study lifelong program optimizations. These ideas were initially published in a 2003 MICRO (International Symposium on Microarchitecture) paper entitled *LLVA: A Low-level Virtual Instruction Set Architecture*, describing its instruction set, and in a 2004 CGO (International Symposium on Code Generation and Optimization) paper entitled *LLVM: A Compilation Framework for Lifelong Program Analysis & Transformation*.

Outside of an academic context, LLVM became a well-designed compiler with the interesting property of writing its intermediate representation to disk. In commercial systems, it was never truly used as a virtual machine such as the Java Virtual Machine (JVM), and thus, it made little sense to continue with the Low Level Virtual Machine name. On the other hand, some other curious names remained as a legacy. The file on the disk that stores a program in the LLVM intermediate representation is referred to as the LLVM bitcode, a parody of the Java bytecode, as a reference to the amount of space necessary to represent programs in the LLVM intermediate representation versus the Java one.

Our goal in writing this book is twofold. First, since the LLVM project grew a lot, we want to present it to you in small pieces, a component at a time, making it as simple as possible to understand while providing you with the joy of working with a powerful compiler library. Second, we want to evoke the spirit of an open source hacker, inspiring you to go far beyond the concepts presented here and never stop expanding your knowledge.

Happy hacking!

What this book covers

Chapter 1, Build and Install LLVM, will show you how to install the Clang/LLVM package on Linux, Windows, or Mac, including a discussion about building LLVM on Visual Studio and Xcode. It will also discuss the different flavors of LLVM distributions and discuss which distribution is best for you: pre-built binaries, distribution packages, or source codes.

Chapter 2, External Projects, will present external LLVM projects that live in separate packages or repositories, such as extra Clang tools, the DragonEgg GCC plugin, the LLVM debugger (LLDB), and the LLVM test suite.

Chapter 3, Tools and Design, will explain how the LLVM project is organized in different tools, working out an example on how to use them to go from source code to assembly language. It will also present how the compiler driver works, and finally, how to write your very first LLVM tool.

Chapter 4, The Frontend, will present the LLVM compiler frontend, the Clang project. It will walk you through all the steps of the frontend while explaining how to write small programs that use each part of the frontend as it is presented. It finishes by explaining how to write a small compiler driver with Clang libraries.

Chapter 5, The LLVM Intermediate Representation, will explain a crucial part of the LLVM design: its intermediate representation. It will show you what characteristics make it special, present its syntax, structure, and how to write a tool that generates the LLVM IR.

Chapter 6, The Backend, will introduce you to the LLVM compiler backend, responsible for translating the LLVM IR to machine code. This chapter will walk you through all the backend steps and provide you with the knowledge to create your own LLVM backend. It finishes by showing you how to create a backend pass.

Chapter 7, The Just-in-Time Compiler, will explain the LLVM Just-in-Time compilation infrastructure, which allows you to generate and execute machine code on demand. This technology is essential in applications where the program source code is only known at runtime, such as JavaScript interpreters in Internet browsers. This chapter walks you through the steps to use the right libraries in order to create your own JIT compiler.

Chapter 8, Cross-platform Compilation, will guide you through the steps for Clang/LLVM to create programs for other platforms such as ARM-based ones. This involves configuring the right environment to correctly compile programs that will run outside the environment where they were compiled.

Chapter 9, The Clang Static Analyzer, will present a powerful tool for discovering bugs in large source code bases without even running the program, but simply by analyzing the code. This chapter will also show you how to extend the Clang Static Analyzer with your own bug checkers.

Chapter 10, Clang Tools with LibTooling, will present the LibTooling framework and a series of Clang tools that are built upon this library, which allow you to perform source code refactoring or simply analyze the source code in an easy way. This chapter finishes by showing you how to write your own C++ source code refactoring tool by using this library.

At the time of this writing, LLVM 3.5 had not been released. While this book focuses on LLVM Version 3.4, we plan to release an appendix updating the examples in this book to LLVM 3.5 by the third week of September 2014, allowing you to exercise the content of the book with the newest versions of LLVM. This appendix will be available at `https://www.packtpub.com/sites/default/files/downloads/6924OS_Appendix.pdf`.

What you need for this book

To begin exploring the world of LLVM, you can use a UNIX system, a Mac OS X system, or a Windows system, as long as they are equipped with a modern C++ compiler. The LLVM source code is very demanding on the C++ compiler used to compile it and uses the newest standards. This means that on Linux, you will need at least GCC 4.8.1; on Max OS X, you will need at least Xcode 5.1; and on Windows, you will need Visual Studio 2012.

Even though we explain how to build LLVM on Windows with Visual Studio, this book does not focus on this platform because some LLVM features are unavailable for it. For example, LLVM lacks loadable module support on Windows, but we show you how to write LLVM plugins that are built as shared libraries. In these cases, the only way to see this in practice is to use either Linux or Mac OS X.

If you do not want to build LLVM for yourself, you can use a prebuilt binary bundle. However, you will be restricted to use the platforms where this convenience is available.

Who this book is for

This book is intended for enthusiasts, computer science students, and compiler engineers interested in learning about the LLVM framework. You need a background in C++ and, although not mandatory, should know at least some compiler theory. Whether you are a newcomer or a compiler expert, this book provides a practical introduction to LLVM and avoids complex scenarios. If you are interested enough and excited about this technology, then this book is definitely for you.

Conventions

In this book, you will find a number of styles of text that distinguish between different kinds of information. Here are some examples of these styles, and an explanation of their meaning.

Code words in text, database table names, folder names, filenames, file extensions, pathnames, dummy URLs, user input, and Twitter handles are shown as follows: "The prebuilt package for Windows comes with an easy-to-use installer that unpacks the LLVM tree structure in a subfolder of your Program Files folder."

A block of code is set as follows:

```
#include <stdio.h>
#include <stdint.h>
#include <stdlib.h>

int main() {
    uint64_t a = 0ULL, b = 0ULL;
    scanf ("%lld %lld", &a, &b);
    printf ("64-bit division is %lld\n", a / b);
    return EXIT_SUCCESS;
}
```

When we wish to draw your attention to a particular part of a code block, the relevant lines or items are set in bold:

```
KEYWORD(float          , KEYALL)
KEYWORD(goto           , KEYALL)
KEYWORD(inline         , KEYC99|KEYCXX|KEYGNU)
```

```
KEYWORD(int          , KEYALL)
KEYWORD(return       , KEYALL)
KEYWORD(short        , KEYALL)
KEYWORD(while        , KEYALL)
```

Any command-line input or output is written as follows:

```
$ sudo mv clang+llvm-3.4-x86_64-linux-gnu-ubuntu-13.10 llvm-3.4
$ export PATH="$PATH:/usr/local/llvm-3.4/bin"
```

New terms and **important words** are shown in bold. Words that you see on the screen, in menus or dialog boxes for example, appear in the text like this: "During installation, make sure to check the **Add CMake to the system PATH for all users** option."

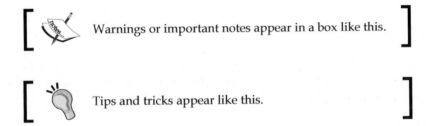

Warnings or important notes appear in a box like this.

Tips and tricks appear like this.

Reader feedback

Feedback from our readers is always welcome. Let us know what you think about this book—what you liked or may have disliked. Reader feedback is important for us to develop titles that you really get the most out of.

To send us general feedback, simply send an e-mail to feedback@packtpub.com, and mention the book title via the subject of your message.

If there is a topic that you have expertise in and you are interested in either writing or contributing to a book, see our author guide on www.packtpub.com/authors.

Customer support

Now that you are the proud owner of a Packt book, we have a number of things to help you to get the most from your purchase.

Downloading the example code

You can download the example code files for all Packt books you have purchased from your account at http://www.packtpub.com. If you purchased this book elsewhere, you can visit http://www.packtpub.com/support and register to have the files e-mailed directly to you.

Errata

Although we have taken every care to ensure the accuracy of our content, mistakes do happen. If you find a mistake in one of our books—maybe a mistake in the text or the code—we would be grateful if you would report this to us. By doing so, you can save other readers from frustration and help us improve subsequent versions of this book. If you find any errata, please report them by visiting http://www.packtpub.com/submit-errata, selecting your book, clicking on the **errata submission form** link, and entering the details of your errata. Once your errata are verified, your submission will be accepted and the errata will be uploaded on our website, or added to any list of existing errata, under the Errata section of that title. Any existing errata can be viewed by selecting your title from http://www.packtpub.com/support.

Piracy

Piracy of copyright material on the Internet is an ongoing problem across all media. At Packt, we take the protection of our copyright and licenses very seriously. If you come across any illegal copies of our works, in any form, on the Internet, please provide us with the location address or website name immediately so that we can pursue a remedy.

Please contact us at copyright@packtpub.com with a link to the suspected pirated material.

We appreciate your help in protecting our authors, and our ability to bring you valuable content.

Questions

You can contact us at questions@packtpub.com if you are having a problem with any aspect of the book, and we will do our best to address it.

1
Build and Install LLVM

The LLVM infrastructure is available for several **Unix** environments (GNU/**Linux**, **FreeBSD, Mac OS X**) and **Windows**. In this chapter, we describe the necessary steps to get LLVM working in all these systems, step by step. LLVM and Clang prebuilt packages are available in some systems but they can be compiled from the source otherwise.

A beginner LLVM user must consider the fact that the basic setup for a LLVM-based compiler includes both LLVM and Clang libraries and tools. Therefore, all the instructions in this chapter are aimed at building and installing both. Throughout this book, we will focus on LLVM Version 3.4. It is important to note, however, that LLVM is a young project and under active development; therefore, it is subject to change.

 At the time of this writing, LLVM 3.5 had not been released. While this book focuses on LLVM Version 3.4, we plan to release an appendix updating the examples in this book to LLVM 3.5 by the third week of September 2014, allowing you to exercise the content of the book with the newest versions of LLVM. This appendix will be available at https://www.packtpub.com/sites/default/files/downloads/6924OS_Appendix.pdf.

This chapter will cover the following topics:

- Understanding LLVM versions
- Installing LLVM with prebuilt binaries
- Installing LLVM using package managers
- Building LLVM from source for Linux
- Building LLVM from source for Windows and Visual Studio
- Building LLVM from source for Mac OS X and Xcode

Understanding LLVM versions

The LLVM project is updated at a fast pace, thanks to the contribution of many programmers. By Version 3.4, its SVN (subversion, the version control system employed) repository tallied over 200,000 commits, while its first release happened over 10 years ago. In 2013 alone, the project had almost 30,000 new commits. As a consequence, new features are constantly being introduced and other features are rapidly getting outdated. As in any big project, the developers need to obey a tight schedule to release stable checkpoints when the project is working well and passes a variety of tests, allowing users to experience the newest features with the comfort of using a well-tested version.

Throughout its history, the LLVM project has employed the strategy of releasing two stable versions per year. Each one of them incremented the minor revision number by 1. For example, an update from version 3.3 to version 3.4 is a minor version update. Once the minor number reaches 9, the next version will then increment the major revision number by 1, as when LLVM 3.0 succeeded LLVM 2.9. Major revision number updates are not necessarily a big change in comparison with its predecessor version, but they represent roughly five years of progress in the development of the compiler if compared with the latest major revision number update.

It is common practice for projects that depend on LLVM to use the *trunk* version, that is, the most updated version of the project available in the SVN repository, at the cost of using a version that is possibly unstable. Recently, beginning with version 3.4, the LLVM community started an effort to produce *point releases*, introducing a new revision number. The first product of this effort was LLVM 3.4.1. The goal of point releases is to *backport* bug fixes from trunk to the latest tagged version with no new features, thus maintaining full compatibility. The point releases should happen after three months of the last release. Since this new system is still in its infancy, we will focus on installing LLVM 3.4 in this chapter. The number of prebuilt packages for LLVM 3.4 is larger, but you should be able to build LLVM 3.4.1, or any other version, with no problems by following our instructions.

Obtaining prebuilt packages

To ease the task of installing the software on your system, LLVM contributors prepare prebuilt packages with the compiled binaries for a specific platform, as opposed to the requirement that you compile the package yourself. Compiling any piece of software can be tricky in some circumstances; it might require some time and should only be necessary if you are using a different platform or actively working on project development. Therefore, if you want a quick way to start with LLVM, explore the available prebuilt packages. In this book, however, we will encourage you to directly hack in to the LLVM source tree. You should be prepared to be able to compile LLVM from source trees yourself.

There are two general ways to obtain prebuilt packages for LLVM; you can obtain packages via distributed binaries in the official website or by third-party GNU/Linux distributions and Windows installers.

Obtaining the official prebuilt binaries

For version 3.4, the following prebuilt packages can be downloaded from the official LLVM website:

Architecture	Version
x86_64	Ubuntu (12.04, 13.10), Fedora 19, Fedora 20, FreeBSD 9.2, Mac OS X 10.9, Windows, and openSUSE 13.1
i386	openSUSE 13.1, FreeBSD 9.2, Fedora 19, Fedora 20, and openSUSE 13.1
ARMv7/ ARMv7a	Linux-generic

To view all the options for a different version, access `http://www.llvm.org/releases/download.html` and check the **Pre-built Binaries** section relative to the version you want to download. For instance, to download and perform a system-wide installation of LLVM on Ubuntu 13.10, we obtain the file's URL at the site and use the following commands:

```
$ sudo mkdir -p /usr/local; cd /usr/local
$ sudo wget http://llvm.org/releases/3.4/clang+llvm-3.4-x86_64-linux-gnu-ubuntu-13.10.tar.xz
$ sudo tar xvf clang+llvm-3.4-x86_64-linux-gnu-ubuntu-13.10.tar.xz
$ sudo mv clang+llvm-3.4-x86_64-linux-gnu-ubuntu-13.10 llvm-3.4
$ export PATH="$PATH:/usr/local/llvm-3.4/bin"
```

LLVM and Clang are now ready to be used. Remember that you need to permanently update your system's PATH environment variable, since the update we did in the last line is only valid for the current shell session. You can test the installation by executing Clang with a simple command, which prints the Clang version you just installed:

```
$ clang -v
```

If you have a problem when running Clang, try to run the binary directly from where it was installed to make sure that you are not running into a misconfigured PATH variable issue. If it still doesn't work, you might have downloaded a prebuilt binary for an incompatible system. Remember that, when compiled, the binaries link against dynamic libraries with specific versions. A link error while running the application is a clear symptom of the use of a binary compiled to a system that is incompatible with yours.

> In Linux, for example, a link error can be reported by printing the name of the binary and the name of the dynamic library that failed to load, followed by an error message. Pay attention when the name of a dynamic library is printed on the screen. It is a clear sign that the system *dynamic linker and loader* failed to load this library because this program was not built for a compatible system.

To install prebuilt packages in other systems, the same steps can be followed, except for Windows. The prebuilt package for Windows comes with an easy-to-use installer that unpacks the LLVM tree structure in a subfolder of your Program Files folder. The installer also comes with the option to automatically update your PATH environment variable to be able to use Clang executables from within any command prompt window.

Using package managers

Package manager applications are available for a variety of systems and are also an easy way to obtain and install LLVM/Clang binaries. For most users, this is usually the recommended way to install LLVM and Clang, since it automatically handles dependency issues and ensures that your system is compatible with the installed binaries.

For example, in Ubuntu (10.04 and later), you should use the following command:

```
$ sudo apt-get install llvm clang
```

In Fedora 18, the command line used is similar but the package manager is different:

```
$ sudo yum install llvm clang
```

Staying updated with snapshot packages

Packages can also be built from nightly source code snapshots, containing the latest commits from the LLVM subversion repository. The snapshots are useful to LLVM developers and users who wish to test the early versions or to third-party users who are interested in keeping their local projects up-to-date with mainline development.

Linux

Debian and Ubuntu Linux (i386 and amd64) repositories are available for you to download the daily compiled snapshots from the LLVM subversion repositories. You can check for more details at http://llvm.org/apt.

For example, to install the daily releases of LLVM and Clang on Ubuntu 13.10, use the following sequence of commands:

```
$ sudo echo "deb http://llvm.org/apt/raring/ llvm-toolchain-raring main"
>> /etc/apt/sources.list
$ wget -O - http://llvm.org/apt/llvm-snapshot.gpg.key | sudo apt-key add -
$ sudo apt-get update
$ sudo apt-get install clang-3.5 llvm-3.5
```

Windows

Windows installers of specific LLVM/Clang snapshots are available for download at http://llvm.org/builds/ in the **Windows snapshot builds** section. The final LLVM/Clang tools are installed by default in C:\Program Files\LLVM\bin (this location may change depending on the release). Note that there is a separate Clang driver that mimics Visual C++ cl.exe named clang-cl.exe. If you intend to use the classic GCC compatible driver, use clang.exe.

 Note that snapshots are not stable releases and might be highly experimental.

Building from sources

In the absence of prebuilt binaries, LLVM and Clang can be built from scratch by obtaining the source code first. Building the project from the source is a good way to start understanding more about the LLVM structure. Additionally, you will be able to fine-tune the configuration parameters to obtain a customized compiler.

System requirements

An updated list of the LLVM-supported platforms can be found at http://llvm.org/docs/GettingStarted.html#hardware. Also, a comprehensive and updated set of software prerequisites to compile LLVM is described at http://llvm.org/docs/GettingStarted.html#software. In Ubuntu systems, for example, the software dependencies can be resolved with the following command:

```
$ sudo apt-get install build-essential zlib1g-dev python
```

If you are using an old version of a Linux distribution with outdated packages, make an effort to update your system. LLVM sources are very demanding on the C++ compiler that is used to build them, and relying on an old C++ compiler is likely to result in a failed build attempt.

Obtaining sources

The LLVM source code is distributed under a BSD-style license and can be downloaded from the official website or through SVN repositories. To download the sources from the 3.4 release, you can either go to the website, `http://llvm.org/ releases/download.html#3.4`, or directly download and prepare the sources for compilation as follows. Note that you will always need Clang and LLVM, but the clang-tools-extra bundle is optional. However, if you intend to exercise the tutorial in *Chapter 10, Clang Tools with LibTooling*, you will need it. Refer to the next chapter for information on building additional projects. Use the following commands to download and install LLVM, Clang, and Clang extra tools:

```
$ wget http://llvm.org/releases/3.4/llvm-3.4.src.tar.gz
$ wget http://llvm.org/releases/3.4/clang-3.4.src.tar.gz
$ wget http://llvm.org/releases/3.4/clang-tools-extra-3.4.src.tar.gz
$ tar xzf llvm-3.4.src.tar.gz; tar xzf clang-3.4.src.tar.gz
$ tar xzf clang-tools-extra-3.4.src.tar.gz
$ mv llvm-3.4 llvm
$ mv clang-3.4 llvm/tools/clang
$ mv clang-tools-extra-3.4 llvm/tools/clang/tools/extra
```

Downloaded sources in Windows can be unpacked using gunzip, WinZip, or any other available decompressing tool.

SVN

To obtain the sources directly from the SVN repositories, make sure you have the subversion package available on your system. The next step is to decide whether you want the latest version stored in the repository or whether you want a stable version. In the case of the latest version (in *trunk*), you can use the following sequence of commands, assuming that you are already in the folder where you want to put the sources:

```
$ svn co http://llvm.org/svn/llvm-project/llvm/trunk llvm
$ cd llvm/tools
```

```
$ svn co http://llvm.org/svn/llvm-project/cfe/trunk clang
$ cd ../projects
$ svn co http://llvm.org/svn/llvm-project/compiler-rt/trunk compiler-rt
$ cd ../tools/clang/tools
$ svn co http://llvm.org/svn/llvm-project/clang-tools-extra/trunk extra
```

If you want to use a stable version (for example, version 3.4), substitute `trunk` for `tags/RELEASE_34/final` in all the commands. You may also be interested in an easy way to navigate the LLVM SVN repository to see the commit history, logs, and source tree structure. For this, you can go to `http://llvm.org/viewvc`.

Git

You can also obtain sources from the Git mirror repositories that sync with the SVN ones:

```
$ git clone http://llvm.org/git/llvm.git
$ cd llvm/tools
$ git clone http://llvm.org/git/clang.git
$ cd ../projects
$ git clone http://llvm.org/git/compiler-rt.git
$ cd ../tools/clang/tools
$ git clone http://llvm.org/git/clang-tools-extra.git
```

Building and installing LLVM

The various approaches to build and install LLVM are explained here.

Using the autotools-generated configure script

A standard way to build LLVM is to generate the platform-specific Makefiles by means of the `configure` script that was created with the GNU autotools. This build system is quite popular, and you are probably familiar with it. It supports several different configuration options.

> You need to install GNU autotools on your machine only if you intend to change the LLVM build system, in which case, you will generate a new `configure` script. Usually, it is unnecessary to do so.

Take out some time to look at the possible options using the following commands:

```
$ cd llvm
$ ./configure --help
```

A few of them deserve a brief explanation:

- `--enable-optimized`: This option allows us to compile LLVM/Clang without debug support and with optimizations. By default, this option is turned off. Debug support, as well as the disabling of optimizations, is recommended if you are using LLVM libraries for development, but it should be discarded for deployment since the lack of optimizations introduces a significant slowdown in LLVM.

- `--enable-assertions`: This option enables assertions in the code. This option is very useful when developing LLVM core libraries. It is turned on by default.

- `--enable-shared`: This option allows us to build LLVM/Clang libraries as shared libraries and link the LLVM tools against them. If you plan to develop a tool outside the LLVM build system and wish to dynamically link against the LLVM libraries, you should turn it on. This option is turned off by default.

- `--enable-jit`: This option enables **Just-In-Time Compilation** for all the targets that support it. It is turned on by default.

- `--prefix`: This is the path to the installation directory where the final LLVM/Clang tools and libraries will be installed; for example, `--prefix=/usr/local/llvm` will install binaries under `/usr/local/llvm/bin` and libraries under `/usr/local/llvm/lib`.

- `--enable-targets`: This option allows us to select the set of targets that the compiler must be able to emit code for. It is worth mentioning that LLVM is able to perform cross-compilation, that is, compile programs that will run on other platforms, such as ARM, MIPS, and so on. This option defines which backends to include in the code generation libraries. By default, all the targets are compiled, but you can save compilation time by specifying only the ones you are interested in.

 This option is not enough to generate a standalone cross-compiler. Refer to *Chapter 8, Cross-platform Compilation*, for the necessary steps to generate one.

After you run `configure` with the desired parameters, you need to complete the build with the classic `make` and `make install` duo. We will give you an example next.

Building and configuring with Unix

In this example, we will build an unoptimized (debug) LLVM/Clang with a sequence of commands that suit any Unix-based system or Cygwin. Instead of installing at /usr/local/llvm, as in the previous examples, we will build and install it in our home directory, explaining how to install LLVM without root privileges. This is customary when working as a developer. In this way, you can also maintain the multiple versions that have been installed. If you want, you can change the installation folder to /usr/local/llvm, making a system-wide installation. Just remember to use sudo when creating the installation directory and to run make install. The sequence of commands to be used is as follows:

```
$ mkdir where-you-want-to-install
$ mkdir where-you-want-to-build
$ cd where-you-want-to-build
```

In this section, we will create a separate directory to hold the object files, that is, the intermediary build byproducts. Do not build in the same folder that is used to keep the source files. Use the following commands with options explained in the previous section:

```
$ /PATH_TO_SOURCE/configure --disable-optimized --prefix=../where-you-want-to-install
$ make && make install
```

 You can optionally use make -jN to allow up to N compiler instances to work in parallel and speed up the build process. For example, you can experiment with make -j4 (or a slightly larger number) if your processor has four cores.

Allow some time for the compilation and installation of all components to finish. Note that the build scripts will also handle the other repositories that you downloaded and put in the LLVM source tree. There is no need to configure Clang or Clang extra tools separately.

To check whether the build succeeded, it is always useful to use the echo $? shell command. The $? shell variable returns the exit code of the last process that you ran in your shell session, while echo prints it to the screen. Thus, it is important to run this command immediately after your make commands. If the build succeeded, the make command will always return 0, as with any other program that has completed its execution successfully:

```
$ echo $?
0
```

Configure your shell's PATH environment variable to be able to easily access the recently installed binaries, and make your first test by asking for the Clang version:

```
$ export PATH="$PATH:where-you-want-to-install/bin"
$ clang -v
clang version 3.4
```

Using CMake and Ninja

LLVM offers an alternative cross-platform build system based on CMake, instead of the traditional configuration scripts. CMake can generate specialized Makefiles for your platform in the same way as the configuration scripts do, but CMake is more flexible and can also generate build files for other systems, such as Ninja, Xcode, and Visual Studio.

Ninja, on the other hand, is a small and fast build system that substitutes GNU Make and its associated Makefiles. If you are curious to read the motivation and the story behind Ninja, visit http://aosabook.org/en/posa/ninja.html. CMake can be configured to generate Ninja build files instead of Makefiles, giving you the option to use either CMake and GNU Make or CMake and Ninja.

Nevertheless, by using the latter, you can enjoy very quick turnaround times when making changes to the LLVM source code and recompiling it. This scenario is especially useful if you intend to develop a tool or a plugin inside the LLVM source tree and depend on the LLVM build system to compile your project.

Make sure that you have CMake and Ninja installed. For example, in Ubuntu systems, use the following command:

```
$ sudo apt-get install cmake ninja-build
```

LLVM with CMake also offers a number of build-customizing options. A full list of options is available at http://llvm.org/docs/CMake.html. The following is a list of options that correspond to the same set that we presented earlier for autotools-based systems. The default values for these flags are the same as those for the corresponding configure script flags:

- CMAKE_BUILD_TYPE: This is a string value that specifies whether the build will be Release or Debug. A Release build is equivalent to use the --enable-optimized flag in the configure script, while a Debug build is equivalent to the --disable-optimized flag.

- CMAKE_ENABLE_ASSERTIONS: This is a Boolean value that maps to the --enable-assertions configure flag.

- `BUILD_SHARED_LIBS`: This is a Boolean value that maps to the `-enable-shared` configure flag, establishing whether the libraries should be shared or static. Shared libraries are not supported on Windows platforms.
- `CMAKE_INSTALL_PREFIX`: This is a string value that maps to the `--prefix` configure flag, providing the installation path.
- `LLVM_TARGETS_TO_BUILD`: This is a semicolon-separated list of targets to build, roughly mapping to the comma-separated list of targets used in the `--enable-targets` configure flag.

To set any of these parameter-value pairs, supply the `-DPARAMETER=value` argument flag to the `cmake` command.

Building with Unix using CMake and Ninja

We will reproduce the same example that we presented earlier for the `configure` scripts, but this time, we will use CMake and Ninja to build it:

First, create a directory to contain the build and installation files:

```
$ mkdir where-you-want-to-build
$ mkdir where-you-want-to-install
$ cd where-you-want-to-build
```

Remember that you need to use a different folder than the one used to hold the LLVM source files. Next, it is time to launch CMake with the set of options that you chose:

```
$ cmake /PATHTOSOURCE -G Ninja -DCMAKE_BUILD_TYPE="Debug" -DCMAKE_
INSTALL_PREFIX="../where-you-want-to-install"
```

You should substitute /PATHTOSOURCE with the absolute location of your LLVM source folder. You can optionally omit the `-G Ninja` argument if you want to use traditional GNU Makefiles. Now, finish the build with either `ninja` or `make`, depending on which you chose. For `ninja`, use the following command:

```
$ ninja && ninja install
```

For `make`, use the following command:

```
$ make && make install
```

As we did earlier in the previous example, we can issue a simple command to check whether the build succeeded. Remember to use it immediately after the last build command, without running other commands in between, because it returns the exit value of the last program that you ran in the current shell session:

```
$ echo $?
0
```

If the preceding command returns zero, we are good to go. Finally, configure your PATH environment variable and use your new compiler:

```
$ export PATH=$PATH:where-you-want-to-install/bin
$ clang -v
```

Solving build errors

If the build commands return a nonzero value, it means that an error has occurred. In this case, either Make or Ninja will print the error to make it visible for you. Make sure to focus on the first error that appeared to find help. LLVM build errors in a stable release typically happen when your system does not meet the criteria for the required software versions. The most common issues come from using an outdated compiler. For example, building LLVM 3.4 with GNU g++ Version 4.4.3 will result in the following compilation error, after successfully compiling more than half of the LLVM source files:

```
[1385/2218] Building CXX object projects/compiler-rt/lib/interception/
CMakeFiles/RTInterception.i386.dir/interception_type_test.cc.o

FAILED: /usr/bin/c++ (...)_test.cc.o -c /local/llvm-3.3/llvm/projects/
compiler-rt/lib/interception/interception_type_test.cc

test.cc:28: error: reference to 'OFF64_T' is ambiguous

interception.h:31: error: candidates are: typedef __sanitizer::OFF64_T
OFF64_T

sanitizer_internal_defs.h:80: error:                    typedef __
sanitizer::u64 __sanitizer::OFF64_T
```

To solve this, you could hack the LLVM source code to work around this issue (and you will find how to do this if you either search online or look at the source yourself), but you will not want to patch every LLVM version that you want to compile. Updating your compiler is far simpler and is certainly the most appropriate solution.

In general, when running into build errors in a stable build, concentrate on what differences your system has in comparison with the recommended setup. Remember that the stable builds have been tested on several platforms. On the other hand, if you are trying to build an unstable SVN release, it is possible that a recent commit broke the build for your system, and it is easier to backtrack to an SVN release that works.

Using other Unix approaches

Some Unix systems provide package managers that automatically build and install applications from the source. They offer a source-compilation counterpart that was previously tested for your system and also try to solve package-dependency issues. We will now evaluate such platforms in the context of building and installing LLVM and Clang:

- For Mac OS X using *MacPorts*, we can use the following command:

  ```
  $ port install llvm-3.4 clang-3.4
  ```

- For Mac OS X using *Homebrew*, we can use the following:

  ```
  $ brew install llvm -with-clang
  ```

- For FreeBSD 9.1 using *ports*, we can use the following (note that starting from FreeBSD 10, Clang is the default compiler, and thus it is already installed):

  ```
  $ cd /usr/ports/devel/llvm34
  $ make install
  $ cd /usr/ports/lang/clang34
  $ make install
  ```

- For Gentoo Linux, we can use the following:

  ```
  $ emerge sys-devel/llvm-3.4 sys-devel/clang-3.4
  ```

Windows and Microsoft Visual Studio

To compile LLVM and Clang on Microsoft Windows, we use Microsoft Visual Studio 2012 and Windows 8. Perform the following steps:

1. Obtain a copy of Microsoft Visual Studio 2012.
2. Download and install the official binary distribution of the CMake tool available at http://www.cmake.org. During installation, make sure to check the **Add CMake to the system PATH for all users** option.

3. CMake will generate the project files needed by Visual Studio to configure and build LLVM. First, run the cmake-gui graphic tool. Then, click on the **Browse Source...** button and select the LLVM source code directory. Next, click on the **Browse Build** button and choose a directory to put the CMake-generated files, which will be used later by Visual Studio, as shown in the following screenshot:

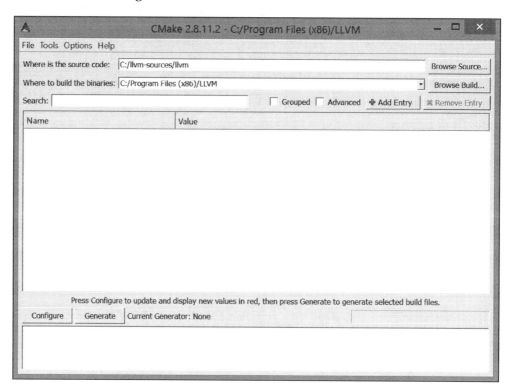

4. Click on **Add Entry** and define CMAKE_INSTALL_PREFIX to contain the installation path for the LLVM tools, as shown in the following screenshot:

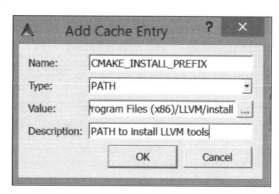

5. Additionally, the set of supported targets can be defined using LLVM_TARGETS_ TO_BUILD, as shown in the following screenshot. You can optionally add any other entry that defines the CMake parameters we previously discussed.

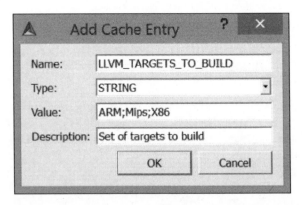

6. Click on the **Configure** button. A pop-up window asks for the *generator* of this project and for the compiler to be used; select **Use default native compilers** and for Visual Studio 2012, select the **Visual Studio 11** option. Click on **Finish**, as shown in the following screenshot:

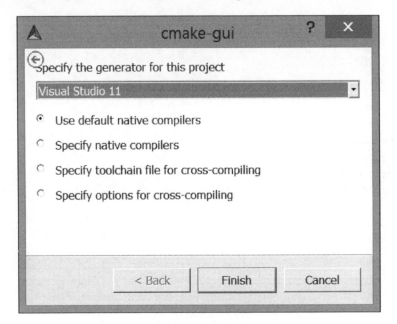

For Visual Studio 2013, use the generator for **Visual Studio 12**. The name of the generator uses the Visual Studio version instead of its commercial name.

7. After the configuration ends, click on the **Generate** button. The Visual Studio solution file, `LLVM.sln`, is then written in the specified build directory. Go to this directory and double-click on this file; it will open the LLVM solution in Visual Studio.

8. To automatically build and install LLVM/Clang, in the **tree view** window on the left, go to **CMakePredefinedTargets**, right-click on **INSTALL**, and select the **Build** option. The predefined **INSTALL** target instructs the system to build and install all the LLVM/Clang tools and libraries, as shown in the following screenshot:

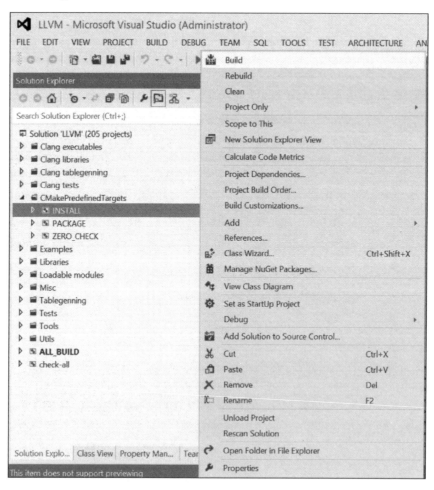

9. To selectively build and install specific tools or libraries, select the corresponding item in the tree list view window on the left-hand side, right-click on the item, and select the **Build** option.

10. Add the LLVM binaries install directory to the system's `PATH` environment variable.

In our example, the install directory is `C:\Program Files (x86)\LLVM\install\bin`. To directly test the installation without updating the PATH environment variable, issue the following command in a command prompt window:

```
C:>"C:\Program Files (x86)\LLVM\install\bin\clang.exe" -v
clang version 3.4…
```

Mac OS X and Xcode

Although LLVM can be compiled for Mac OS X by using regular Unix instructions described earlier, Xcode can also be used:

1. Obtain a copy of Xcode.

2. Download and install the official binary distribution of the CMake tool available at `http://www.cmake.org`. Make sure to check the **Add CMake to the system PATH for all users** option.

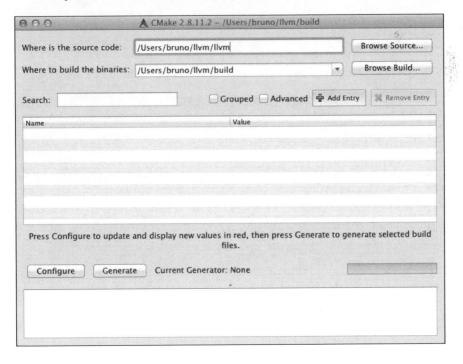

3. CMake is able to generate the project files used by Xcode. First, run the `cmake-gui` graphic tool. Then, as shown in the preceding screenshot, click on the **Browse Source** button and select the LLVM source code directory. Next, click on the **Browse Build** button and choose a directory to add the CMake-generated files, which will be used by Xcode.

4. Click on **Add Entry** and define `CMAKE_INSTALL_PREFIX` to contain the installation path for the LLVM tools.

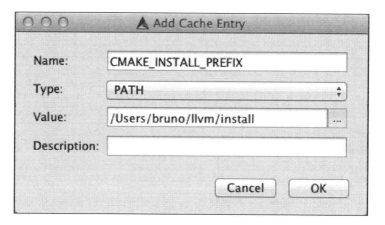

5. Additionally, the set of supported targets can be defined using `LLVM_TARGETS_TO_BUILD`. You can optionally add any other entries that define the CMake parameters we previously discussed.

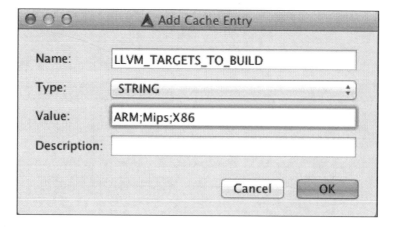

6. Xcode does not support the generation of LLVM **Position Independent Code** (**PIC**) libraries. Click on **Add Entry** and add the `LLVM_ENABLE_PIC` variable, which was the **BOOL** type, leaving the checkbox unmarked, as shown in the following screenshot:

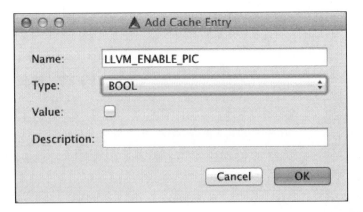

7. Click on the **Configure** button. A pop-up window asks for the generator for this project and the compiler to be used. Select **Use default native compilers** and **Xcode**. Click on the **Finish** button to conclude the process, as shown in the following screenshot:

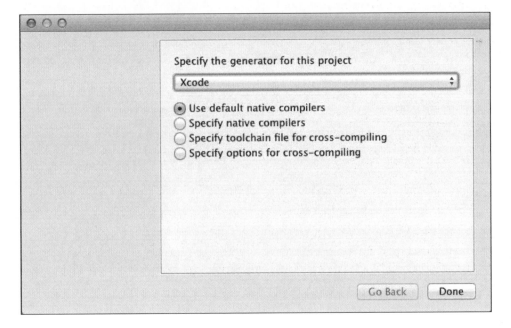

8. After the configuration ends, click on the **Generate** button. The `LLVM.xcodeproj` file is then written in the build directory that was specified earlier. Go to this directory and double-click on this file to open the LLVM project in Xcode.

9. To build and install LLVM/Clang, select the **install** scheme.

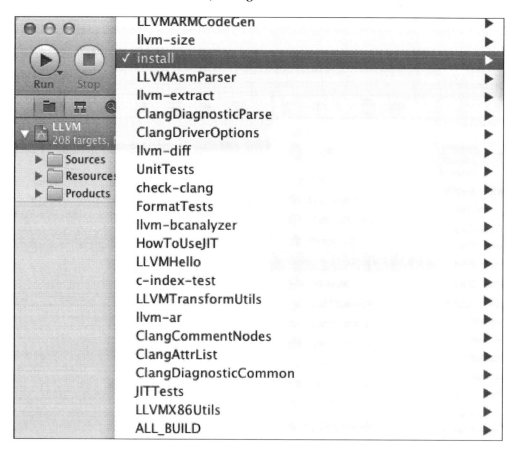

10. Next, click on the **Product** menu and then select the **Build** option, as shown in the following screenshot:

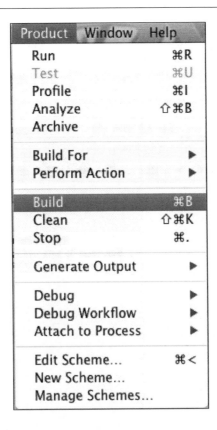

11. Add the LLVM binaries install directory to the system's PATH environment variable.

In our example, the folder with the installed binaries is /Users/Bruno/llvm/ install/bin. To test the installation, use the clang tool from the install directory as follows:

```
$ /Users/Bruno/llvm/install/bin/clang -v
clang version 3.4…
```

Summary

This chapter provided detailed instructions on how to install LLVM and Clang by showing you how to use prebuilt binaries via officially built packages, third-party package managers, and daily snapshots. Moreover, we detailed how to build the project from sources by using standard Unix tools and IDEs in different operating system environments.

In the next chapter, we will cover how to install other LLVM-based projects that may be very useful for you. These external projects typically implement tools that are developed outside the main LLVM SVN repository and are shipped separately.

2

External Projects

Projects that live outside the core LLVM and Clang repositories need to be separately downloaded. In this chapter, we introduce a variety of other official LLVM projects and explain how to build and install them. Readers only interested in core LLVM tools may skip this chapter or come back when required.

In this chapter, we will cover what are and how to install the following projects:

- Clang extra tools
- Compiler-RT
- DragonEgg
- LLVM test suite
- LLDB
- libc++

Beyond the projects covered in this chapter, there are two official LLVM projects outside the scope of this book: Polly, the polyhedral optimizer, and lld, the LLVM linker, which is currently in development.

Prebuilt binary packages do not include any of the external projects presented in this chapter, except for Compiler-RT. Therefore, unlike the previous chapter, we will only cover techniques that involve downloading the source code and build them ourselves.

Do not expect the same level of maturity as that of the core LLVM/Clang project from all of these projects. Some of them are experimental or in their infancy.

Introducing Clang extras

The most noticeable design decision of LLVM is its segregation between backend and frontend as two separate projects, LLVM core and Clang. LLVM started as a set of tools orbiting around the LLVM intermediate representation (IR) and depended on a hacked GCC to translate high-level language programs to its particular IR, stored in *bitcode* files. Bitcode is a term coined as a parody of Java *bytecode* files. An important milestone of the LLVM project happened when Clang appeared as the first frontend specifically designed by the LLVM team, bringing with it the same level of quality, clear documentation, and library organization as the core LLVM. It is not only able to convert C and C++ programs into LLVM IR but also to supervise the entire compilation process as a flexible compiler driver that strives to stay compatible with GCC.

We will henceforth refer to Clang as a frontend program rather than a driver, responsible for translating C and C++ programs to the LLVM IR. The exciting aspect of Clang libraries is the possibility to use them to write powerful tools, giving the C++ programmer freedom to work with hot topics of C++ such as C++ code refactoring tools and source-code analysis tools. Clang comes prepackaged with some tools that may give you an idea of what we can do with its libraries:

- **Clang Check**: It is able to perform syntax checks, apply quick fixes to solve common issues, and also dump the internal Clang Abstract Syntax Tree (AST) representation of any program
- **Clang Format**: It comprises both a tool and a library, `LibFormat`, that are able to not only indent code but also format any piece of C++ code to conform with LLVM coding standards, Google's style guide, Chromium's style guide, Mozilla's style guide, and WebKit's style guide

The `clang-tools-extra` repository is a collection of more applications that are built on top of Clang. They are able to read large C or C++ code bases and perform all sorts of code refactoring and analysis. We enumerate below some of the tools of this package, but it is not limited to them:

- **Clang Modernizer**: It is a code refactoring tool that scans C++ code and changes old-style constructs to conform with more modern styles proposed by newer standards, such as the C++-11 standard
- **Clang Tidy**: It is a *linter tool* that checks for common programming mistakes that violate either LLVM or Google coding standards
- **Modularize**: It helps you in identifying C++ header files that are suitable to compose a module, a new concept that is being currently discussed by C++ standardization committees (for more information, please refer to *Chapter 10, Clang Tools with LibTooling*)

- **PPTrace**: It is a simple tool that tracks the activity of the Clang C++ preprocessor

More information on how to use these tools and how to build your own tool is available in *Chapter 10, Clang Tools with LibTooling.*

Building and installing Clang extra tools

You can obtain an official snapshot of version 3.4 of this project at `http://llvm.org/releases/3.4/clang-tools-extra-3.4.src.tar.gz`. If you want to scan through all available versions, check `http://llvm.org/releases/download.html`. To compile this set of tools without difficulty, build it together with the source of the core LLVM and Clang, relying on the LLVM build system. To do this, you must put the source directory into the Clang source tree as follows:

```
$ wget http://llvm.org/releases/3.4/clang-tools-extra-3.4.src.tar.gz
$ tar xzf clang-tools-extra-3.4.src.tar.gz
$ mv clang-tools-extra-3.4 llvm/tools/clang/tools/extra
```

You may also obtain sources directly from the official LLVM subversion repository:

```
$ cd llvm/tools/clang/tools
$ svn co http://llvm.org/svn/llvm-project/clang-tools-extra/trunk extra
```

Recall from the previous chapter that you can replace `trunk` with `tags/RELEASE_34/final` if you want to obtain the stable sources for version 3.4. Alternatively, if you prefer using the GIT version control software, you can download it with the following command lines:

```
$ cd llvm/tools/clang/tools
$ git clone http://llvm.org/git/clang-tools-extra.git extra
```

After placing the sources into the Clang tree, you must proceed with the compilation instructions from *Chapter 1, Build and Install LLVM,* using either CMake or the autotools-generated `configure` script. To test for a successful install, run the `clang-modernize` tool as follows:

```
$ clang-modernize -version
clang-modernizer version 3.4
```

Understanding Compiler-RT

The Compiler-RT (runtime) project provides target-specific support for low-level functionality that is not supported by the hardware. For example, 32-bit targets usually lack instructions to support 64-bit division. Compiler-RT solves this problem by providing a target-specific and optimized function that implements 64-bit division while using 32-bit instructions. It provides the same functionalities and thus is the LLVM equivalent of `libgcc`. Moreover, it has runtime support for the address and memory sanitizer tools. You can download Compiler-RT Version 3.4 at `http://llvm. org/releases/3.4/compiler-rt-3.4.src.tar.gz` or look for more versions at `http://llvm.org/releases/download.html`.

Since it is a crucial component in a working LLVM-based compiler tool chain, we have already presented how to install Compiler-RT in the previous chapter. If you still do not have it, remember to put its sources into the `projects` folder inside the LLVM source tree, such as in the following command sequence:

```
$ wget http://llvm.org/releases/3.4/compiler-rt-3.4.src.tar.gz.

$ tar xzf compiler-rt-3.4.src.tar.gz

$ mv compiler-rt-3.4 llvm/projects/compiler-rt
```

If you prefer, you can rely instead on its SVN repository:

```
$ cd llvm/projects

$ svn checkout http://llvm.org/svn/llvm-project/compiler-rt/trunk
compiler-rt
```

You can also download it via a GIT mirror as an alternative to SVN:

```
$ cd llvm/projects

$ git clone http://llvm.org/git/compiler-rt.git
```

 Compiler-RT works, among others, in GNU/Linux, Darwin, FreeBSD, and NetBSD. The supported architectures are the following: i386, x86_64, PowerPC, SPARC64, and ARM.

Seeing Compiler-RT in action

To see a typical situation where the compiler runtime library kicks in, you can perform a simple experiment by writing a C program that performs 64-bit division:

```
#include <stdio.h>
#include <stdint.h>
#include <stdlib.h>
int main() {
```

```
    uint64_t a = 0ULL, b = 0ULL;
    scanf ("%lld %lld", &a, &b);
    printf ("64-bit division is %lld\n", a / b);
    return EXIT_SUCCESS;
}
```

> **Downloading the example code**
>
> You can download the example code files for all Packt books you
> have purchased from your account at http://www.packtpub.
> com. If you purchased this book elsewhere, you can visit http://
> www.packtpub.com/support and register to have the files
> e-mailed directly to you.

If you have a 64-bit x86 system, experiment with two commands by using your
LLVM compiler:

```
$ clang -S -m32 test.c -o test-32bit.S
$ clang -S test.c -o test-64bit.S
```

The -m32 flag instructs the compiler to generate a 32-bit x86 program, while the -S
flag produces the x86 assembly language file for this program in test-32bit.S.
If you look at this file, you will see a curious call whenever the program needs to
perform the division:

```
    call    __udivdi3
```

This function is defined by Compiler-RT and demonstrates where the library will be
used. However, if you omit the -m32 flag and use the 64-bit x86 compiler, as in the
second compiler command that generated the test-64bit.S assembly language file,
you will no longer see a program that requires the assistance of Compiler-RT because
it can easily perform this division with a single instruction:

```
    divq -24(%rbp)
```

Using the DragonEgg plugin

As explained earlier, LLVM started as a project that was dependent on GCC when it still lacked its own C/C++ frontend. In those instances, to use LLVM, you needed to download a hacked GCC source tree called `llvm-gcc` and compile it in its entirety. Since the compilation involved the full GCC package, it was a very time-consuming and tricky task, requiring knowledge of all the necessary GNU lore to rebuild GCC by yourself. The DragonEgg project appeared as a clever solution to leverage the GCC plugin system, separating the LLVM logic in its own and much smaller code tree. In this way, the users no longer needed to rebuild the entire GCC package, but just a plugin, and then load it into GCC. DragonEgg is also the sole project under the LLVM project umbrella that is licensed under GPL.

Even with the rise of Clang, DragonEgg persists today because Clang only handles the C and C++ languages, while GCC is able to parse a wider variety of languages. By using the DragonEgg plugin, you can use GCC as a frontend to the LLVM compiler, being able to compile most of the languages supported by GCC: Ada, C, C++, and FORTRAN, with partial support for Go, Java, Obj-C, and Obj-C++.

The plugin acts by substituting the middle- and backend of GCC with the LLVM ones and performs all the compilation steps automatically, as you would expect from a first-class compiler driver. The compilation pipeline for this new scenario is represented in the following illustration:

If you wish, you can use the `-fplugin-arg-dragonegg-emit-ir -S` set of flags to stop the compilation pipeline at the LLVM IR generation phase and use LLVM tools to analyze and investigate the result of the frontend, or use the LLVM tools to finish the compilation yourself. We will see an example shortly.

As it is an LLVM side project, maintainers do not update DragonEgg at the same pace as the LLVM main project. The most recent stable version of DragonEgg at the time of this writing was version 3.3, which is bound to the toolset of LLVM 3.3. Therefore, if you generate LLVM bitcodes, that is, programs written on disk by using the LLVM IR, you cannot use LLVM tools of a version other than 3.3 to analyze this file, optimize, or proceed with the compilation. You can find the official DragonEgg website at `http://dragonegg.llvm.org`.

Building DragonEgg

To compile and install DragonEgg, first get the source from `http://llvm.org/releases/3.3/dragonegg-3.3.src.tar.gz`. For Ubuntu, use the following commands:

```
$ wget http://llvm.org/releases/3.3/dragonegg-3.3.src.tar.gz.
$ tar xzvf dragonegg-3.3.src.tar.gz
$ cd dragonegg-3.3.src
```

If you wish to explore the current but unstable sources from SVN, use the following command:

```
$ svn checkout http://llvm.org/svn/llvm-project/dragonegg/trunk dragonegg
```

For the GIT mirror, use the following:

```
$ git clone http://llvm.org/git/dragonegg.git
```

To compile and install, you need to provide the LLVM installation path. The LLVM version must match the version of DragonEgg being installed. Assuming the same install prefix, /usr/local/llvm, from *Chapter 1*, *Build and Install LLVM*, and assuming GCC 4.6 is installed and present in your shell PATH variable, you should use the following commands:

```
$ GCC=gcc-4.6 LLVM_CONFIG=/usr/local/llvm/bin/llvm-config make
$ cp -a dragonegg.so /usr/local/llvm/lib
```

Note that the project lacks autotools or CMake project files. You should build directly by using the make command. If your gcc command already supplies the correct GCC version that you want to use, you can omit the GCC=gcc-4.6 prefix when running make. The plugin is the resulting shared library named dragonegg.so, and you can invoke it using the following GCC command line. Consider that you are compiling a classic "Hello, World!" C code.

```
$ gcc-4.6 -fplugin=/usr/local/llvm/lib/dragonegg.so hello.c -o hello
```

 Although DragonEgg theoretically supports GCC version 4.5 and higher, GCC 4.6 is highly recommended. DragonEgg is not extensively tested and maintained in other GCC versions.

Understanding the compilation pipeline with DragonEgg and LLVM tools

If you wish to see the frontend in action, use the `-S -fplugin-arg-dragonegg-emit-ir` flag, which will emit a human-readable file with the LLVM IR code:

```
$ gcc-4.6 -fplugin=/usr/local/llvm/lib/dragonegg.so -S -fplugin-arg-
dragonegg-emit-ir hello.c -o hello.ll
$ cat hello.ll
```

The ability to stop the compilation once the compiler translates the program to IR and serializing the in-memory representation to disk is a particular characteristic of LLVM. Most other compilers are unable to do this. After appreciating how LLVM IR represents your program, you can manually proceed with the compilation process by using several LLVM tools. The following command invokes a special assembler that converts LLVM in textual form to binary form, still stored on disk:

```
$ llvm-as hello.ll -o hello.bc
$ file hello.bc
hello.bc: LLVM bitcode
```

If you want, you can translate it back to human-readable form by using a special IR disassembler (`llvm-dis`). The following tool will apply target-independent optimizations while displaying to you statistics about successful code transformations:

```
$ opt -stats hello.bc -o hello.bc
```

The `-stats` flag is optional. Afterwards, you can use the LLVM backend tool to translate it to target-machine assembly language:

```
$ llc -stats hello.bc -o hello.S
```

Again, the `-stats` flag is optional. Since it is an assembly file, you can use either your GNU `binutils` assembler or the LLVM assembler. In the following command, we will use the LLVM assembler:

```
$ llvm-mc -filetype=obj hello.S -o hello.o
```

LLVM defaults to use your system linker because the LLVM linker project, `lld`, is currently in development and is not integrated into the core LLVM project. Therefore, if you do not have `lld`, you can finish the compilation by using your regular compiler driver, which will activate your system linker:

```
$ gcc hello.o -o hello
```

Keep in mind that, for performance reasons, the real LLVM compiler driver never serializes the program representation to disk in any stage, except for the object file, since it still lacks an integrated linker. It uses the in-memory representation and coordinates several LLVM components to carry on compilation.

Understanding the LLVM test suite

The LLVM test suite consists of an official set of programs and benchmarks used to test the LLVM compiler. The test suite is very useful to LLVM developers, which validates optimizations and compiler improvements by compiling and running such programs. If you are using an unstable release of LLVM, or if you hacked into LLVM sources and suspect that something is not working as it should, it is very useful to run the test suite by yourself. However, keep in mind that simpler LLVM regression and unit tests live in the LLVM main tree, and you can easily run them with make check-all. The test suite differs from the classic regression and unit tests because it contains entire benchmarks.

You must place the LLVM test suite in the LLVM source tree to allow the LLVM build system to recognize it. You can find the sources for version 3.4 at http://llvm.org/releases/3.4/test-suite-3.4.src.tar.gz.

To fetch the sources, use the following commands:

```
$ wget http://llvm.org/releases/3.4/test-suite-3.4.src.tar.gz
$ tar xzf test-suite-3.4.src.tar.gz
$ mv test-suite-3.4 llvm/projects/test-suite
```

If you otherwise prefer downloading it via SVN to get the most recent and possibly unstable version, use the following:

```
$ cd llvm/projects
$ svn checkout http://llvm.org/svn/llvm-project/test-suite/trunk test-suite
```

If you prefer GIT instead, use the following commands:

```
$ cd llvm/projects
$ git clone http://llvm.org/git/llvm-project/test-suite.git
```

You need to regenerate the build files of LLVM to use the test suite. In this special case, you cannot use CMake. You must stick with the classic configure script to work with the test suite. Repeat the configuration steps described in *Chapter 1, Build and Install LLVM*.

The test suite has a set of Makefiles that test and check benchmarks. You can also provide a custom Makefile that evaluates custom programs. Place the custom Makefile in the test suite's source directory using the naming template `llvm/projects/test-suite/TEST.<custom>.Makefile`, where the `<custom>` tag must be replaced by any name you want. Check `llvm/projects/test-suite/TEST.example.Makefile` for an example.

 You need to regenerate LLVM build files to allow for a custom or changed Makefile to work.

During configuration, a directory for the test suite is created in the LLVM object directory where programs and benchmarks will run. To run and test the example Makefile, enter the object directory path from *Chapter 1, Build and Install LLVM*, and execute the following command lines:

```
$ cd your-llvm-build-folder/projects/test-suite
$ make TEST="example" report
```

Using LLDB

The LLDB (Low Level Debugger) project is a debugger built with the LLVM infrastructure, being actively developed and shipped as the debugger of Xcode 5 on Mac OS X. Since its development began in 2011, outside the scope of Xcode, LLDB had not yet released a stable version until the time of this writing. You can obtain LLDB sources at `http://llvm.org/releases/3.4/lldb-3.4.src.tar.gz`. Like many projects that depend on LLVM, you can easily build it by integrating it in the LLVM build system. To accomplish this, just put its source code in the LLVM `tools` folder, as in the following example:

```
$ wget http://llvm.org/releases/3.4/lldb-3.4.src.tar.gz
$ tar xvf lldb-3.4.src.tar.gz
$ mv lldb-3.4 llvm/tools/lldb
```

You can alternatively use its SVN repository to get the latest revision:

```
$ cd llvm/tools
$ svn checkout http://llvm.org/svn/llvm-project/lldb/trunk lldb
```

If you prefer, you can use its GIT mirror instead:

```
$ cd llvm/tools
$ git clone http://llvm.org/git/llvm-project/lldb.git
```

[LLDB is still experimental for GNU/Linux systems.]

Before building it, note that LLDB has some software prerequisites: Swig, libedit (only for Linux), and Python. On Ubuntu systems, for example, you can solve these dependencies with the following command:

```
$ sudo apt-get install swig libedit-dev python
```

Remember that, as with other projects presented in this chapter, you need to regenerate LLVM build files to allow for LLDB compilation. Follow the same steps for building LLVM from source that we saw in *Chapter 1, Build and Install LLVM*.

To perform a simple test on your recent `lldb` installation, just run it with the `-v` flag to print its version:

```
$ lldb -v
lldb version 3.4 ( revision )
```

Exercising a debug session with LLDB

To see how it looks to use LLDB, we will start a debug session to analyze the Clang binary. The Clang binary contains many C++ symbols you can inspect. If you compiled the LLVM/Clang project with the default options, you have a Clang binary with debug symbols. This happens when you omit the `--enable-optimized` flag when running the `configure` script to generate LLVM Makefiles, or use `-DCMAKE_BUILD_TYPE="Debug"` when running CMake, which is the default build type.

If you are familiar with GDB, you may be interested in referring to the table at `http://lldb.llvm.org/lldb-gdb.html`, which maps common GDB commands to the LLDB counterpart.

In the same way as GDB, we start LLDB by passing as a command-line argument the path to the executable we want to debug:

```
$ lldb where-your-llvm-is-installed/bin/clang
Current executable set to 'where-your-llvm-is-installed/bin/clang'
(x86_64).
(lldb) break main
Breakpoint 1: where = clang`main + 48 at driver.cpp:293, address =
0x000000001000109e0
```

To start debugging, we provide the command-line arguments to the Clang binary. We will use the -v argument, which should print the Clang version:

```
(lldb) run -v
```

After LLDB hits our breakpoint, feel free to step through each C++ line of code with the next command. As with GDB, LLDB accepts any command abbreviation, such as n instead of next, as long as it stays unambiguous:

```
(lldb) n
```

To see how LLDB prints C++ objects, step until you reach the line after declaring the argv or the ArgAllocator object and print it:

```
(lldb) n
(lldb) p ArgAllocator
(llvm::SpecificBumpPtrAllocator<char>) $0 = {
 Allocator = {
   SlabSize = 4096
   SizeThreshld = 4096
   DefaultSlabAllocator = (Allocator = llvm::MallocAllocator @
0x00007f85f1497f68)
   Allocator = 0x0000007fffbff200
   CurSlab = 0x0000000000000000
    CurPtr = 0x0000000000000000
   End = 0x0000000000000000
   BytesAllocated = 0
 }
}
```

After you are satisfied, quit the debugger with the q command:

```
(lldb) q
Quitting LLDB will kill one or more processes. Do you really want to
proceed: [Y/n] y
```

Introducing the libc++ standard library

The libc++ library is a C++ standard library rewrite for the LLVM project umbrella that supports the most recent C++ standards, including C++11 and C++1y, and that is dual-licensed under the MIT license and the UIUC license. The libc++ library is an important companion of Compiler-RT, being part of the runtime libraries used by Clang++ to build your final C++ executable, along with libclc (the OpenCL runtime library) when necessary. It differs from Compiler-RT because it is not crucial for you to build libc++. Clang is not limited to it and may link your program with the GNU libstdc++ in the absence of libc++. If you have both, you can choose which library Clang++ should use with the -stdlib switch. The libc++ library supports x86 and x86_64 processors and it was designed as a replacement to the GNU libstdc++ for Mac OS X and GNU/Linux systems.

libc++ support on GNU/Linux is still under way, and is not as stable as the Mac OS X one.

One of the major impediments to continue working in the GNU libstdc++, according to libc++ developers, is that it would require a major code rewrite to support the newer C++ standards, and that the mainline libstdc++ development switched to a GPLv3 license that some companies that back the LLVM project are unable to use. Notice that LLVM projects are routinely used in commercial products in a way that is incompatible with the GPL philosophy. In the face of these challenges, the LLVM community decided to work on a new C++ standard library chiefly for Mac OS X, with support for Linux.

The easiest way to get libc++ in your Apple computer is to install Xcode 4.2 or later.

If you intend to build the library yourself for your GNU/Linux machine, bear in mind that the C++ standard library is composed of the library itself and a lower-level layer that implements functionalities dealing with exception handling and **Run-Time Type Information (RTTI)**. This separation of concerns allow the C++ standard library to be more easily ported to other systems. It also gives you different options when building your C++ standard library. You can build libc++ linked with either libsupc++, the GNU implementation of this lower-level layer, or with libc++abi, the implementation of the LLVM team. However, libc++abi currently only supports Mac OS X systems.

To build libc++ with libsupc++ in a GNU/Linux machine, start by downloading the source packages:

```
$ wget http://llvm.org/releases/3.4/libcxx-3.4.src.tar.gz
$ tar xvf libcxx-3.4.src.tar.gz
$ mv libcxx-3.4 libcxx
```

You still could not rely, until the time of this writing, on the LLVM build system to build the library for you as we did with other projects. Therefore, notice that we did not put libc++ sources into the LLVM source tree this time.

Alternatively, the SVN repository with the experimental top-of-trunk version is also available:

```
$ svn co http://llvm.org/svn/llvm-project/libcxx/trunk libcxx
```

You can also use the GIT mirror:

```
$ git clone http://llvm.org/git/llvm-project/libcxx.git
```

As soon as you have a working LLVM-based compiler, you need to generate the libc++ build files that specifically use your new LLVM-based compiler. In this example, we will assume that we have a working LLVM 3.4 compiler in our path.

To use libsupc++, we first need to find where you have its headers installed in your system. Since it is part of the regular GCC compiler for GNU/Linux, you can discover this by using the following commands:

```
$ echo | g++ -Wp,-v -x c++ - -fsyntax-only
#include "..." search starts here:
#include <...> search starts here:
/usr/include/c++/4.7.0
/usr/include/c++/4.7.0/x86_64-pc-linux-gnu
(Subsequent entries omitted)
```

In general, the first two paths indicate where the libsupc++ headers are. To confirm this, look for the presence of a libsupc++ header file such as bits/exception_ptr.h:

```
$ find /usr/include/c++/4.7.0 | grep bits/exception_ptr.h
```

Afterwards, generate libc++ build files to compile it with your LLVM-based compiler. To perform this, override the shell CC and CXX environment variables, which define the system C and C++ compilers, respectively, to use the LLVM compiler you want to embed with libc++. To use CMake to build libc++ with libsupc++, you will need to define the CMake parameters LIBCXX_CXX_ABI, which define the lower-level library to use, and LIBCXX_LIBSUPCXX_INCLUDE_PATHS, which is a semicolon-separated list of paths pointing to the folders with the libsupc++ include files that you just discovered:

```
$ mkdir where-you-want-to-build

$ cd where-you-want-to-build

$ CC=clang CXX=clang++ cmake -DLIBCXX_CXX_ABI=libstdc++
  -DLIBCXX_LIBSUPCXX_INCLUDE_PATHS="/usr/include/c++/4.7.0;/usr/
  include/c++/4.7.0/x86_64-pc-linux-gnu" -DCMAKE_INSTALL_PREFIX=
  "/usr" ../libcxx
```

At this stage, make sure that `../libcxx` is the correct path to reach your libc++ source folder. Run the `make` command to build the project. Use `sudo` for the installation command, since we will install the library in `/usr` to allow `clang++` to find the library later:

```
$ make && sudo make install
```

You can experiment with the new library and the newest C++ standards by using the `-stdlib=libc++` flag when calling `clang++` to compile your C++ project.

To see your new library in action, compile a simple C++ application with the following command:

```
$ clang++ -stdlib=libc++ hello.cpp -o hello
```

It is possible to perform a simple experiment with the `readelf` command to analyze the `hello` binary and confirm that it is indeed linked with your new libc++ library:

```
$ readelf d hello

Dynamic section at offset 0x2f00 contains 25 entries:
  Tag          Type                Name/Value
  0x00000001   (NEEDED)            Shared library: [libc++.so.1]
```

Subsequent entries are omitted in the preceding code. We see right at the first ELF dynamic section entry a specific request to load the `libc++.so.1` shared library that we just compiled, confirming that our C++ binaries now use the new C++ standard library of LLVM. You can find additional information at the official project site, `http://libcxx.llvm.org/`.

Summary

The LLVM umbrella is composed of several projects; some of them are not necessary for the main compiler driver to work but are useful tools and libraries. In this chapter, we showed how one can build and install such components. Further chapters will explore in detail some of those tools. We advise the reader to come back to this chapter again for build and install instructions.

In the next chapter, we will introduce you to the design of the LLVM core libraries and tools.

3
Tools and Design

The LLVM project consists of several libraries and tools that, together, make a large compiler infrastructure. A careful design is the key to connecting all these pieces together. Throughout, LLVM emphasizes the philosophy that *everything is a library*, leaving a relatively small amount of code that is not immediately reusable and is exclusive of a particular tool. Still, a large number of tools allows the user to exercise the libraries from a command terminal in many ways. In this chapter, we will cover the following topics:

- An overview and design of LLVM core libraries
- How the compiler driver works
- Beyond the compiler driver: meeting LLVM intermediary tools
- How to write your first LLVM tool
- General advice on navigating the LLVM source code

Introducing LLVM's basic design principles and its history

LLVM is a notoriously didactic framework because of a high degree of organization in its several tools, which allows the curious user to observe many steps of the compilation. The design decisions go back to its first versions more than 10 years ago when the project, which had a strong focus on backend algorithms, relied on GCC to translate high-level languages, such as C, to the LLVM **intermediate representation (IR)**. Today, a central aspect of the design of LLVM is its IR. It uses **Single-Static Assignments (SSA)**, with two important characteristics:

- Code is organized as three-address instructions
- It has an infinite number of registers

This does not mean, however, that LLVM has a single form of representing the program. Throughout the compilation process, other intermediary data structures hold the program logic and help its translation across major checkpoints. Technically, they are also intermediate forms of program representation. For example, LLVM employs the following additional data structures across different compilation stages:

- When translating C or C++ to the LLVM IR, Clang will represent the program in the memory by using an **Abstract Syntax Tree (AST)** structure (the `TranslationUnitDecl` class)

- When translating the LLVM IR to a machine-specific assembly language, LLVM will first convert the program to a **Directed Acyclic Graph (DAG)** form to allow easy instruction selection (the `SelectionDAG` class) and then it will convert it back to a three-address representation to allow the instruction scheduling to happen (the `MachineFunction` class)

- To implement assemblers and linkers, LLVM uses a fourth intermediary data structure (the `MCModule` class) to hold the program representation in the context of object files

Besides other forms of program representation in LLVM, the LLVM IR is the most important one. It has the particularity of being not only an in-memory representation, but also being stored on disk. The fact that LLVM IR enjoys a specific encoding to live in the outside world is another important decision that was made early in the project lifetime and that reflected, at that time, an academic interest to study lifelong program optimizations.

In this philosophy, the compiler goes beyond applying optimizations at compile time, exploring optimization opportunities at the installation time, runtime, and idle time (when the program is not running). In this way, the optimization happens throughout its entire life, thereby explaining the name of this concept. For example, when the user is not running the program and the computer is idle, the operating system can launch a compiler daemon to process the profiling data collected during runtime to reoptimize the program for the specific use cases of this user.

Notice that by being able to be stored on disk, the LLVM IR, which is a key enabler of lifelong program optimizations, offers an alternative way to encode entire programs. When the whole program is stored in the form of a compiler IR, it is also possible to perform a new range of very effective inter-procedural optimizations that cross the boundary of a single translation unit or a C file. Thus, this also allows powerful link-time optimizations to happen.

On the other hand, before lifelong program optimizations become a reality, program distribution needs to happen at the LLVM IR level, which does not happen. This would imply that LLVM will run as a platform or virtual machine and will compete with Java, which too has serious challenges. For example, the LLVM IR is not target-independent like Java. LLVM has also not invested in powerful feedback-directed optimizations for the post-installation time. For the reader who is interested in reading more about these technical challenges, we suggest reading a helpful **LLVMdev** discussion thread at http://lists.cs.uiuc. edu/pipermail/llvmdev/2011-October/043719.html.

As the project matured, the design decision of maintaining an on-disk representation of the compiler IR remained as an enabler of link-time optimizations, giving less attention to the original idea of lifelong program optimizations. Eventually, LLVM's core libraries formalized their lack of interest in becoming a platform by renouncing the acronym Low Level Virtual Machine, adopting just the name LLVM for historical reasons, making it clear that the LLVM project is geared to being a strong and practical C/C++ compiler rather than a Java platform competitor.

Still, the on-disk representation alone has promising applications, besides link-time optimizations, that some groups are fighting to bring to the real world. For example, the FreeBSD community wants to embed program executables with its LLVM program representation to allow install-time or offline microarchitectural optimizations. In this scenario, even if the program was compiled to a generic x86, when the user installs the program, for example, on the specific Intel Haswell x86 processor, the LLVM infrastructure can use the LLVM representation of the binary and specialize it to use new instructions supported on Haswell. Even though this is a new idea that is currently being assessed, it demonstrates that the on-disk LLVM representation allows for radical new solutions. The expectations are for microarchitectural optimizations because the full platform independence seen in Java looks impractical in LLVM and this possibility is currently explored only on external projects (see PNaCl, Chromium's Portable Native Client).

As a compiler IR, the two basic principles of the LLVM IR that guided the development of the core libraries are the following:

- SSA representation and infinite registers that allow fast optimizations
- Easy link-time optimizations by storing entire programs in an on-disk IR representation

Understanding LLVM today

Nowadays, the LLVM project has grown and holds a huge collection of compiler-related tools. In fact, the name LLVM might refer to any of the following:

- **The LLVM project/infrastructure**: This is an umbrella for several projects that, together, form a complete compiler: frontends, backends, optimizers, assemblers, linkers, libc++, compiler-rt, and a JIT engine. The word "LLVM" has this meaning, for example, in the following sentence: "LLVM is comprised of several projects".

- **An LLVM-based compiler**: This is a compiler built partially or completely with the LLVM infrastructure. For example, a compiler might use LLVM for the frontend and backend but use GCC and GNU system libraries to perform the final link. LLVM has this meaning in the following sentence, for example: "I used LLVM to compile C programs to a MIPS platform".

- **LLVM libraries**: This is the reusable code portion of the LLVM infrastructure. For example, LLVM has this meaning in the sentence: "My project uses LLVM to generate code through its Just-in-Time compilation framework".

- **LLVM core**: The optimizations that happen at the intermediate language level and the backend algorithms form the LLVM core where the project started. LLVM has this meaning in the following sentence: "LLVM and Clang are two different projects".

- **The LLVM IR**: This is the LLVM compiler intermediate representation. LLVM has this meaning when used in sentences such as "I built a frontend that translates my own language to LLVM".

To understand the LLVM project, you need to be aware of the most important parts of the infrastructure:

- **Frontend**: This is the compiler step that translates computer-programming languages, such as C, C++, and Objective-C, into the LLVM compiler IR. This includes a lexical analyzer, a syntax parser, a semantic analyzer, and the LLVM IR code generator. The Clang project implements all frontend-related steps while providing a plugin interface and a separate static analyzer tool to allow deep analyses. For details, you can go through *Chapter 4, The Frontend*, *Chapter 9, The Clang Static Analyzer*, and *Chapter 10, Clang Tools with LibTooling*.

- **IR**: The LLVM IR has both human-readable and binary-encoded representations. Tools and libraries provide interfaces to IR construction, assembling, and disassembling. The LLVM optimizer also operates on the IR where most part of optimizations is applied. We explain the IR in detail in *Chapter 5, The LLVM Intermediate Representation*.

- **Backend**: This is the step that is responsible for code generation. It converts LLVM IR to target-specific assembly code or object code binaries. Register allocation, loop transformations, peephole optimizers, and target-specific optimizations/transformations belong to the backend. We analyze this in depth in *Chapter 6, The Backend*.

The following diagram illustrates the components and gives us an overview of the entire infrastructure when used in a specific configuration. Notice that we can reorganize the components and utilize them in a different arrangement, for example, not using the LLVM IR linker if we do not want to explore link-time optimizations.

The interaction between each of these compiler parts can happen in the following two ways:

- **In memory**: This happens via a single supervisor tool, such as Clang, that uses each LLVM component as a library and depends on the data structures allocated in the memory to feed the output of a stage to the input of another

- **Through files**: This happens via a user who launches smaller standalone tools that write the result of a particular component to a file on disk, depending on the user to launch the next tool with this file as the input

Hence, higher-level tools, such as Clang, can incorporate the usage of several other smaller tools by linking together the libraries that implement their functionality. This is possible because LLVM uses a design that emphasizes the reuse of the maximum amount of code, which then lives in libraries. Moreover, standalone tools that incarnate a smaller number of libraries are useful because they allow a user to interact directly with a specific LLVM component via the command line.

For example, consider the following diagram. We show you the names of tools in boxes in boldface and libraries that they use to implement their functionality in separated boxes in regular font. In this example, the LLVM backend tool, `llc`, uses the `libLLVMCodeGen` library to implement part of its functionality while the `opt` command, which launches only the LLVM IR-level optimizer, uses another library—called `libLLVMipa`—to implement target-independent interprocedural optimizations. Yet, we see `clang`, a larger tool that uses both libraries to override `llc` and `opt` and present a simpler interface to the user. Therefore, any task performed by such higher-level tools can be decomposed into a chain of lower-level tools while yielding the same results. The next sections illustrate this concept. In practice, Clang is able to carry on the entire compilation and not just the work of `opt` and `llc`. That explains why, in a static build, the Clang binary is often the largest, since it links with and exercises the entire LLVM ecosystem.

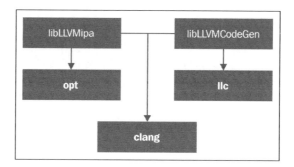

Interacting with the compiler driver

A compiler driver is similar to the clerk at a burger place who interfaces with you, recognizes your order, passes it to the backend that builds your burger, and then delivers it back to you with coke and perhaps some ketchup sachets, thereby completing your order. The driver is responsible for integrating all necessary libraries and tools in order to provide the user with a friendlier experience, freeing the user from the need to use individual compiler stages such as the frontend, backend, assembler, and linker. Once you feed your program source code to a compiler driver, it can generate an executable. In LLVM and Clang, the compiler driver is the `clang` tool.

Consider the simple C program, `hello.c`:

```
#include <stdio.h>

int main() {
  printf("Hello, World!\n");
  return 0;
}
```

To generate an executable for this simple program, use the following command:

```
$ clang hello.c -o hello
```

 Use instructions from *Chapter 1, Build and Install LLVM*, to obtain a ready-to-use version of LLVM.

For people who are familiar with GCC, note that the preceding command is very similar to the one used for GCC. In fact, the Clang compiler driver was designed to be compatible with GCC flags and command structure, allowing LLVM to be used as a replacement for GCC in many projects. For Windows, Clang also has a version called `clang-cl.exe` that mimics the Visual Studio C++ compiler command-line interface. The Clang compiler driver implicitly invokes all other tools from the frontend to the linker.

In order to see all subsequent tools called by the driver to complete your order, use the `-###` command argument:

```
$ clang -### hello.c -o hello
clang version 3.4 (tags/RELEASE_34/final)
Target: x86_64-apple-darwin11.4.2
Thread model: posix
"/bin/clang" -cc1 -triple x86_64-apple-macosx10.7.0 … -main-file-name
hello.c (...) /examples/hello/hello.o -x c hello.c
"/opt/local/bin/ld" (...) -o hello /examples/hello/hello.o (...)
```

The first tool the Clang driver calls is the `clang` tool itself with the `-cc1` parameter, which disables the compiler-driver mode while enabling the compiler mode. It also uses a myriad of arguments to tweak the C/C++ options. Since LLVM components are libraries, the `clang -cc1` is linked with the IR generation, the code generator for the target machine, and assembler libraries. Therefore, after parsing, `clang -cc1` itself is able to call other libraries and supervise the compilation pipeline in the memory until the object file is ready. Afterwards, the Clang driver (different from the compiler `clang -cc1`) invokes the linker, which is an external tool, to generate the executable file, as shown in the preceding output line. It uses the system linker to complete the compilation because the LLVM linker, `lld`, is still under development.

Notice that it is much faster to use the memory than the disk, making intermediary compilation files unattractive. This explains why Clang, the LLVM frontend and the first tool to interact with the input, is responsible for carrying on the rest of the compilation in the memory rather than writing an intermediary output file to be read by another tool.

Using standalone tools

We can also exercise the compilation workflow described previously through the usage of LLVM standalone tools, linking the output of one tool into the output of another. Although this slows downs the compilation due to the use of the disk to write intermediary files, it is an interesting didactic exercise to observe the compilation pipeline. This also allows you to fine-tune the parameters given to intermediary tools. Some of these tools are as follows:

- `opt`: This is a tool that is aimed at optimizing a program at the IR level. The input must be an LLVM bitcode file (encoded LLVM IR) and the generated output file must have the same type.

- `llc`: This is a tool that converts the LLVM bitcode to a target-machine assembly language file or object file via a specific backend. You can pass arguments to select an optimization level, to turn on debugging options, and to enable or disable target-specific optimizations.

- `llvm-mc`: This tool is able to assemble instructions and generate object files for several object formats such as ELF, MachO, and PE. It can also disassemble the same objects, dumping the equivalent assembly information and the internal LLVM machine instruction data structures for such instructions.

- `lli`: This tool implements both an interpreter and a JIT compiler for the LLVM IR.

- `llvm-link`: This tool links together several LLVM bitcodes to produce a single LLVM bitcode that encompasses all inputs.

- `llvm-as`: This tool transforms human-readable LLVM IR files, called LLVM assemblies, into LLVM bitcodes.

- `llvm-dis`: This tool decodes LLVM bitcodes into LLVM assemblies.

Let's consider a simple C program composed of functions among multiple source files. The first source file is `main.c`, and it is reproduced as follows:

```
#include <stdio.h>

int sum(int x, int y);

int main() {
    int r = sum(3, 4);
    printf("r = %d\n", r);
    return 0;
}
```

The second file is `sum.c`, and it is reproduced as follows:

```
int sum(int x, int y) {
    return x+y;
}
```

We can compile this C program with the following command:

```
$ clang main.c sum.c -o sum
```

However, we can achieve the same result using the standalone tools. First, we change the `clang` command to generate LLVM bitcode files for each C source file and stop there instead of proceeding with the entire compilation:

```
$ clang -emit-llvm -c main.c -o main.bc
$ clang -emit-llvm -c sum.c -o sum.bc
```

The `-emit-llvm` flag tells `clang` to generate either the LLVM bitcode or LLVM assembly files, depending on the presence of the `-c` or `-s` flag. In the preceding example, `-emit-llvm`, together with the `-c` flag, tells `clang` to generate an object file in the LLVM bitcode format. Using the `-flto -c` combination of flags yields the same result. If you intend to generate the LLVM assembly, which is human readable, use the following pair of commands instead:

```
$ clang -emit-llvm -S -c main.c -o main.ll
$ clang -emit-llvm -S -c sum.c -o sum.ll
```

> Notice that without the `-emit-llvm` or `-flto` flags, the `-c` flag generates an object file with the target machine language while the `-S`, generates the target assembly language file. This behavior is compatible with GCC.

The `.bc` and `.ll` are the file extensions that are used for the LLVM bitcode and assembly files, respectively. In order to continue with the compilation, we can proceed in the following two ways:

- Generate target-specific object files from each LLVM bitcode and build the program executable by linking them with the system linker (part **A** of the next diagram):

```
$ llc -filetype=obj main.bc -o main.o
$ llc -filetype=obj sum.bc -o sum.o
$ clang main.o sum.o -o sum
```

- First, link the two LLVM bitcodes into a final LLVM bitcode. Then, build the target-specific object file from the final bitcode and generate the program executable by calling the system linker (part **B** of the following diagram):

```
$ llvm-link main.bc sum.bc -o sum.linked.bc
$ llc -filetype=obj sum.linked.bc -o sum.linked.o
$ clang sum.linked.o -o sum
```

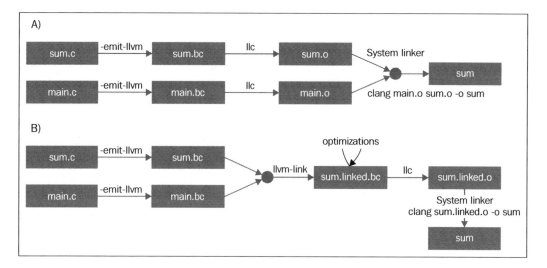

The `-filetype=obj` parameter specifies an object file output instead of the target assembly file. We use the Clang driver, `clang`, to invoke the linker, but the system linker can be used directly if you know all parameters that your system linker requires to link with your system libraries.

Linking IR files prior to the backend invocation (`llc`) allows the final produced IR to be further optimized with link-time optimizations provided by the `opt` tool (for examples, see *Chapter 5, The LLVM Intermediate Representation*). Alternatively, the `llc` tool can generate an assembly output, which can be further assembled using `llvm-mc`. We show you more details of this interface in *Chapter 6, The Backend*.

Delving into the LLVM internal design

In order to decouple the compiler into several tools, the LLVM design typically enforces component interaction to happen at a high level of abstraction. It segregates different components into separate libraries; it is written in C++ using object-oriented paradigms and a pluggable pass interface is available, allowing easy integration of transformations and optimizations throughout the compilation pipeline.

Getting to know LLVM's basic libraries

The LLVM and Clang logic is carefully organized into the following libraries:

- `libLLVMCore`: This contains all the logic related to the LLVM IR: IR construction (data layout, instructions, basic blocks, and functions) and the IR verifier. It also provides the pass manager.

- `libLLVMAnalysis`: This groups several IR analysis passes, such as alias analysis, dependence analysis, constant folding, loop info, memory dependence analysis, and instruction simplify.

- `libLLVMCodeGen`: This implements target-independent code generation and machine level—the lower level version of the LLVM IR—analyses and transformations.

- `libLLVMTarget`: This provides access to the target machine information by generic target abstractions. These high-level abstractions provide the communication gateway between generic backend algorithms implemented in `libLLVMCodeGen` and the target-specific logic that is reserved for the next library.

- `libLLVMX86CodeGen`: This has the x86 target-specific code generation information, transformation, and analysis passes, which compose the x86 backend. Note that there is a different library for each machine target, such as `LLVMARMCodeGen` and `LLVMMipsCodeGen`, implementing ARM and MIPS backends, respectively.

- `libLLVMSupport`: This comprises a collection of general utilities. Error, integer and floating point handling, command-line parsing, debugging, file support, and string manipulation are examples of algorithms that are implemented in this library, which is universally used across LLVM components.

- `libclang`: This implements a C interface, as opposed to C++, which is the default implementation language of LLVM code, to access much of Clang's frontend functionalities—diagnostic reporting, AST traversing, code completion, mapping between cursors, and source code. Since it is a C, simpler interface, it allows projects written in other languages, such as Python, to use the Clang functionality more easily, albeit the C interface is designed to be more stable and allow external projects to depend on it. This only covers a subset of the C++ interface used by internal LLVM components.

- `libclangDriver`: This contains the set of classes used by the compiler driver tool to understand GCC-like command-line parameters to prepare jobs and to organize adequate parameters for external tools to finish different steps of the compilation. It can manage different strategies for the compilation, depending on the target platform.

- `libclangAnalysis`: This is a set of frontend level analyses provided by Clang. It features CFG and call-graph construction, reachable code, format string security, among others.

As an example of how these libraries can be used to compose LLVM tools, Figure 3.3 shows you the `llc` tool's dependence upon `libLLVMCodeGen`, `libLLVMTarget`, and others as well as the dependence of these libraries on others. Still, notice that the preceding list is not complete.

We will leave other libraries that were omitted from this initial overview to later chapters. For Version 3.0, the LLVM team wrote a nice document showing the dependency relationship between all LLVM libraries. Even though the document is outdated, it still provides an interesting overview of the organization of the libraries and is accessible at `http://llvm.org/releases/3.0/docs/UsingLibraries.html`.

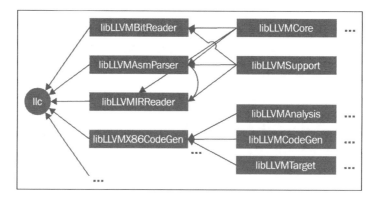

Introducing LLVM's C++ practices

The LLVM libraries and tools are written in C++ to take advantage of object-oriented programming paradigms and to enhance interoperability between its parts. Additionally, good C++ programming practices are enforced in an attempt to avoid inefficiencies in the code as much as possible.

Seeing polymorphism in practice

Inheritance and polymorphism abstracts common tasks of the backends by leaving generic code-generation algorithms to base classes. In this scheme, each specific backend can focus on implementing its particularities by writing fewer necessary methods that override superclass generic operations. LibLLVMCodeGen contains the common algorithms, and LibLLVMTarget contains the interface that abstracts individual machines. The following code snippet (from llvm/lib/Target/Mips/MipsTargetMachine.h) shows you how a MIPS target-machine description class is declared as a subclass of the LLVMTargetMachine class and illustrates this concept. This code is part of the LLVMMipsCodeGen library:

```
class MipsTargetMachine : public LLVMTargetMachine {
  MipsSubtarget       Subtarget;
  const DataLayout    DL;
...
```

To further clarify this design choice, we show you another backend example in which the target-independent register allocator, which is common to all backends, needs to know which registers are reserved and cannot be used for allocation. This information depends upon the specific target and cannot be encoded into generic superclasses. It performs this task through the use of MachineRegisterInfo::getReservedRegs(), which is a generic method that must be overridden by each target. The following code snippet (from llvm/lib/Target/Sparc/SparcRegisterInfo.cpp) shows you an example of how the SPARC target overrides this method:

```
BitVector SparcRegisterInfo::getReservedRegs(...) const {
  BitVector Reserved(getNumRegs());
  Reserved.set(SP::G1);
  Reserved.set(SP::G2);
...
```

In this code, the SPARC backend individually selects which registers cannot be used for general register allocation by building a bit vector.

Introducing C++ templates in LLVM

LLVM frequently uses C++ templates, although special caution is taken to control the long compilation times that are typical of C++ projects that abuse templates. Whenever possible, it employs template specialization to allow the implementation of fast and recurrently used common tasks. As a template example in the LLVM code, let's present the function that checks whether an integer, passed as a parameter, fits into the given bit width, which is the template parameter (code from llvm/include/llvm/Support/MathExtras.h):

```
template<unsigned N>
inline bool isInt(int64_t x) {
```

```
    return N >= 64 ||
(-(INT64_C(1)<<(N-1))) <= x && x < (INT64_C(1)<<(N-1)));
}
```

In this code, notice how the template has code that handles all bit width values, N. It features an early comparison to return `true` whenever the bit width is greater than 64 bits. If not, it builds two expressions, which are the lower and upper bounds for this bit width, checking whether x is between these bounds. Compare this code to the following template specialization, which is used to get faster code for the common case where the bit width is 8:

`llvm/include/llvm/Support/MathExtras.h`:

```
template<>
inline bool isInt<8>(int64_t x) {
  return static_cast<int8_t>(x) == x;
}
```

This code brings down the number of comparisons from three to one, thereby justifying the specialization.

Enforcing C++ best practices in LLVM

It is common to introduce bugs unintentionally when programming, but the difference is in how you manage your bugs. The LLVM philosophy advises you to use the assertion mechanism implemented in `libLLVMSupport` whenever possible. Notice that debugging a compiler can be particularly difficult, because the product of the compilation is another program. Therefore, if you can detect erratic behavior earlier, before writing a complicated output that is not trivial in order to determine whether it is correct, you are saving a lot of your time. For example, let's see the code of an ARM backend pass that changes the layout of constant pools, redistributing them across several smaller pools "islands" across a function. This strategy is commonly used in ARM programs to load large constants with a limited PC-relative addressing mechanism because a single, larger pool can be placed in a location that is too far away from the instruction that uses it. This code lives at `llvm/lib/Target/ARM/ARMConstantIslandPass.cpp` and we show an excerpt of it next:

```
const DataLayout &TD = *MF->getTarget().getDataLayout();
for (unsigned i = 0, e = CPs.size(); i != e; ++i) {
  unsigned Size = TD.getTypeAllocSize(CPs[i].getType());
  assert(Size >= 4 && "Too small constant pool entry");
  unsigned Align = CPs[i].getAlignment();
  assert(isPowerOf2_32(Align) && "Invalid alignment");
  // Verify that all constant pool entries are a multiple of their
     alignment.
  // If not, we would have to pad them out so that instructions
     stay aligned.
```

```
assert((Size % Align) == 0 && "CP Entry not multiple of 4
    bytes!");
```

In this fragment, the code iterates through a data structure that represents ARM constant pools, and the programmer expects each field of this object to respect specific constraints. Notice how the programmer keeps the data semantics under his control by using `assert` calls. If something is different from what he expected when writing this code, his program will immediately quit execution and print the assertion call that failed. The programmer uses the idiom of suffixing the Boolean expression with `&& "error cause!"`, which does not interfere in the evaluation of the Boolean expression of `assert` but will give a short textual explanation about the assertion failure when this expression is printed in the event of its failure. The use of asserts has a performance impact that is completely removed once the LLVM project is compiled in a release build because it disables the assertions.

Another common practice that you will see with frequency in the LLVM code is the use of smart pointers. They provide automatic memory deallocation once the symbol goes out of scope and is used in the LLVM code base to, for example, hold the target information and modules. In the past, LLVM provided a special smart pointer class called `OwningPtr`, which is defined in `llvm/include/llvm/ADT/OwningPtr.h`. As of LLVM 3.5, this class has been deprecated in favor of `std::unique_ptr()`, introduced with the C++11 standard.

If you are interested in the full list of C++ best practices adopted in the LLVM project, visit `http://llvm.org/docs/CodingStandards.html`. It is a worthwhile read for every C++ programmer.

Making string references lightweight in LLVM

The LLVM project has an extensive library of data structures that support common algorithms, and strings have a special place in the LLVM libraries. They belong to a class in C++ that leads to a heated discussion: when should we use a simple `char*` versus the `string` class of the C++ standard library? To discuss this in the context of LLVM, consider the intensive use of string references throughout LLVM libraries to reference the name of LLVM modules, functions, and values, among others. In some cases, the strings LLVM handles can contain null characters, rendering the approach of passing constant string references as `const char*` pointers to be impossible, since the null character terminates a C-style string. On the other hand, working with `const std::string&` frequently introduces extra heap allocations, because the `string` class needs to own the character buffer. We see this in the following example:

```
bool hasComma (const std::string &a) {
  // code
}
void myfunc() {
```

```
    char buffer [40];
    // code to create our string in our own buffer
    hasComma(buffer); // C++ compiler is forced to create a new
      string object, duplicating the buffer
    hasComma("hello, world!"); // Likewise
}
```

Notice that every time we try to create a string in our own buffer, we will spend an extra heap allocation to copy this string to the internal buffer of the string object, which must own its buffer. In the first case, we have a stack-allocated string while in the second case, the string is held as a global constant. What C++ is missing, for these cases, is a simple class that avoids unnecessary allocations when we only need a reference to a string. Even if we work strictly with string objects, saving unnecessary heap allocations, a reference to a string object imposes two indirections. Since the string class already works with an internal pointer to hold its data, passing a pointer to a string object introduces the overhead of a double reference when we access the actual data.

We can make this more efficient with an LLVM class to work with string references: StringRef. This is a lightweight class that can be passed by value in the same way as const char*, but it also stores the size of the string, allowing null characters. However, contrary to string objects, it does not own the buffer and, thus, never allocates heap space but merely refers to a string that lives outside it. This concept is also explored in other C++ projects: Chromium, for instance, uses the StringPiece class to implement the same idea.

LLVM also introduces yet another string-manipulation class. To build a new string out of several concatenations, LLVM provides the Twine class. It defers the actual concatenation by storing only references to the strings that will compose the final product. This was created in the pre-C++11 era when string concatenation was expensive.

If you are interested in finding out about other generic classes that LLVM provides to help its programmers, a very important document you should keep in your bookmarks is the LLVM Programmer's Manual, which discusses all LLVM generic data structures that might be useful for any code. The manual is located at http://llvm.org/docs/ProgrammersManual.html.

Demonstrating the pluggable pass interface

A pass is a transformation analysis or optimization. LLVM APIs allow you to easily register any pass during different parts of the program compilation lifetime, which is an appreciated point of the LLVM design. A pass manager is used to register, schedule, and declare dependencies between passes. Hence, instances of the PassManager class are available throughout different compiler stages.

For example, targets are free to apply custom optimizations at several points during code generation, such as prior to and after register allocation or before the assembly emission. To illustrate this, we show you an example where the X86 target conditionally registers a pair of custom passes prior to the assembly emission (from `lib/Target/X86/X86TargetMachine.cpp`):

```
bool X86PassConfig::addPreEmitPass() {
    ...
    if (getOptLevel() != CodeGenOpt::None &&          getX86Subtarget().
    hasSSE2()) {
        addPass(createExecutionDependencyFixPass(&X86::VR128RegClass));
        ...
    }

    if (getOptLevel() != CodeGenOpt::None &&
        getX86Subtarget().padShortFunctions()) {
        addPass(createX86PadShortFunctions());
    }
    ...
```

Note how the backend reasons about whether the pass should be added by using specific target information. Before adding the first pass, the X86 target is checked to see whether it supports SSE2 multimedia extensions. For the second pass, it checks whether it was specifically asked for padding.

Part **A** of the following diagram shows you an example of how optimization passes are inserted in the `opt` tool and part **B** illustrates the several target hooks in the code generation where custom target optimizations can be inserted. Note that the insertion points are spread during different code generation stages. This diagram is especially useful when you write your first passes and need to decide where to run them. The `PassManager` interface is described in detail in *Chapter 5, The LLVM Intermediate Representation*.

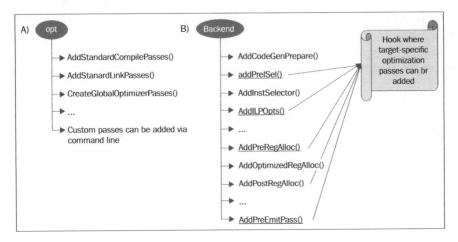

Writing your first LLVM project

In this section, we will show you how to write your first project that uses LLVM libraries. In the previous sections, we presented how to use LLVM tools to produce an intermediary language file that corresponds to a program, a bitcode file. We will now create a program that reads this bitcode file and prints the name of the functions defined within it and their number of basic blocks, showing how easy it is to use LLVM libraries.

Writing the Makefile

Linking with LLVM libraries requires the use of long command lines that are not practical to write without the help of a build system. We show you a Makefile in the following code, based on the one used in DragonEgg, to accomplish this task, explaining each part as we present it. If you copy and paste this code, you will lose the tab character; remember that Makefiles depend on using the tab character to specify the commands that define a rule. Thus, you should manually insert them:

```
LLVM_CONFIG?=llvm-config

ifndef VERBOSE
QUIET:=@
endif

SRC_DIR?=$(PWD)
LDFLAGS+=$(shell $(LLVM_CONFIG) --ldflags)
COMMON_FLAGS=-Wall -Wextra
CXXFLAGS+=$(COMMON_FLAGS) $(shell $(LLVM_CONFIG) --cxxflags)
CPPFLAGS+=$(shell $(LLVM_CONFIG) --cppflags) -I$(SRC_DIR)
```

This first part defines the first Makefile variables that will be used as the compiler flags. The first variable determines the location of the llvm-config program. In this case, it needs to be in your path. The llvm-config tool is an LLVM program that prints a variety of useful information to build an external project that needs to be linked with the LLVM libraries.

When defining the set of flags to be used in the C++ compiler, for instance, notice that we ask Make to launch the llvm-config --cxxflags shell command line, which prints the set of C++ flags that you used to compile the LLVM project. This way, we make the compilation of the sources of our project compatible with LLVM sources. The last variable defines the set of flags that are to be passed to the compiler preprocessor.

```
HELLO=helloworld
HELLO_OBJECTS=hello.o
```

```
default: $(HELLO)

%.o : $(SRC_DIR)/%.cpp
    @echo Compiling $*.cpp
    $(QUIET)$(CXX) -c $(CPPFLAGS) $(CXXFLAGS) $<

$(HELLO) : $(HELLO_OBJECTS)
    @echo Linking $@
    $(QUIET)$(CXX) -o $@ $(CXXFLAGS) $(LDFLAGS) $^ `$(LLVM_CONFIG)
--libs bitreader core support`
```

In this second fragment, we defined our Makefile rules. The first rule is always the default one, which we bound to build our hello-world executable. The second one is a generic rule that compiles all of our C++ files into object files. We pass the preprocessor flags and the C++ compiler flags to it. We also use the $(QUIET) variable to omit the full command line from appearing on the screen, but if you want a verbose build log, you can define VERBOSE when running GNU Make.

The last rule links all object files—in this case, just one—to build our project executable that is linked with LLVM libraries. This part is accomplished by the linker, but some C++ flags might also take effect. Thus, we pass both C++ and linker flags to the command line. We finish this with the `command` construct, which instructs the shell to substitute this part with the output of `command`. In our case, the command is llvm-config --libs bitreader core support. The --libs flag asks llvm-config to provide us with the list of linker flags that are used to link with the requested LLVM libraries. Here, we asked for libLLVMBitReader, libLLVMCore, and libLLVMSupport.

This list of flags, returned by llvm-config, is a series of -l linker parameters, as in -lLLVMCore -lLLVMSupport. Note, however, that the order of the parameters passed to the linker matters and requires that you put libraries that depend on others first. For example, since libLLVMCore uses the generic functionality provided by libLLVMSupport, the correct order is -lLLVMCore -lLLVMSupport.

The order matters because a library is a collection of object files, and when linking a project against a library, the linker only selects those object files that are known to resolve undefined symbols seen so far. Thus, if it is processing the last library in your command-line argument and this library happens to use a symbol from a library that was already processed, most linkers (including GNU ld) will not go back to include a potentially missing object file, thus ruining the build.

If you want to avoid this responsibility and force the linker to iteratively visit each library until all necessary object files are resolved, you must use the `--start-group` and `--end-group` flags at the start and end of the list of libraries, but this can slow down the linker. In order to avoid headaches in building the entire dependency graph to figure out the order of the linker arguments, you can simply use `llvm-config --libs` and let it do this for you, as we did previously.

The last part of the Makefile defines a clean rule to delete all compiler-generated files, allowing us to restart the build from scratch. The clean rule is written as follows:

```
clean::
    $(QUIET)rm -f $(HELLO) $(HELLO_OBJECTS)
```

Writing the code

We present the code of our pass in its entirety. It is relatively short because it builds upon the LLVM pass infrastructure, which does most of the work for us.

```cpp
#include "llvm/Bitcode/ReaderWriter.h"
#include "llvm/IR/Function.h"
#include "llvm/IR/Module.h"
#include "llvm/Support/CommandLine.h"
#include "llvm/Support/MemoryBuffer.h"
#include "llvm/Support/raw_os_ostream.h"
#include "llvm/Support/system_error.h"
#include <iostream>

using namespace llvm;

static cl::opt<std::string> FileName(cl::Positional, cl::desc("Bitcode
file"), cl::Required);

int main(int argc, char** argv) {
  cl::ParseCommandLineOptions(argc, argv, "LLVM hello world\n");
  LLVMContext context;
  std::string error;
  OwningPtr<MemoryBuffer> mb;
  MemoryBuffer::getFile(FileName, mb);
  Module *m = ParseBitcodeFile(mb.get(), context, &error);
  if (m == 0) {
    std::cerr << "Error reading bitcode: " << error << std::end;
    return -1;
  }
  raw_os_ostream O(std::cout);
```

```
    for (Module::const_iterator i = m->getFunctionList().begin(),
        e = m->getFunctionList().end(); i != e; ++i) {
      if (!i->isDeclaration()) {
        O << i->getName() << " has " << i->size() << " basic
  block(s).\n";
      }
    }
    return 0;
}
```

Our program uses the LLVM facilities from the `cl` namespace (`cl` stands for command line) to implement the command-line interface for us. We just call the `ParseCommandLineOptions` function and declare a global variable of the `cl::opt<string>` type to show that our program receives a single parameter, which is a `string` type that holds the bitcode filename.

Later, we instantiate an `LLVMContext` object to hold all the data that pertains to an LLVM compilation, allowing LLVM to be thread-safe. The `MemoryBuffer` class defines a read-only interface for a block of memory. The `ParseBitcodeFile` function will use this to read the contents of our input file and parse the contents of the LLVM IR in this file. After performing checks against errors and ensuring that everything went fine, we iterate through all functions of the module in this file. An LLVM module is a concept that is similar to a translation unit and contains everything encoded into the bitcode file, being the highest entity in the LLVM hierarchy, followed by functions, then by basic blocks and finally, by instructions. If the function is only a declaration, we discard it, since we want to check for function definitions. When we find these function definitions, we print their name and the number of basic blocks it has.

Compile this program and run it with `-help` to see what the LLVM command-line functionalities that have already been prepared for your program are. Afterwards, look for a C or C++ file that you want to convert to the LLVM IR, convert it, and analyze it using your program:

```
$ clang -c -emit-llvm mysource.c -o mysource.bc
$ helloworld mysource.bc
```

If you want to further explore what you can extract from functions, refer to the LLVM doxygen documentation about the `llvm::Function` class at http://llvm.org/docs/doxygen/html/classllvm_1_1Function.html. As an exercise, try to extend this example to print the list of arguments of each function.

Navigating the LLVM source – general advice

Before proceeding with learning more about the LLVM implementation, note that there are points that are worth understanding, chiefly for new programmers in the world of open source software. If you were working in a closed-source project inside a company, you would probably get lot of help from fellow programmers who are older than you in the project and have a deeper understanding about many design decisions that might sound obscure to you at first. If you run into problems, the author of a component will probably be willing to explain it to you orally. The efficacy of his oral explanations comes when while doing so, he might even be able to read your facial expressions, figure out when you do not understand a specific point, and adapt his discourse to create a custom explanation for you.

However, when working remotely, as happens with most community projects, there is no physical presence, and thus, less oral communication. Therefore, there is more incentive for stronger documentation in open source communities. On the other hand, documentation might not be what most usually expect, as in an English-written document that clearly states all design decisions. Much of the documentation is the code itself, and in this sense, there is pressure to write clear code in order to help others understand what is happening without the English documentation.

Understanding the code as a documentation

Even though the most important parts of LLVM have an English documentation and we refer to them throughout this book, our final goal is to prepare you to read the code directly because this is a prerequisite to go deeper into the LLVM infrastructure. We will provide you with the basic concepts that are necessary to help you understand how LLVM works, and with it, you will find the joy of understanding LLVM code without the need to read an English documentation or to be able to read the many parts of LLVM that lack any English documentation at all. Even though this can be challenging, when you start doing it, you will grow inside of yourself a deeper sense of understanding about the project and will be increasingly more confident about hacking into it. Before you realize it, you will be a programmer with advanced knowledge about LLVM internals and will be helping others in the e-mail lists.

Asking the community for help

The e-mail lists are there to remind you that you are not alone. They are the `cfe-dev` lists for the Clang frontend and the `llvmdev` list for LLVM core. Take a moment to subscribe to these lists at the following addresses:

- Clang Front End Developer List (`http://lists.cs.uiuc.edu/mailman/listinfo/cfe-dev`)
- LLVM core Developer List (`http://lists.cs.uiuc.edu/mailman/listinfo/llvmdev`)

There are many people working in the project, trying to implement things that you are also interested in. Therefore, there is a high probability that you might ask something that others have already dealt with.

Before asking for help, it is best to exercise your brain and try to hack into the code without assistance. See how high you can fly on your own and try your best to evolve your knowledge. If you run into something that looks puzzling to you, write an e-mail to the list, making it clear that you have previously investigated the matter before soliciting for help. By following these guidelines, you have a far better chance of receiving the best answers to your problem.

Coping with updates – using the SVN log as a documentation

The LLVM project is constantly changing, and in effect, a very common scenario you might find yourself in is to update the LLVM version and see that the portion of your software that interfaces with LLVM libraries is broken. Before trying to read the code again to see how it has changed, use the code revision that is in your favor.

To see how this works in practice, let's exercise the update of the frontend Clang from 3.4 to 3.5. Suppose that you wrote a code for the static analyzer that instantiates a `BugType` object:

```
BugType *bugType = new BugType("This is a bug name",
                              "This is a bug category name");
```

This object is used to make your own checkers (more details in *Chapter 9, The Clang Static Analyzer*) report specific kinds of bugs. Now, let's update the entire LLVM and Clang codebases to the 3.5 Version and compile the lines. This gives us the following output:

```
error: no matching constructor for initialization of
     'clang::ento::BugType'
  BugType *bugType = new BugType("This is a bug name",
              ^              ~~~~~~~~~~~~~~~~~~~~~~
```

This error happened because the `BugType` constructor method changed from one version to the other. If you have difficulty in figuring out how to adapt your code to the newer version, you need to have access to a change log, which is an important documentation that states code changes from a specific period. Luckily, for every open source project that uses a code-revision system, we can easily obtain it by querying the code revision server for the commit messages that affected a particular file. In the case of LLVM, you can even do this by using your browser through **ViewVC** at `http://llvm.org/viewvc`.

In this case, we are interested in looking at what changed in the header file that defines this constructor method. We look into the LLVM source tree and find it at `include/clang/StaticAnalyzer/Core/BugReporter/BugType.h`.

If you are using a text-mode editor, be sure to use a tool that helps you navigate in the LLVM source code. For instance, take a moment to look at how to use CTAGS in your editor. You will easily find each file in the LLVM source tree that defines the classes that you are interested in. If you are stubborn and want to live without CTAGS or any other tool that helps you navigate large C/C++ projects, (such as Visual Studio's IntelliSense or Xcode), you can always resort to a command such as `grep -re "keyword" *`, which is issued at the root folder of the project to list all files that contain the keyword. By using smart keywords, you can easily find definition files.

To look at the commit messages that affect this specific header file, we can access `http://llvm.org/viewvc/llvm-project/cfe/trunk/include/clang/StaticAnalyzer/Core/BugReporter/BugType.h?view=log`, which will print the log in our browser. Now, we see a particular revision that happened three months ago at the time of writing this book, when LLVM was being updated to v3.5:

```
Revision 201186 - (view) (download) (annotate) - [select for diffs]
Modified Tue Feb 11 15:49:21 2014 CST (3 months, 1 week ago) by alexfh
File length: 2618 byte(s)
Diff to previous 198686 (colored)
```

```
Expose the name of the checker producing each diagnostic message.

Summary: In clang-tidy we'd like to know the name of the checker
producing each diagnostic message. PathDiagnostic has BugType and
Category fields, which are both arbitrary human-readable strings, but we
need to know the exact name of the checker in the form that can be used
in the CheckersControlList option to enable/disable the specific checker.
This patch adds the CheckName field to the CheckerBase class, and sets it
in the CheckerManager::registerChecker() method, which gets them from the
CheckerRegistry.  Checkers that implement multiple checks have to store
the names of each check in the respective registerXXXChecker method.

Reviewers: jordan_rose, krememek  Reviewed By: jordan_rose  CC: cfe-
commits

Differential Revision: http://llvm-reviews.chandlerc.com/D2557
```

This commit message is very thorough and explains all the reasoning behind the change of the BugType constructor: previously, instantiating this object with two strings was not enough to know which checker discovered a specific bug. Therefore, you must now instantiate the object by passing an instance of your checker object, which will be stored in the BugType object and make it easy to discover which checker produces each bug.

Now, we change our code to conform to the following updated interface. We assume that this code runs as part of a function member of a Checker class, as is usually the case when implementing static analyzer checkers. Therefore, the this keyword should return a Checker object:

```
BugType *bugType = new BugType(this, "This is a bug name",
                               "This is a bug category name");
```

Concluding remarks

When you hear that the LLVM project is well documented, do not expect to find an English page that precisely describes all bits and pieces of the code. What this means is that when you rely on reading the code, the interfaces, the comments, and commit messages, you will be able to progress with your understanding about the LLVM project and get yourself updated with the latest changes. Do not forget to practice hacking into the source code to discover how things are done, which means that you need your CTAGS ready for exploration!

Summary

In this chapter, we presented you with a historical perspective of the design decisions used in the LLVM project and gave you an overview of the most important ones. We also showed you how to use the LLVM components in two different ways. First, by using the compiler driver, which is a high-level tool that performs the entire compilation for you in a single command. Second, by using separate LLVM standalone tools. Besides storing intermediary results on the disk, which slows down compilation, the tools allow us to interface with specific fragments of the LLVM libraries via the command line, giving us finer control over the compilation process. They are an excellent way to learn how LLVM works. We also showed you a few of the C++ coding styles used in LLVM and explained how you should face the LLVM code documentation and use the community to ask for help.

In the next chapter, we will present details about the Clang frontend implementation and its libraries.

4

The Frontend

The compiler frontend converts source code into the compiler's intermediate representation prior to target-specific code generation. Since programming languages have distinct syntax and semantic domains, frontends usually handle either a single language or a group of similar ones. Clang, for instance, handles C, C++, and objective-C source code inputs. In this chapter, we will cover the following topics:

- How to link programs with Clang libraries and use `libclang`
- Clang diagnostics and the Clang frontend stages
- Lexical, syntactical, and semantic analyses with `libclang` examples
- How to write a simplified compiler driver that uses the C++ Clang libraries

Introducing Clang

The Clang project is known as the official LLVM frontend for C, C++, and Objective-C. You can access the Clang official website at `http://clang.llvm.org`, and we cover Clang configuration, build, and install in *Chapter 1, Build and Install LLVM*.

Similar to the confusion over the name LLVM owing to its multiple meanings, Clang may also refer to up to three distinct entities:

1. The frontend (implemented in Clang libraries).
2. The compiler driver (implemented in the `clang` command and the Clang Driver library).
3. The actual compiler (implemented in the `clang -cc1` command). The compiler in `clang -cc1` is not implemented solely with Clang libraries, but also makes extensive use of LLVM libraries to implement the middle- and backends of the compiler, as well as the integrated assembler.

In this chapter, we focus on Clang libraries and the C-family frontend for LLVM.

To understand how the driver and compiler work, we start by analyzing the command line invocation for the `clang` compiler driver:

```
$ clang hello.c -o hello
```

After parsing the command-line arguments, the Clang driver invokes the internal compiler by spawning another instance of itself with the `-cc1` option. By using `-Xclang <option>` in the compiler driver, you can pass specific arguments to this tool, which, unlike the driver, has no obligation of mimicking the GCC command-line interface. For example, the `clang -cc1` tool has a special option to print the Clang Abstract Syntax Tree (AST). To activate it, you can use the following command structure:

```
$ clang -Xclang -ast-dump hello.c
```

You can also directly call `clang -cc1` instead of the driver:

```
$ clang -cc1 -ast-dump hello.c
```

However, remember that one of the tasks of the compiler driver is to initialize the call of the compiler with all the necessary parameters. Run the driver with the `-###` flag to see which parameters it uses to call the `clang -cc1` compiler. For example, if you call `clang -cc1` manually, you will also need to provide all the system headers' locations by yourself via the `-I` flag.

Frontend actions

An important aspect (and source of confusion) of the `clang -cc1` tool is that it implements not only the compiler frontend but also instantiates, by means of the LLVM libraries, all other LLVM components necessary to carry on the compilation up to the point where LLVM can. Thus, it implements an *almost* complete compiler. Typically, for x86 targets, `clang -cc1` stops at the object file frontier because the LLVM linker is still experimental and is not integrated. At this point, it relinquishes control back to the driver, which will call an external tool to link the project. The `-###` flag shows the list of programs called by the Clang driver and illustrates this:

```
$ clang hello.c -###
clang version 3.4 (tags/RELEASE_34/final 211335)
Target: i386-pc-linux-gnu
Thread model: posix
 "clang" "-cc1" (...parameters) "hello.c" "-o" "/tmp/hello-dddafc1.o"
 "/usr/bin/ld" (...parameters) "/tmp/hello-ddafc1.o" "-o" "hello"
```

We omitted the full list of parameters used by the driver. The first line shows that `clang -cc1` carries on the compilation from the C source file up to the object code emission. Afterwards, the last line shows that Clang still depends on the system linker to finish the compilation.

Internally, each invocation of `clang -cc1` is controlled by one main frontend action. The complete set of actions is defined in the source file `include/clang/Frontend/FrontendOptions.h`. The following table contains a few examples and describes different tasks that the `clang -cc1` tool may execute:

Action	Description
ASTView	Parse ASTs and view them in Graphviz
EmitBC	Emit an LLVM bitcode `.bc` file
EmitObj	Emit a target-specific `.o` file
FixIt	Parse and apply any fixits to the source
PluginAction	Run a plugin action
RunAnalysis	Run one or more source code analyses

The `-cc1` option triggers the execution of the `cc1_main` function (check the source code file `tools/driver/cc1_main.cpp` for details). For example, when indirectly calling `-cc1` via `clang hello.c -o hello`, this function initializes target-specific information, sets up the diagnostic infrastructure, and performs the `EmitObj` action. This action is implemented in `CodeGenAction`, a subclass of `FrontendAction`. This code will instantiate all Clang and LLVM components and orchestrate them to build the object file.

The existence of different frontend actions allows Clang to run the compilation pipeline for purposes other than compilation, such as static analysis. Still, depending on the target that you specify for `clang` via the `-target` command-line argument, it will load a different `ToolChain` object. This will change which tasks should be performed by `-cc1` by means of the execution of a different frontend action, which ones should be performed by external tools, and which external tools to use. For example, a given target may use the GNU assembler and the GNU linker to finish the compilation, while another may use the LLVM integrated assembler and the GNU linker. If you are in doubt about which external tools Clang is using for your target, you may always resort to the `-###` switch to print the driver commands. We discuss more about different targets in *Chapter 8, Cross-platform Compilation.*

Libraries

From this point on, we will focus on Clang as a set of libraries that implements a compiler frontend rather than the driver and compiler applications. In this sense, Clang is designed to be modular and is composed of several libraries. The libclang (http://clang.llvm.org/doxygen/group__CINDEX.html) is one of the most important interfaces for external Clang users and provides extensive frontend functionality through a C API. It includes several Clang libraries, which can also be used individually and linked together into your projects. A list of the most relevant libraries for this chapter follows:

- libclangLex: This library is used for preprocessing and lexical analysis, handling macros, tokens, and pragma constructions

- libclangAST: This library adds functionality to build, manipulate, and traverse Abstract Syntax Trees

- libclangParse: This library is used for parsing logic using the results from the lexical phase

- libclangSema: This library is used for semantic analysis, which provides actions for AST verification

- libclangCodeGen: This library handles LLVM IR code generation using target-specific information

- libclangAnalysis: This library contains the resources for static analysis

- libclangRewrite: This library allows support for code rewriting and providing an infrastructure to build code-refactoring tools (more details in *Chapter 10, Clang Tools with LibTooling*)

- libclangBasic: This library provides a set of utilities – memory allocation abstractions, source locations, and diagnostics, among others.

Using libclang

Throughout this chapter, we will explain parts of the Clang frontend and give you examples by using the libclang C interface. Even though it is not a C++ API that directly accesses the internal Clang classes, a big advantage of using libclang comes from its stability; since many clients rely on it, the Clang team designed it considering backwards compatibility with previous versions. However, you should feel free to use the regular C++ LLVM interfaces whenever you want, in the same way as when you used the regular C++ LLVM interface for reading bitcode function names in the example from *Chapter 3, Tools and Design*.

In your LLVM installation folder, in the `include` subfolder, check for the subfolder `clang-c`, that is, where the `libclang` C headers are located. To run the examples from this chapter, you will need to include the `Index.h` header, the main entry point of the Clang C interface. Originally, developers created this interface to help integrated development environments, such as Xcode, to navigate a C source file and produce quick code fixes, code completion, and indexing, which gave the name `Index.h` for the main header file. We will also illustrate how to use Clang with the C++ interface, but we will leave that for the end of the chapter.

Different from the example in *Chapter 3, Tools and Design*, where we used `llvm-config` to help us build the list of LLVM libraries to link with, we do not have such a tool for Clang libraries. To link against `libclang`, you can change the `Makefile` from *Chapter 3, Tools and Design*, to the following listing. In the same way as in the previous chapter, remember to manually insert the tab characters to allow the `Makefile` to work properly. Since this is a generic Makefile intended for all examples, notice that we used the `llvm-config --libs` flag without any argument, which returns the full list of LLVM libraries.

```
LLVM_CONFIG?=llvm-config

ifndef VERBOSE
QUIET:=@
endif

SRC_DIR?=$(PWD)
LDFLAGS+=$(shell $(LLVM_CONFIG) --ldflags)
COMMON_FLAGS=-Wall -Wextra
CXXFLAGS+=$(COMMON_FLAGS) $(shell $(LLVM_CONFIG) --cxxflags)
CPPFLAGS+=$(shell $(LLVM_CONFIG) --cppflags) -I$(SRC_DIR)

CLANGLIBS = \
   -Wl,--start-group\
   -lclang\
   -lclangFrontend\
   -lclangDriver\
   -lclangSerialization\
   -lclangParse\
   -lclangSema\
   -lclangAnalysis\
   -lclangEdit\
   -lclangAST\
   -lclangLex\
   -lclangBasic\
   -Wl,--end-group
```

```
LLVMLIBS=$(shell $(LLVM_CONFIG) --libs)

PROJECT=myproject
PROJECT_OBJECTS=project.o

default: $(PROJECT)

%.o : $(SRC_DIR)/%.cpp
    @echo Compiling $*.cpp
    $(QUIET)$(CXX) -c $(CPPFLAGS) $(CXXFLAGS) $<

$(PROJECT) : $(PROJECT_OBJECTS)
    @echo Linking $@
    $(QUIET)$(CXX) -o $@ $(CXXFLAGS) $(LDFLAGS) $^ $(CLANGLIBS)
$(LLVMLIBS)

clean::
    $(QUIET)rm -f $(PROJECT) $(PROJECT_OBJECTS)
```

If you are using dynamic libraries and have installed your LLVM in a nonstandard location, remember that it is not enough to configure your PATH environment variable, but your dynamic linker and loader also need to know where the LLVM shared libraries are located. Otherwise, when you run your projects, it will not find the requested shared libraries, if it is linked with any. Configure the library path in the following way:

```
$ export
  LD_LIBRARY_PATH=$(LD_LIBRARY_PATH):/your/llvm/installation/lib
```

Substitute /your/llvm/installation with the full path to where you installed LLVM in *Chapter 1, Build and Install LLVM*.

Understanding Clang diagnostics

Diagnostics are an essential part of the interaction of a compiler with its users. They are the messages that a compiler gives to the user to signal errors, warnings, or suggestions. Clang features very good compilation diagnostics with pretty printing and C++ error messages with improved readability. Internally, Clang divides diagnostics as per kind: each different frontend phase has a distinct kind and its own diagnostics set. For example, it defines diagnostics from the parsing phase in the file include/clang/Basic/DiagnosticParseKinds.td. Clang also classifies diagnostics according to the severity of the reported issue: NOTE, WARNING, EXTENSION, EXTWARN, and ERROR. It maps these severities as Diagnostic::Level enum.

You can introduce new diagnostics by adding new TableGen definitions in the files `include/clang/Basic/Diagnostic*Kinds.td` and by writing code that is able to check the desired condition, emitting the diagnostic accordingly. All `.td` files in the LLVM source code are written using the TableGen language.

TableGen is an LLVM tool used in the LLVM build system to generate C++ code for parts of the compiler that can be synthesized in a mechanical fashion. The idea started with LLVM backends, which has plenty of code that can be generated based on descriptions of the target machine and now is present throughout the entire LLVM project as well. TableGen is designed to represent information in a straightforward way: through records. For example, `DiagnosticParseKinds.td` contains definitions of records that represent diagnostics:

```
def err_invalid_sign_spec : Error<"'%0'
    cannot be signed or unsigned">;
def err_invalid_short_spec : Error<"'short %0' is invalid">;
```

In this example, `def` is the TableGen keyword to define a new record. Which fields must be conveyed in these records depends entirely on which TableGen backend will be used, and there is a specific backend for each type of generated file. The output of TableGen is always a `.inc` file that is included in another LLVM source file. In this case, TableGen needs to generate `DiagnosticsParseKinds.inc` with macro definitions explaining each diagnostic.

The `err_invalid_sign_spec` and `err_invalid_short_spec` are record identifiers, while `Error` is a TableGen class. Notice that the semantics is slightly different from C++ and does not correspond exactly to C++ entities. Each TableGen class, different from C++, is a record template defining fields of information that other records can inherit. However, like C++, TableGen also allows for a hierarchy of classes.

The template-like syntax is used to specify parameters for the definition based on the `Error` class, which receives a single string as a parameter. All definitions deriving from this class will be diagnostics of type ERROR and the specific message is encoded in the class parameter, for example, `"'short %0' is invalid"`. While the TableGen syntax is quite simple, it can easily confuse readers due to the high amount of information encoded in TableGen entries. Refer to `http://llvm.org/docs/TableGen/LangRef.html` when in doubt.

Reading diagnostics

We now present a C++ example that uses the `libclang` C interface to read and dump all the diagnostics produced by Clang when reading a given source file.

```cpp
extern "C" {
#include "clang-c/Index.h"
}
#include "llvm/Support/CommandLine.h"
#include <iostream>

using namespace llvm;

static cl::opt<std::string>
FileName(cl::Positional, cl::desc("Input file"), cl::Required);

int main(int argc, char** argv)
{
  cl::ParseCommandLineOptions(argc, argv, "Diagnostics Example");
  CXindex index = clang_createIndex(0, 0);
  const char *args[] = {
    "-I/usr/include",
    "-I."
  };
  CXTranslationUnit translationUnit = clang_parseTranslationUnit
    (index, FileName.c_str(), args, 2, NULL, 0,
    CXTranslationUnit_None);
  unsigned diagnosticCount = clang_getNumDiagnostics(translationUnit);
  for (unsigned i = 0; i < diagnosticCount; ++i) {
    CXDiagnostic diagnostic = clang_getDiagnostic(translationUnit, i);
    CXString category = clang_getDiagnosticCategoryText(diagnostic);
    CXString message = clang_getDiagnosticSpelling(diagnostic);
    unsigned severity = clang_getDiagnosticSeverity(diagnostic);
    CXSourceLocation loc = clang_getDiagnosticLocation(diagnostic);
    CXString fName;
    unsigned line = 0, col = 0;
    clang_getPresumedLocation(loc, &fName, &line, &col);
    std::cout << "Severity: " << severity << " File: "
            << clang_getCString(fName) << " Line: "
            << line << " Col: " << col << " Category: \""
            << clang_getCString(category) << "\" Message: "
            << clang_getCString(message) << std::endl;
```

```
        clang_disposeString(fName);
        clang_disposeString(message);
        clang_disposeString(category);
        clang_disposeDiagnostic(diagnostic);
    }
    clang_disposeTranslationUnit(translationUnit);
    clang_disposeIndex(index);
    return 0;
}
```

Before including the `libclang` C header file in this C++ source, we use the `extern "C"` environment to allow the C++ compiler to compile this header as C code.

We repeat the use of the `cl` namespace, from the previous chapter, to help us parse the command-line arguments of our program. We then use several functions from the `libclang` interface (`http://clang.llvm.org/doxygen/group__CINDEX.html`). First, we create an index, the top-level context structure used by `libclang`, by calling the `clang_createIndex()` function. It receives two integer-encoded Booleans as parameters: the first is `true` if we want to exclude declarations from **precompiled headers (PCH)** and the second is `true` if we want to display diagnostics. We set both to `false` (zero) because we want to display the diagnostics by ourselves.

Next, we ask Clang to parse a translation unit via `clang_parseTranslationUnit()` (see `http://clang.llvm.org/doxygen/group__CINDEX__TRANSLATION__UNIT.html`). It receives as an argument the name of the source file to parse, which we retrieve from the `FileName` global. This variable corresponds to the string parameter used to launch our tool. We also need to specify a set of two arguments defining where to find include files — you are free to adjust these arguments to suit your system.

> The tough part of implementing our own Clang tool is the lack of the driver's parameter-guessing abilities, which supplies the adequate parameters to process source files in your system. You would not have to worry about this if you were creating a Clang plugin, for example. To solve this issue, you can use a compile commands database, discussed in *Chapter 10, Clang Tools with LibTooling*, which gives the exact set of parameters used to process each input source file you want to analyze. In this case, we can generate the database with CMake. However, in our example, we provide these arguments ourselves.

After parsing and putting all the information in the CXTranslationUnit C data structure, we implement a loop that iterates through all diagnostics generated by Clang and dump them to the screen. To do this, we first use clang_getNumDiagnostics() to retrieve the number of diagnostics generated when parsing this file and determine the bounds of the loop (see http://clang.llvm.org/doxygen/group__CINDEX__DIAG.html). Second, for each loop iteration, we use clang_getDiagnostic() to retrieve the current diagnostic, clang_getDiagnosticCategoryText() to retrieve a string describing the type of this diagnostic, clang_getDiagnosticSpelling() to retrieve the message to display to the user, and clang_getDiagnosticLocation() to retrieve the exact code location where it occurred. We also use clang_getDiagnosticSeverity() to retrieve the enum member that represents the severity of this diagnostic (NOTE, WARNING, EXTENSION, EXTWARN, or ERROR), but we convert it to an unsigned value and print it as a number for simplicity.

Since this is a C interface that lacks the C++ string class, when dealing with strings, the functions usually return a special CXString object that requires you to call clang_getCString() to access the internal char pointer to print it and clang_disposeString() to later delete it.

Remember that your input source file may include other files, requiring the diagnostic engine to also record the filename besides line and column. The triple attributes set of file, line, and column allows you to locate which part of the code is being referred. A special object, CXSourceLocation, represents this triple set. To translate this to filename, line, and column number, you must use the clang_getPresumedLocation() function with CXString and int as by-reference parameters that will be filled accordingly.

After we are done, we delete our objects by means of clang_disposeDiagnostic(), clang_disposeTranslationUnit(), and clang_disposeIndex().

Let's test it with the file hello.c as follows:

```
int main() {
  printf("hello, world!\n")
}
```

There are two mistakes in this C source file: it lacks the inclusion of the correct header file and is missing a semicolon. Let us build our project and then run it to see which diagnostics Clang will provide us:

```
$ make
$ ./myproject hello.c
```

```
Severity: 2 File: hello.c Line: 2 Col: 9 Category: "Semantic Issue"
Message: implicitly declaring library function 'printf' with type 'int
(const char *, ...)'
Severity: 3 File: hello.c Line: 2 Col: 24 Category: "Parse Issue"
Message: expected ';' after expression
```

We see that these two diagnostics are produced by different phases of the frontend, semantic and parser (syntactical). We will explore each phase in the next sections.

Learning the frontend phases with Clang

To transform a source code program into LLVM IR bitcode, there are a few intermediate steps the source code must pass through. The following figure illustrates all of them, and they are the topics of this section:

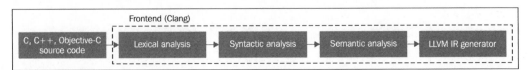

Lexical analysis

The very first frontend step processes the source code's textual input by splitting language constructs into a set of words and tokens, removing characters such as comments, white spaces, and tabs. Each word or token must be part of the language subset, and reserved language keywords are converted into internal compiler representations. The reserved words are defined in include/clang/Basic/ TokenKinds.def. For example, see the definition of the while reserved word and the < symbol, two known C/C++ tokens, highlighted in the TokenKinds.def excerpt here:

```
TOK(identifier)          // abcde123
// C++11 String Literals.
TOK(utf32_string_literal) // U"foo"
...
PUNCTUATOR(r_paren,              ")")
PUNCTUATOR(l_brace,              "{")
PUNCTUATOR(r_brace,              "}")
PUNCTUATOR(starequal,            "*=")
PUNCTUATOR(plus,                 "+")
PUNCTUATOR(plusplus,             "++")
PUNCTUATOR(arrow,                "->")
```

```
PUNCTUATOR(minusminus,          "--")
PUNCTUATOR(less,                "<")
...
KEYWORD(float                   , KEYALL)
KEYWORD(goto                    , KEYALL)
KEYWORD(inline                  , KEYC99|KEYCXX|KEYGNU)
KEYWORD(int                     , KEYALL)
KEYWORD(return                  , KEYALL)
KEYWORD(short                   , KEYALL)
KEYWORD(while                   , KEYALL)
```

The definitions on this file populates the `tok` namespace. In this way, whenever the compiler needs to check for the presence of reserved words after lexical processing, they can be accessed using this namespace. For instance, the {, <, `goto`, and `while` constructs are accessed by the `enum` elements `tok::l_brace`, `tok::less`, `tok::kw_goto`, and `tok::kw_while`.

Consider the following C code in `min.c`:

```c
int min(int a, int b) {
  if (a < b)
    return a;
  return b;
}
```

Each token contains an instance of the `SourceLocation` class, which is used to hold a location within a program source code. Remember that you worked with the C counterpart `CXSourceLocation`, but both refer to the same data. We can dump the tokens and their `SourceLocation` results from lexical analysis by using the following `clang -cc1` command line:

```
$ clang -cc1 -dump-tokens min.c
```

For instance, the output of the highlighted `if` statement is:

```
if 'if'   [StartOfLine] [LeadingSpace] Loc=<min.c:2:3>
l_paren '('   [LeadingSpace] Loc=<min.c:2:6>
identifier 'a'   Loc=<min.c:2:7>
less '<'   [LeadingSpace] Loc=<min.c:2:9>
identifier 'b'   [LeadingSpace] Loc=<min.c:2:11>
r_paren ')'   Loc=<min.c:2:12>
return 'return'   [StartOfLine] [LeadingSpace] Loc=<min.c:3:5>
identifier 'a'   [LeadingSpace] Loc=<min.c:3:12>
semi ';'   Loc=<min.c:3:13>
```

Note that each language construct is prefixed by its type: `r_paren` for), `less` for <, `identifier` for strings not matching reserved words, and so on.

Exercising lexical errors

Let's consider the source code `lex-err.c`:

```
int a = 08000;
```

The error in the preceding code comes from the wrong spelling of octal constants: a constant in octal must not have digits above 7. This triggers a lexical error, as shown here:

```
$ clang -c lex.c
lex.c:1:10: error: invalid digit '8' in octal constant
int a = 08000;
         ^
1 error generated.
```

Now, let's run this same example with the project we crafted in the diagnostics section:

```
$ ./myproject lex.c
Severity: 3 File: lex.c Line: 1 Col: 10 Category: "Lexical or
Preprocessor Issue" Message: invalid digit '8' in octal constant
```

We see that our project identifies it as being a lexer issue, which is what we were expecting.

Writing libclang code that uses the lexer

We show here an example that uses `libclang` to tokenize, using the LLVM lexer, the stream of the first 60 characters of a source code file:

```
extern "C" {
#include "clang-c/Index.h"
}
#include "llvm/Support/CommandLine.h"
#include <iostream>

using namespace llvm;

static cl::opt<std::string>
FileName(cl::Positional ,cl::desc("Input file"),
         cl::Required);

int main(int argc, char** argv)
{
```

```
  cl::ParseCommandLineOptions(argc, argv, "My tokenizer\n");
  CXIndex index = clang_createIndex(0,0);
  const char *args[] = {
    "-I/usr/include",
    "-I."
  };
  CXTranslationUnit translationUnit = clang_
parseTranslationUnit(index, FileName.c_str(),
                                                              args,
2, NULL, 0, CXTranslationUnit_None);
  CXFile file = clang_getFile(translationUnit, FileName.c_str());
  CXSourceLocation loc_start = clang_getLocationForOffset
(translationUnit, file, 0);
  CXSourceLocation loc_end = clang_getLocationForOffset
(translationUnit, file, 60);
  CXSourceRange range = clang_getRange(loc_start, loc_end);
  unsigned numTokens = 0;
  CXToken *tokens = NULL;
  clang_tokenize (translationUnit, range, &tokens, &numTokens);
  for (unsigned i = 0; i < numTokens; ++i) {
    enum CXTokenKind kind = clang_getTokenKind(tokens[i]);
    CXString name = clang_getTokenSpelling(translationUnit,
tokens[i]);
    switch (kind) {
    case CXToken_Punctuation:
      std::cout << "PUNCTUATION(" << clang_getCString(name) << ") ";
      break;
    case CXToken_Keyword:
      std::cout << "KEYWORD(" << clang_getCString(name) << ") ";
      break;
    case CXToken_Identifier:
      std::cout << "IDENTIFIER(" << clang_getCString(name) << ") ";
      break;
    case CXToken_Literal:
      std::cout << "COMMENT(" << clang_getCString(name) << ") ";
      break;
    default:
      std::cout << "UNKNOWN(" << clang_getCString(name) << ") ";
      break;
    }
    clang_disposeString(name);
  }
```

```
      std::cout << std::endl;
      clang_disposeTokens (translationUnit, tokens, numTokens);
      clang_disposeTranslationUnit(translationUnit);
      return 0;
  }
```

To build this code, we start with the same boilerplate code to initialize the command-line parameters and calls to `clang_createIndex()`/`clang_parseTranslationUnit()` seen in the previous example. The difference comes next. Instead of querying for diagnostics, we prepare the arguments of the `clang_tokenize()` function, which will run the Clang lexer and return a stream of tokens for us. To do this, we must build a `CXSourceRange` object specifying the range of source code (begin and end) where we want to run the lexer. This object can be composed of two `CXSourceLocation` objects, one for the start and the other for the end. We create them with `clang_getLocationForOffset()`, which returns a `CXSourceLocation` for a specific offset from a `CXFile` obtained using `clang_getFile()`.

To build `CXSourceRange` out of two `CXSourceLocation`, we use the `clang_getRange()` function. With it, we are ready to call `clang_tokenize()` with two important parameters passed by reference: a pointer to `CXToken`, which will store the token stream, and an `unsigned` type that will return the number of tokens in the stream. With this number, we build a loop structure and iterate through all tokens.

For each token, we get its kind via `clang_getTokenKind()` and also the fragment of code that corresponds to it via `clang_getTokenSpelling()`. We then use a `switch` construct to print a different text depending on the token kind, as well as the fragment of code corresponding to this token. You can see the result in the example that follows.

We will use the following input to this project:

```
  #include <stdio.h>
  int main() {
    printf("hello, world!");
  }
```

After running our tokenizer, we obtain the following output:

```
PUNCTUATION(#) IDENTIFIER(include) PUNCTUATION(<) IDENTIFIER(stdio)
  PUNCTUATION(.) IDENTIFIER(h) PUNCTUATION(>) KEYWORD(int)
  IDENTIFIER(main) PUNCTUATION(() PUNCTUATION()) PUNCTUATION({)
  IDENTIFIER(printf) PUNCTUATION(() COMMENT("hello, world!")
  PUNCTUATION()) PUNCTUATION(;) PUNCTUATION(})
```

Preprocessing

The C/C++ preprocessor acts before any semantic analysis takes place and is responsible for expanding macros, including files, or skipping parts of the code by means of the preprocessor directives, which start with #. The preprocessor works in a tight dependence with the lexer, and they interact with each other continuously. Since it works early in the frontend, before the semantic analysis tries to extract any meaning from your code, you can do bizarre things with macros, such as change a function declaration with macro expansions. Notice that this allows us to promote a radical change in the syntax of the language. If it pleases you, you can even code like this:

```
⊖ ○ ○                          c File.c — Edited
      ◀  ▶   c File.c › No Selection
      #include "SDL.h"

      #define $ for(0=9
      #define CX M+=(T%3+2*!(!T*t-6))
      #define x ,A=4*!T,O=t,W=h=T<37u(Q?p:D(A+3),D(A),D(A+1)[i]+D(A+2)*g+):K(t),U=V=K(a),o
        ?U=h,W=V:V,
      #define C B*-~L
      #define Z short
      #define y a(Z)Y[++0]
      #define B ),a--||(
      #define _ ),e--||(

      #define V(I,D,E)(0=a(I)h[r])&&!(A=(D)(V={1[E+L]<<16)+*i)/0,A-(I)A)?1[E+L]=V-0*(*E=A
        ):H(0)
      #define i(B,M)B(o){return M;}
      #define R(O,M,_){S=L?a(I Z)0:0,N=L?a(I Z)0 M(f=a(I Z)_):(0 M(f=a(I n)_)}}
      #define T(_)R(r[u(10,L=4,--}],=,_}
      #define u(a,r,T)16*i[a]+(I Z)(T i[r])
      #define a(_)*(_*)&
      #define L(_)M(W,_,U)

      #define M(S,F,T)R(r[S],F,r[T])
      #define A(_){i[L=4]+=2,R(_,=,r[u(10,4,-2+)])}}
      #define c(R,T)(1[u=19,L+T]=(N=a(R)h[r]*(R)*T)>>16,*i=N,G(F(N-(R)N)))
      #define h(_){1&{L?a(Z)_:_}>>C-1)
      #define I unsigned
      #define n char
      #define e(_)v(F{40[L(_##=40[E]+),E]&N==5|_ N<_(int)S))

      I n t,e,l[80186],*E,m,u,L,a,T,o,r[1<<21],X,*Y,b,Q=0,R=0;I Z*i,M,p,q=3;I*localtime(),
        f,S,kb=0,h,W,U,c,g,d,V,A;N,0,P=983040,j[5];SDL_Surface*k=0;i(K,P+(L?2*o:2+o+o/4&
        7))i(D,r[a(I)E[259+4*o]+0])}i(w,i[o]+=~(-2*47[E])*~L}i(v,(z{(f^=S^N)&16},G(N-S&&1
        &(40[E]^f>C-1))}}J(){V=61442;$;0--;}V+=40[E+0]<<D(25);}i(H,(46[u=76,J(),T(V),T
        (9[i]),T(M),M(P+18,=,4*o+2),R(M,=,r[4*o]),E]=0))s(o){$;0--;}40[E+0]=1&&1<<D(25)&
        o;}i(BP,(*i+=262*o*z{F({*E&15)>9|42[E])),*E&=15})i(SP,(w(7),R&&--1[i]&&o?R++,Q&&
        Q++,M--:0))DX(){$,0*=27840;0--;}0[([I*)k->pixels]=-!!(1<<7-0%8&r[0/2880*90+0%720/
        8+(88+952[l]/128*4+0/720%4<<13)]);SDL_Flip(k);}main(BX,nE)n**nE;{9[i=E=r+P]=P>>4
        ;$;q;)j[--q]=*++nE?open(*nE,32898):0;read(2[a(I)*i=*j?lseek(*j,0,2)>>9:0,j],E+(M
        =256),P};$;Y=r+16*9[i]+M,Y-r;Q|R||kb&46[E]&&KB}--64[T=1[0=32[L=(X=*Y&7)&1,o=X/2&
        1,l]=0,t=(c=y)&7,a=c/8&7,Y]>>6,g=~-T?y:(n)y,d=BX=y,l],!T*t-6&&T-2?T-17d=g:0:(d=y
        ),Q&&Q--,R&&R--x(O=*Y,0=u=D(51),e=D(8),m=D(14)_ 0=*Y/2&7,M+=(n)c*(L^(D(m)[E]|D
        (22)[E]|D(23)[E]^D(24)[E]))_ L=*Y&8,R(K(X)[r],=,c)_ L=e+=3,o=0,a=X x a=m _ T(X[i
```

This is the code of Adrian Cable, one of the winners of the 22nd **International Obfuscated C Code Contest (IOCCC)**, which, for our amusement, allows us to reproduce the contestants' source code under the Creative Commons Attribution-ShareAlike 3.0 license. It is an 8086 emulator. If you want to learn how to deobfuscate this code, read the *ClangFormat* section in *Chapter 10, Clang Tools with LibTooling*. To expand the macros, you can also run the compiler driver with the -E option, which will only run the preprocessor and then interrupt the compilation, without any further analyses.

The fact that the preprocessor allows us to transform our source code into unintelligible pieces of text is a warning message to use macros with moderation. Good advice aside, the token stream is preprocessed by the lexer to handle preprocessor directives such as macros and pragmas. The preprocessor uses a symbol table to hold the defined macros and, whenever a macro instantiation occurs, the tokens saved in the symbol table replace the current ones.

If you have Clang extra tools installed (*Chapter 2, External Projects*), you will have pp-trace available at your command prompt. This tool exposes the preprocessor activity.

Consider the following example of pp.c:

```
#define EXIT_SUCCESS 0
int main() {
  return EXIT_SUCCESS;
}
```

If we run the compiler driver with the -E option, we will see the following output:

```
$ clang -E pp.c -o pp2.c && cat pp2.c
...
int main() {
  return 0;
}
```

If we run the pp-trace tool, we will see the following output:

```
$ pp-trace pp.c
...
- Callback: MacroDefined
  MacroNameTok: EXIT_SUCCESS
  MacroDirective: MD_Define
- Callback: MacroExpands
  MacroNameTok: EXIT_SUCCESS
  MacroDirective: MD_Define
  Range: ["/examples/pp.c:3:10", "/examples/pp.c:3:10"]
  Args: (null)
- Callback: EndOfMainFile
```

We omitted the long list of built-in macros that pp-trace dumps before starting the preprocessing of the actual file. In fact, this list can be very useful if you want to know which macros your compiler driver defines by default when building your sources. The pp-trace tool is implemented by overriding preprocessor callbacks, which means that you can implement functionality in your tool that happens each time the preprocessor manifests itself. In our example, it acted twice: to read the EXIT_SUCCESS macro definition and later by expanding it in line 3. The pp-trace tool also prints the parameters that your tool will receive if it implements the MacroDefined callback. The tool is also quite small and, if you wish to implement preprocessor callbacks, reading its source is a good first step.

Syntactic analysis

After the lexical analysis tokenizes the source code, the syntactic analysis takes place and groups together the tokens to form expressions, statements, and function bodies, among others. It checks whether a group of tokens makes sense together with respect to their physical layout, but the meaning of this code is not yet analyzed, in the same way as the syntactic analysis of the English language is not worried with what your text says, but whether the sentences are correct or not. This analysis is also called parsing, which receives a stream of tokens as input and outputs an Abstract Syntax Tree (AST).

Understanding Clang AST nodes

An AST node represents declarations, statements, and types. Hence, there are three core classes to represent AST nodes: Decl, Stmt, and Type. Each C or C++ language construct is represented in Clang by a C++ class, which must inherit from one of these core classes. The following diagram illustrates part of the class hierarchy. For example, the IfStmt class (representing a complete if statement body) directly inherits from the Stmt class. On the other hand, the FunctionDecl and VarDecl classes—used to hold function and variable declarations or definitions—inherits from more than one class and only reaches Decl indirectly.

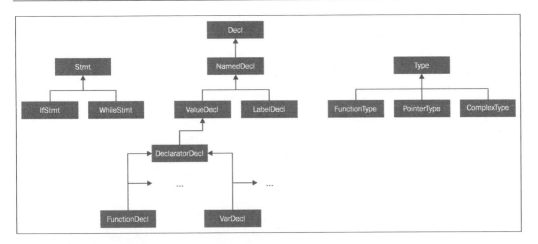

To view the full diagram, navigate the doxygen pages for each class. For example, for `Stmt`, visit `http://clang.llvm.org/doxygen/classclang_1_1Stmt.html`; click on the subclasses to discover their immediate derived classes.

The top-level AST node is `TranslationUnitDecl`. It is the root of all other AST nodes and represents an entire translation unit. Using the `min.c` source code as an example, remember that we can dump its AST nodes with the `-ast-dump` switch:

```
$ clang -fsyntax-only -Xclang -ast-dump min.c
TranslationUnitDecl …
|-TypedefDecl … __int128_t '__int128'
|-TypedefDecl … __uint128_t 'unsigned __int128'
|-TypedefDecl … __builtin_va_list '__va_list_tag [1]'
`-FunctionDecl … <min.c:1:1, line:5:1> min 'int (int, int)'
  |-ParmVarDecl … <line:1:7, col:11> a 'int'
  |-ParmVarDecl … <col:14, col:18> b 'int'
  `-CompoundStmt … <col:21, line:5:1>

. . .
```

Note the presence of the top-level translation unit declaration, `TranslationUnitDecl`, and the `min` function declaration, represented by `FunctionDecl`. The `CompoundStmt` declaration contains other statements and expressions. It is illustrated in a graphical view of the ASTs in the following diagram, obtained with the following command:

```
$ clang -fsyntax-only -Xclang -ast-view min.c
```

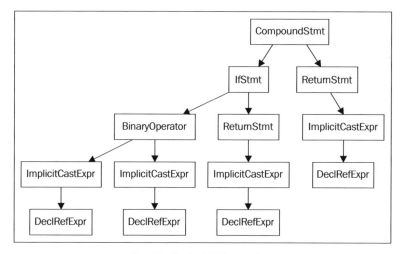

Function body AST from min.c

The AST node `CompoundStmt` contains the `if` and `return` statements, `IfStmt` and `ReturnStmt`. Every use of a and b generates an `ImplicitCastExpr` expression to the `int` type, as required by C standards.

The `ASTContext` class contains the whole AST for a translation unit. Any AST node can be reached by starting at the top-level `TranslationUnitDecl` instance through the `ASTContext::getTranslationUnitDecl()` interface.

Understanding the parser actions with a debugger

The set of tokens generated in the lexer phase are processed and consumed during the parsing, generating an AST node whenever a group of required tokens are seen together. For example, whenever the token `tok::kw_if` is found, the function `ParseIfStatement` is called, consuming all the tokens that are part of an `if` body, while generating all the necessary children AST nodes and an `IfStmt` root for them. See the following snippet from the file `lib/Parse/ParseStmt.cpp` (line 212):

```
...
   case tok::kw_if: // C99 6.8.4.1: if-statement
     return ParseIfStatement(TrailingElseLoc);
   case tok::kw_switch:  // C99 6.8.4.2: switch-statement
     return ParseSwitchStatement(TrailingElseLoc);
...
```

We can better understand how Clang reaches the `ParseIfStatement` method in `min.c` by dumping the call `backtrace` through a debugger:

```
$ gdb clang
$ b ParseStmt.cpp:213
$ r -cc1 -fsyntax-only min.c
...
213      return ParseIfStatement(TrailingElseLoc);
(gdb) backtrace
#0   clang::Parser::ParseStatementOrDeclarationAfterAttributes
#1   clang::Parser::ParseStatementOrDeclaration
#2   clang::Parser::ParseCompoundStatementBody
#3   clang::Parser::ParseFunctionStatementBody
#4   clang::Parser::ParseFunctionDefinition
#5   clang::Parser::ParseDeclGroup
#6   clang::Parser::ParseDeclOrFunctionDefInternal
#7   clang::Parser::ParseDeclarationOrFunctionDefinition
#8   clang::Parser::ParseExternalDeclaration
#9   clang::Parser::ParseTopLevelDecl
#10  clang::ParseAST
#11  clang::ASTFrontendAction::ExecuteAction
#12  clang::FrontendAction::Execute
#13  clang::CompilerInstance::ExecuteAction
#14  clang::ExecuteCompilerInvocation
#15  cc1_main
#16  main
```

The `ParseAST()` function starts the translation unit parsing by reading the top-level declarations through `Parser::ParseTopLevelDecl()`. Then, it processes all subsequent AST nodes and consumes the associated tokens, attaching each new AST node to its parent AST node. The execution only returns to `ParseAST()` when the parser has consumed all tokens. Afterwards, a user of the parser can access the AST nodes from the top-level `TranslationUnitDecl`.

Exercising a parser error

Consider the following `for` statement in `parse.c`:

```
void func() {
  int n;
  for (n = 0 n < 10; n++);
}
```

The error in the code comes from a missing semicolon after `n = 0`. Here is the diagnostic message that Clang outputs during compilation:

```
$ clang -c parse.c
parse.c:3:14: error: expected ';' in 'for' statement specifier
  for (n = 0 n < 10; n++);
             ^
1 error generated.
```

Now let's run our diagnostics project:

```
$ ./myproject parse.c
Severity: 3 File: parse.c Line: 3 Col: 14 Category: "Parse Issue"
Message: expected ';' in 'for' statement specifier
```

Since all tokens in this example are correct, the lexer finishes successfully and produces no diagnostics. However, when grouping the tokens together to see if they make sense when building the AST, the parser notices that the `for` structure is missing a semicolon. In this case, our diagnostic category is *Parse Issue*.

Writing code that traverses the Clang AST

The `libclang` interface allows you to walk the Clang AST by means of a cursor object, which points to a node of the current AST. To get the top-level cursor, you can use the `clang_getTranslationUnitCursor()` function. In this example, we will write a tool that outputs the name of all C functions or C++ methods contained in a C or C++ source file:

```
extern "C" {
#include "clang-c/Index.h"
}
#include "llvm/Support/CommandLine.h"
#include <iostream>

using namespace llvm;
static cl::opt<std::string>
```

```
FileName(cl::Positional, cl::desc("Input file"), cl::Required);

enum CXChildVisitResult visitNode (CXCursor cursor, CXCursor parent,
                                   CXClientData client_data) {
  if (clang_getCursorKind(cursor) == CXCursor_CXXMethod ||
      clang_getCursorKind(cursor) == CXCursor_FunctionDecl) {
    CXString name = clang_getCursorSpelling(cursor);
    CXSourceLocation loc = clang_getCursorLocation(cursor);
    CXString fName;
    unsigned line = 0, col = 0;
    clang_getPresumedLocation(loc, &fName, &line, &col);
    std::cout << clang_getCString(fname) << ":"
              << line << ":"<< col << " declares "
              << clang_getCString(name) << std::endl;
    return CXChildVisit_Continue;
  }
  return CXChildVisit_Recurse;
}

int main(int argc, char** argv)
{
  cl::ParseCommandLineOptions(argc, argv, "AST Traversal Example");
  CXindex index = clang_createIndex(0, 0);
  const char *args[] = {
    "-I/usr/include",
    "-I."
  };
  CXTranslationUnit translationUnit = clang_parseTranslationUnit
    (index, FileName.c_str(), args, 2, NULL, 0,
    CXTranslationUnit_None);
  CXCursor cur = clang_getTranslationUnitCursor(translationUnit);
  clang_visitChildren(cur, visitNode, NULL);
  clang_disposeTranslationUnit(translationUnit);
  clang_disposeIndex(index);
  return 0;
}
```

The most important function in this example is `clang_visitChildren()`, which will recursively visit all child nodes of the cursor passed as a parameter, calling a callback function on each visit. We start our code by defining this callback function, which we name `visitNode()`. This function must return a value that is a member of the `CXChildVisitResult` enum, which gives us only three possibilities:

- Return CXChildVisit_Recurse when we want clang_visitChildren() to continue its AST traversal by visiting the children of the node we are currently in

- Return CXChildVisit_Continue when we want it to continue visiting, but skip the children of the current node we are in

- Return CXChildVisit_Break when we are satisfied and want clang_visitChildren() to no longer visit any more nodes

Our callback function receives three parameters: the cursor that represents the AST node we are currently visiting; another cursor that represents the parent of this node; and a CXClientData object, which is a typedef to a void pointer. This pointer allows you to pass any data structure whose state you want to maintain across your callback calls. This can be useful if you want to build an analysis.

While this code structure can be used to build analyses, if you feel that your analysis is more complex and needs a structure like **control flow graph (CFG)**, do not use cursors or libclang—it is more adequate to implement your analysis as a Clang plugin that directly uses the Clang C++ API to create a CFG out of the AST (see http://clang.llvm.org/docs/ClangPlugins.html and the CFG::buildCFG method). It is usually much more difficult to build analyses directly out of the AST than with a CFG. You should also look at *Chapter 9, The Clang Static Analyzer*, which explains how to build powerful Clang static analyses.

In our example, we ignore the client_data and parent parameters. We simply ask whether the current cursor is pointing to a C function declaration (CXCursor_FunctionDecl) or C++ method (CXCursor_CXXMethod) by means of the clang_getCursorKind() function. When we are sure that we are visiting the right cursor, we use a couple of functions to extract information from the cursor: clang_getCursorSpelling() to get the code fragment corresponding to this AST node and clang_getCursorLocation() to get the CXSourceLocation object associated with it. Afterwards, we print them in a similar way to what we used when we implemented the diagnostics project and finish the function by returning CXChildVisit_Continue. We use this option because we are sure there are no nested function declarations, and it does not make sense to continue the traversal by visiting the children of this cursor.

If the cursor is not what we are expecting, we simply continue the AST recursive traversal by returning CXChildVisit_Recurse.

With the `visitNode` callback function implemented, the remainder of the code is quite simple. We use the initial boilerplate code to parse command-line parameters and to parse the input file. Afterwards, we call `visitChildren()` with the top-level cursor and our callback. The last parameter is the client data that we do not use and set to NULL.

We will run this project in the following input file:

```
#include <stdio.h>
int main() {
  printf("hello, world!");
}
```

The output is as follows:

```
$ ./myproject hello.c

hello.c:2:5 declares main
```

This project also prints a tremendous amount of information by pointing out each line of the `stdio.h` header file that declares a function, but we omitted it here for brevity.

Serializing the AST with precompiled headers

We can serialize the Clang AST and save it in a PCH extension file. This feature speeds up compilation time by avoiding processing the same header files every time they are included in the source files of a project. When choosing to use PCH files, all header files are precompiled into a single PCH file and, during the compilation of a translation unit, information from the precompiled headers are lazily fetched.

To generate PCH files for C, for example, you should use the same syntax seen in GCC for precompiled header generation, which relies on the `-x c-header` flag, as seen here:

```
$ clang -x c-header myheader.h -o myheader.h.pch
```

To use your new PCH file, you should employ the `-include` flag as follows:

```
$ clang -include myheader.h myproject.c -o myproject
```

Semantic analysis

The semantic analysis ensures that the code does not violate the language type system by means of a symbol table. This table stores, among other things, mappings between identifiers (symbols) and their respective types. An intuitive approach for type checking is to perform it after parsing by traversing the AST while gathering information about types from the symbol table.

Clang, on the other hand, does not traverse the AST after parsing. Instead, it performs type checking on the fly, together with AST node generation. Let us go back to the `min.c` parsing example. In this case, the `ParseIfStatement` function invokes the semantic action `ActOnIfStmt` to perform semantic checking for the `if` statement, emitting diagnostics accordingly. In `lib/Parse/ParseStmt.cpp`, line 1082, we can observe the transfer of control to allow the semantic analysis to happen:

```
...
return Actions.ActOnIfStmt(IfLoc, FullCondExp, ...);
...
```

To aid the semantic analysis, the `DeclContext` base class contains references from the first to the last `Decl` node for each scope. This eases the semantic analysis because, to perform symbol lookup of name references and check both the symbol type and whether the symbol actually exists, the semantic analysis engine can find the symbol declarations by looking into AST nodes derived from `DeclContext`. Examples of such AST nodes are `TranslationUnitDecl`, `FunctionDecl`, and `LabelDecl`.

Using the `min.c` example, you can use Clang to dump declaration contexts as follows:

```
$ clang -fsyntax-only -Xclang -print-decl-contexts min.c
[translation unit] 0x7faf320288f0
        <typedef> __int128_t
        <typedef> __uint128_t
        <typedef> __builtin_va_list
        [function] f(a, b)
            <parameter> a
            <parameter> b
```

Note that only declarations inside `TranslationUnitDecl` and `FunctionDecl` appear on the results, since they are the only nodes that derive from `DeclContext`.

Exercising a semantic error

The following `sema.c` file contains two definitions using the identifier `a`:

```
int a[4];
int a[5];
```

The preceding error comes from the use of the same name for two distinct variables, which have different types. This error must be caught during semantic analysis, and Clang reports the problem accordingly:

```
$ clang -c sema.c
sema.c:3:5: error: redefinition of 'a' with a different type
int a[5];
    ^
sema.c:2:5: note: previous definition is here
int a[4];
    ^
1 error generated.
```

If we run our diagnostics project, we get the following output:

```
$ ./myproject sema.c
Severity: 3 File: sema.c Line: 2 Col: 5 Category: "Semantic Issue"
Message: redefinition of 'a' with a different type: 'int [5]' vs 'int
[4]'
```

Generating the LLVM IR code

After the combined parsing and semantic analysis, the `ParseAST` function invokes the method `HandleTranslationUnit` to trigger any client that is interested in consuming the final AST. If the compiler driver used the `CodeGenAction` frontend action, this client will be `BackendConsumer`, which will traverse the AST while generating LLVM IR that implements the exact same behavior that is represented in the tree. The translation to LLVM IR starts at the top-level declaration, `TranslationUnitDecl`.

If we continue with our `min.c` example, the `if` statement is converted to LLVM IR in the file `lib/CodeGen/CGStmt.cpp`, line 130, by the function `EmitIfStmt`. Using the debugger backtrace, we can see the calling path from the `ParseAST` function to `EmitIfStmt`:

```
$ gdb clang
(gdb) b CGStmt.cpp:130
(gdb) r -cc1 -emit-obj min.c
...
130    case Stmt::IfStmtClass: EmitIfStmt(cast<IfStmt>(*S));
break;
(gdb) backtrace
#0   clang::CodeGen::CodeGenFunction::EmitStmt
#1   clang::CodeGen::CodeGenFunction::EmitCompoundStmtWithoutScope
#2   clang::CodeGen::CodeGenFunction::EmitFunctionBody
#3   clang::CodeGen::CodeGenFunction::GenerateCode
#4   clang::CodeGen::CodeGenModule::EmitGlobalFunctionDefinition
#5   clang::CodeGen::CodeGenModule::EmitGlobalDefinition
#6   clang::CodeGen::CodeGenModule::EmitGlobal
#7   clang::CodeGen::CodeGenModule::EmitTopLevelDecl
#8   (anonymous namespace)::CodeGeneratorImpl::HandleTopLevelDecl
#9   clang::BackendConsumer::HandleTopLevelDecl
#10  clang::ParseAST
```

As the code is translated to LLVM IR, we finish our frontend tour. If we proceed with the regular pipeline, next, LLVM IR libraries are used to optimize the LLVM IR code and the backend performs target-code generation. If you want to implement a frontend for your own language, the *Kaleidoscope* frontend tutorial is an excellent read at `http://llvm.org/docs/tutorial`. In the next section, we will present how to write a simplified Clang driver that will put to use the same frontend stages discussed in our tour.

Putting it together

In this example, we will take the opportunity to introduce you to the Clang C++ interface and will not rely on the `libclang` C interface anymore. We will create a program that will apply the lexer, the parser, and the semantic analysis to input files by using the internal Clang C++ classes; thus, we will have the opportunity to do the work of a simple `FrontendAction` object. You can continue using the Makefile that we presented at the beginning of this chapter. However, you may be interested in turning off the `-Wall -Wextra` compiler flags because it will generate a large volume of warnings for Clang headers regarding unused parameters.

The source code for this example is reproduced as follows:

```
#include "llvm/ADT/IntrusiveRefCntPtr.h"
#include "llvm/Support/CommandLine.h"
#include "llvm/Support/Host.h"
#include "clang/AST/ASTContext.h"
#include "clang/AST/ASTConsumer.h"
#include "clang/Basic/Diagnostic.h"
#include "clang/Basic/DiagnosticOptions.h"
#include "clang/Basic/FileManager.h"
#include "clang/Basic/SourceManager.h"
#include "clang/Basic/LangOptions.h"
#include "clang/Basic/TargetInfo.h"
#include "clang/Basic/TargetOptions.h"
#include "clang/Frontend/ASTConsumers.h"
#include "clang/Frontend/CompilerInstance.h"
#include "clang/Frontend/TextDiagnosticPrinter.h"
#include "clang/Lex/Preprocessor.h"
#include "clang/Parse/Parser.h"
#include "clang/Parse/ParseAST.h"
#include <iostream>

using namespace llvm;
using namespace clang;

static cl::opt<std::string>
FileName(cl::Positional, cl::desc("Input file"), cl::Required);

int main(int argc, char **argv)
{
    cl::ParseCommandLineOptions(argc, argv, "My simple front end\n");
    CompilerInstance CI;
    DiagnosticOptions diagnosticOptions;
    CI.createDiagnostics();

    IntrusiveRefCntPtr<TargetOptions> PTO(new TargetOptions());
    PTO->Triple = sys::getDefaultTargetTriple();
    TargetInfo *PTI = TargetInfo::CreateTargetInfo(CI.
getDiagnostics(), PTO.getPtr());
    CI.setTarget(PTI);
```

```
CI.createFileManager();
CI.createSourceManager(CI.getFileManager());
CI.createPreprocessor();
CI.getPreprocessorOpts().UsePredefines = false;
ASTConsumer *astConsumer = CreateASTPrinter(NULL, "");
CI.setASTConsumer(astConsumer);

CI.createASTContext();
CI.createSema(TU_Complete, NULL);
const FileEntry *pFile = CI.getFileManager().getFile(FileName);
if (!pFile) {
    std::cerr << "File not found: " << FileName << std::endl;
    return 1;
}
CI.getSourceManager().createMainFileID(pFile);
CI.getDiagnosticsClient().BeginSourceFile(CI.getLangOpts(), 0);
ParseAST(CI.getSema());
// Print AST statistics
CI.getASTContext().PrintStats();
CI.getASTContext().Idents.PrintStats();

return 0;
}
```

The preceding code runs the lexer, the parser, and the semantic analysis over the input source file that you specify via the command line. It finishes by printing the parsed source code and AST statistics. This code performs the following steps:

1. The CompilerInstance class manages the entire infrastructure to handle compilation (see http://clang.llvm.org/doxygen/ classclang_1_1CompilerInstance.html). The first step instantiates this class and saves it to CI.

2. Usually, the clang -cc1 tool will instantiate a specific FrontendAction, which will perform all the steps covered here. Since we want to expose these steps to you, we will not use FrontendAction; instead, we will configure CompilerInstance ourselves. We use a CompilerInstance method to create the diagnostic engine and set the current target by getting a target triple from the system.

3. We now instantiate three new resources: a file manager, a source manager, and the preprocessor. The first is necessary to read source files, while the second is responsible for managing SourceLocation instances used in the lexer and parser.

4. We create an `ASTConsumer` reference and push it to `CI`. This allows a frontend client to consume the final AST (after parsing and semantic analysis) in its own way. For example, if we wanted this driver to generate LLVM IR code, we would have to provide a specific code generation `ASTConsumer` instance (called `BackendConsumer`), which is precisely how `CodeGenAction` sets up `ASTConsumer` of its `CompilerInstance`. In this example, we include the header `ASTConsumers.h`, which provides assorted consumers for us to experiment with, and we use a consumer that merely prints the AST to the console. We create it by means of the `CreateASTPrinter()` call. If you are interested, take some time to implement your own `ASTConsumer` subclass to perform any kind of frontend analysis you are interested in (start by looking at `lib/Frontend/ASTConsumers.cpp`, which has some implementation examples).

5. We create a new `ASTContext`, used by the parser, and `Sema`, used by the semantic analysis, and push them to our `CI` object. We also initialize the diagnostics consumer (in this case, our standard consumer will also merely print the diagnostics to the screen).

6. We call `ParseAST` to perform the lexical and syntactic analysis, which will call our `ASTConsumer` afterwards by means of the `HandleTranslationUnit` function call. Clang will also print the diagnostics and interrupt the pipeline if there is a serious error in any frontend phase.

7. We print AST statistics to standard output.

Let's test our simple frontend tool in the following file:

```
int main() {
    char *msg = "Hello, world!\n";
    write(1, msg, 14);
    return 0;
}
```

The output generated is as follows:

```
$ ./myproject test.c
int main() {
    char *msg = "Hello, world!\n";
    write(1, msg, 14);
    return 0;
}
```

```
*** AST Context Stats:
  39 types total.
    31 Builtin types
    3 Complex types
    3 Pointer types
    1 ConstantArray types
    1 FunctionNoProto types
Total bytes = 544
0/0 implicit default constructors created
0/0 implicit copy constructors created
0/0 implicit copy assignment operators created
0/0 implicit destructors created

Number of memory regions: 1
Bytes used: 1594
Bytes allocated: 4096
Bytes wastes: 2502 (includes alignment, etc)
```

Summary

In this chapter, we described the Clang frontend. We explained the distinction between the Clang frontend libraries, the compiler driver, and the actual compiler in the `clang -cc1` tool. We also talked about diagnostics and introduced a small `libclang` program to dump them. Next, we went touring through all steps of the frontend: lexer, parser, semantic analysis, and code generation by showing how Clang implements these stages. Finally, we finished the chapter with an example of how to write a simple compiler driver that activates all frontend stages. If you are interested in reading more about the AST, a good community document is at `http://clang.llvm.org/docs/IntroductionToTheClangAST.html`. If you are interested in reading more about the Clang design, you should check out `http://clang.llvm.org/docs/InternalsManual.html` before diving into the actual source code.

In the next chapter, we will move on to the next step of the compilation pipeline: the LLVM intermediate representation.

5

The LLVM Intermediate Representation

The LLVM **Intermediate Representation (IR)** is the backbone that connects frontends and backends, allowing LLVM to parse multiple source languages and generate code to multiple targets. Frontends produce the IR, while backends consume it. The IR is also the point where the majority of LLVM target-independent optimizations takes place. In this chapter, we will cover the following topics:

- The characteristics of the LLVM IR
- The LLVM IR language syntax
- How to write a tool that generates the LLVM IR
- The LLVM IR pass structure
- How to write your own IR pass

Overview

The choice of the compiler IR is a very important decision. It determines how much information the optimizations will have to make the code run faster. On one hand, a very high-level IR allows optimizers to extract the original source code intent with ease. On the other hand, a low-level IR allows the compiler to generate code tuned for a particular hardware more easily. The more information you have about the target machine, the more opportunities you have to explore machine idiosyncrasies. Moreover, the task at lower levels must be done with care. As the compiler translates the program to a representation that is closer to machine instructions, it becomes increasingly difficult to map program fragments to the original source code. Furthermore, if the compiler design is exaggerated using a representation that represents a specific target machine very closely, it becomes awkward to generate code for other machines that have different constructs.

This design trade-off has led to different choices among compilers. Some compilers, for instance, do not support code generation for multiple targets and focus on only one machine architecture. This enables them to use specialized IRs throughout their entire pipeline that make the compiler efficient with respect to a single architecture, which is the case of the Intel C++ Compiler (`icc`). However, writing compilers that generate code for a single architecture is an expensive solution if you aim to support multiple targets. In these cases, it is unfeasible to write a different compiler for each architecture, and it is best to design a single compiler that performs well on a variety of targets, which is the goal of compilers such as GCC and LLVM.

For these projects, called *retargetable compilers*, there are substantially more challenges to coordinate the code generation for multiple targets. The key to minimizing the effort to build a retargetable compiler lies in using a common IR, the point where different backends share the same understanding about the source program to translate it to a divergent set of machines. Using a common IR, it is possible to share a set of target-independent optimizations among multiple backends, but this puts pressure on the designer to raise the level of the common IR to not overrepresent a single machine. Since working at higher levels precludes the compiler from exploring target-specific trickery, a good retargetable compiler also employs other IRs to perform optimizations at different, lower levels.

The LLVM project started with an IR that operated at a lower level than the Java bytecode, thus, the initial acronym was Low Level Virtual Machine. The idea was to explore low-level optimization opportunities and employ link-time optimizations. The link-time optimizations were made possible by writing the IR to disk, as in a bytecode. The bytecode allows the user to amalgamate multiple modules in the same file and then apply interprocedural optimizations. In this way, the optimizations will act on multiple compilation units as if they were in the same module.

In *Chapter 3, Tools and Design*, we explained that LLVM, nowadays, is neither a Java competitor nor a virtual machine, and it has other intermediate representations to achieve efficiency. For example, besides the LLVM IR, which is the common IR where target-independent optimizations work, each backend may apply target-dependent optimizations when the program is represented with the `MachineFunction` and `MachineInstr` classes. These classes represent the program using target-machine instructions.

On the other hand, the `Function` and `Instruction` classes are, by far, the most important ones because they represent the common IR that is shared across multiple targets. This intermediate representation is mostly target-independent (but not entirely) and the *official* LLVM intermediate representation. To avoid confusion, while LLVM has other levels to represent a program, which technically makes them IRs as well, we do not refer to them as LLVM IRs; however, we reserve this name for the official, common intermediate representation by the `Instruction` class, among others. This terminology is also adopted by the LLVM documentation.

The LLVM project started as a set of tools that orbit around the LLVM IR, which justifies the maturity of the optimizers and the number of optimizers that act at this level. This IR has three equivalent forms:

- An in-memory representation (the `Instruction` class, among others)
- An on-disk representation that is encoded in a space-efficient form (the bitcode files)
- An on-disk representation in a human-readable text form (the LLVM assembly files)

LLVM provides tools and libraries that allow you to manipulate and handle the IR in all forms. Hence, these tools can transform the IR back and forth, from memory to disk as well as apply optimizations, as illustrated in the following diagram:

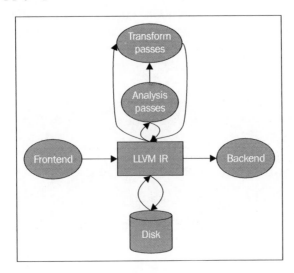

Understanding the LLVM IR target dependency

The LLVM IR is designed to be as target-independent as possible, but it still conveys some target-specific aspects. Most people blame the C/C++ language for its inherent, target-dependent nature. To understand this, consider that when you use standard C headers in a Linux system, for instance, your program implicitly imports some header files from the `bits` Linux headers folder. This folder contains target-dependent header files, including macro definitions that constrain some entities to have a particular type that matches what the **syscalls** of this kernel-machine expect. Afterwards, when the frontend parses your source code, it needs to also use different sizes for `int`, for example, depending on the intended target machine where this code will run.

Therefore, both library headers and C types are already target-dependent, which makes it challenging to generate an IR that can later be translated to a different target. If you consider only the target-dependent, C standard library headers, the parsed AST for a given compilation unit is already target-dependent, even before the translation to the LLVM IR. Furthermore, the frontend generates IR code using type sizes, calling conventions, and special library calls that match the ones defined by each target ABI. Still, the LLVM IR is quite versatile and is able to cope with distinct targets in an abstract way.

Exercising basic tools to manipulate the IR formats

We mention that the LLVM IR can be stored on disk in two formats: bitcode and assembly text. We will now learn how to use them. Consider the sum.c source code:

```
int sum(int a, int b) {
  return a+b;
}
```

To make Clang generate the bitcode, you can use the following command:

```
$ clang sum.c -emit-llvm -c -o sum.bc
```

To generate the assembly representation, you can use the following command:

```
$ clang sum.c -emit-llvm -S -c -o sum.ll
```

You can also assemble the LLVM IR assembly text, which will create a bitcode:

```
$ llvm-as sum.ll -o sum.bc
```

To convert from bitcode to IR assembly, which is the opposite, you can use the disassembler:

```
$ llvm-dis sum.bc -o sum.ll
```

The llvm-extract tool allows the extraction of IR functions, globals, and also the deletion of globals from the IR module. For instance, extract the sum function from sum.bc with the following command:

```
$ llvm-extract -func=sum sum.bc -o sum-fn.bc
```

Nothing changes between sum.bc and sum-fn.bc in this particular example since sum is already the sole function in this module.

Introducing the LLVM IR language syntax

Observe the LLVM IR assembly file, sum.ll:

```
target datalayout = "e-p:64:64:64-i1:8:8-i8:8:8-i16:16:16-
    i32:32:32-i64:64:64-f32:32:32-f64:64:64-v64:64:64-v128:128:128-
    a0:0:64-s0:64:64-f80:128:128-n8:16:32:64-S128"
target triple = "x86_64-apple-macosx10.7.0"

define i32 @sum(i32 %a, i32 %b) #0 {
entry:
  %a.addr = alloca i32, align 4
  %b.addr = alloca i32, align 4
  store i32 %a, i32* %a.addr, align 4
  store i32 %b, i32* %b.addr, align 4
  %0 = load i32* %a.addr, align 4
  %1 = load i32* %b.addr, align 4
  %add = add nsw i32 %0, %1
  ret i32 %add
}

attributes #0 = { nounwind ssp uwtable ... }
```

The contents of an entire LLVM file, either assembly or bitcode, are said to define an LLVM module. The module is the LLVM IR top-level data structure. Each module contains a sequence of functions, which contains a sequence of basic blocks that contain a sequence of instructions. The module also contains peripheral entities to support this model, such as global variables, the target data layout, and external function prototypes as well as data structure declarations.

LLVM local values are the analogs of the registers in the assembly language and can have any name that starts with the % symbol. Thus, %add = add nsw i32 %0, %1 will add the local value %0 to %1 and put the result in the new local value, %add. You are free to give any name to the values, but if you are short on creativity, you can just use numbers. In this short example, we can already see how LLVM expresses its fundamental properties:

- It uses the **Static Single Assignment (SSA)** form. Note that there is no value that is reassigned; each value has only a single assignment that defines it. Each use of a value can immediately be traced back to the sole instruction responsible for its definition. This has an immense value to simplify optimizations, owing to the trivial use-def chains that the SSA form creates, that is, the list of definitions that reaches a user. If LLVM had not used the SSA form, we would need to run a separate data flow analysis to compute the use-def chains, which are mandatory for classical optimizations such as constant propagation and common subexpression elimination.

- Code is organized as three-address instructions. Data processing instructions have two source operands and place the result in a distinct destination operand.

- It has an infinite number of registers. Note how LLVM local values can be any name that starts with the `%` symbol, including numbers that start at zero, such as `%0`, `%1`, and so on, that have no restriction on the maximum number of distinct values.

The `target datalayout` construct contains information about endianness and type sizes for `target triple` that is described in `target host`. Some optimizations depend on knowing the specific data layout of the target to transform the code correctly. Observe how the layout declaration is done:

```
target datalayout = "e-p:64:64:64-i1:8:8-i8:8:8-i16:16:16-
    i32:32:32-i64:64:64-f32:32:32-f64:64:64-v64:64:64-v128:128:128-
    a0:0:64-s0:64:64-f80:128:128-n8:16:32:64-S128"
target triple = "x86_64-apple-macosx10.7.0"
```

We can extract the following facts from this string:

- The target is an `x86_64` processor with `macOSX 10.7.0`. It is a little-endian target, which is denoted by the first letter in the layout (a lowercase `e`). Big-endian targets need to use an uppercase `E`.

- The information provided about types is in the format `type:<size>:<abi>:<preferred>`. In the preceding example, `p:64:64:64` represents a pointer that is 64 bits wide in `size`, with the `abi` and `preferred` alignments set to the 64-bit boundary. The ABI alignment specifies the minimum required alignment for a type, while the preferred alignment specifies a potentially larger value, if this will be beneficial. The 32-bit integer types `i32:32:32` are 32 bits wide in `size`, 32-bit `abi` and `preferred` alignment, and so on.

The function declaration closely follows the C syntax:

```
define i32 @sum(i32 %a, i32 %b) #0 {
```

This function returns a value of the type `i32` and has two `i32` arguments, `%a` and `%b`. Local identifiers always need the `%` prefix, whereas global identifiers use `@`. LLVM supports a wide range of types, but the most important ones are the following:

- Arbitrary-sized integers in the `iN` form; common examples are `i32`, `i64`, and `i128`.

- Floating-point types, such as the 32-bit single precision `float` and 64-bit double precision `double`.

- Vectors types in the format `<<# elements> x <elementtype>>`. A vector with four `i32` elements is written as `<4 x i32>`.

The `#0` tag in the function declaration maps to a set of function attributes, also very similar to the ones used in C/C++ functions and methods. The set of attributes is defined at the end of the file:

```
attributes #0 = { nounwind ssp uwtable "less-precise-
   fpmad"="false" "no-frame-pointer-elim"="true" "no-frame-pointer-
      elim-non-leaf"="true" "no-infs-fp-math"="false" "no-nans-fp-
         math"="false" "unsafe-fp-math"="false" "use-soft-
            float"="false" }
```

For instance, `nounwind` marks a function or method as not throwing exceptions, and `ssp` tells the code generator to use a *stack smash protector* in an attempt to increase the security of this code against attacks.

The function body is explicitly divided into **basic blocks (BBs)**, and a label is used to start a new BB. A label relates to a basic block in the same way that a value identifier relates to an instruction. If a label declaration is omitted, the LLVM assembler automatically generates one using its own naming scheme. A basic block is a sequence of instructions with a single entry point at its first instruction, and a single exit point at its last instruction. In this way, when the code jumps to the label that corresponds to a basic block, we know that it will execute all of the instructions in this basic block until the last instruction, which will change the control flow by jumping to another basic block. Basic blocks and their associated labels need to adhere to the following conditions:

- Each BB needs to end with a terminator instruction, one that jumps to other BBs or returns from the function

- The first BB, called the entry BB, is special in an LLVM function and must not be the target of any branch instructions

Our LLVM file, `sum.11`, has only one BB because it has no jumps, loops, or calls. The function start is marked with the `entry` label, and it ends with the return instruction, `ret`:

```
entry:
   %a.addr = alloca i32, align 4
   %b.addr = alloca i32, align 4
   store i32 %a, i32* %a.addr, align 4
   store i32 %b, i32* %b.addr, align 4
   %0 = load i32* %a.addr, align 4
   %1 = load i32* %b.addr, align 4
   %add = add nsw i32 %0, %1
   ret i32 %add
```

The `alloca` instruction reserves space on the stack frame of the current function. The amount of space is determined by element type size, and it respects a specified alignment. The first instruction, `%a.addr = alloca i32, align 4`, allocates a 4-byte stack element, which respects a 4-byte alignment. A pointer to the stack element is stored in the local identifier, `%a.addr`. The `alloca` instruction is commonly used to represent local (automatic) variables.

The `%a` and `%b` arguments are stored in the stack locations `%a.addr` and `%b.addr` by means of `store` instructions. The values are loaded back from the same memory locations by `load` instructions, and they are used in the addition, `%add = add nsw i32 %0, %1`. Finally, the addition result, `%add`, is returned by the function. The `nsw` flag specifies that this add operation has "no signed wrap", which indicates instructions that are known to have no overflow, allowing for some optimizations. If you are interested in the history behind the `nsw` flag, a worthwhile read is the LLVMdev post at `http://lists.cs.uiuc.edu/pipermail/llvmdev/2011-November/045730.html` by Dan Gohman.

In fact, the `load` and `store` instructions are redundant, and the function arguments can be used directly in the `add` instruction. Clang uses `-O0` (no optimizations) by default, and the unnecessary loads and stores are not removed. If we compile with `-O1` instead, the outcome is a much simpler code, which is reproduced here:

```
define i32 @sum(i32 %a, i32 %b) ... {
entry:
  %add = add nsw i32 %b, %a
  ret i32 %add
}
...
```

Using the LLVM assembly directly is very handy when writing small examples to test target backends and as a means to learn basic LLVM concepts. However, a library is the recommended interface for frontend writers to build the LLVM IR, which is the subject of our next section. You can find a complete reference to the LLVM IR assembly syntax at `http://llvm.org/docs/LangRef.html`.

Introducing the LLVM IR in-memory model

The in-memory representation closely models the LLVM language syntax that we just presented. The header files for the C++ classes that represent the IR are located at `include/llvm/IR`. The following is a list of the most important classes:

- The `Module` class aggregates all of the data used in the entire translation unit, which is a synonym for "module" in LLVM terminology. It declares the `Module::iterator` typedef as an easy way to iterate across the functions inside this module. You can obtain these iterators via the `begin()` and `end()` methods. View its full interface at `http://llvm.org/docs/doxygen/html/classllvm_1_1Module.html`.

- The `Function` class contains all objects related to a function definition or declaration. In the case of a declaration (use the `isDeclaration()` method to check whether it is a declaration), it contains only the function prototype. In both cases, it contains a list of the function parameters accessible via the `getArgumentList()` method or the pair of `arg_begin()` and `arg_end()`. You can iterate through them using the `Function::arg_iterator` typedef. If your `Function` object represents a function definition, and you iterate through its contents via the `for (Function::iterator i = function.begin(), e = function.end(); i != e; ++i)` idiom, you will iterate across its basic blocks. View its full interface at `http://llvm.org/docs/doxygen/html/classllvm_1_1Function.html`.

- The `BasicBlock` class encapsulates a sequence of LLVM instructions, accessible via the `begin()`/`end()` idiom. You can directly access its last instruction using the `getTerminator()` method, and you also have a few helper methods to navigate the CFG, such as accessing predecessor basic blocks via `getSinglePredecessor()`, when the basic block has a single predecessor. However, if it does not have a single predecessor, you need to work out the list of predecessors yourself, which is also not difficult if you iterate through basic blocks and check the target of their terminator instructions. View its full interface at `http://llvm.org/docs/doxygen/html/classllvm_1_1BasicBlock.html`.

- The `Instruction` class represents an atom of computation in the LLVM IR, a single instruction. It has some methods to access high-level predicates, such as `isAssociative()`, `isCommutative()`, `isIdempotent()`, or `isTerminator()`, but its exact functionality can be retrieved with `getOpcode()`, which returns a member of the `llvm::Instruction` enumeration, which represents the LLVM IR opcodes. You can access its operands via the `op_begin()` and `op_end()` pair of methods, which are inherited from the `User` superclass that we will present shortly. View its full interface at `http://llvm.org/docs/doxygen/html/classllvm_1_1Instruction.html`.

We have still not presented the most powerful aspect of the LLVM IR (enabled by the SSA form): the `Value` and `User` interfaces; these allow you to easily navigate the use-def and def-use chains. In the LLVM in-memory IR, a class that inherits from `Value` means that it defines a result that can be used by others, whereas a subclass of `User` means that this entity uses one or more `Value` interfaces. `Function` and `Instruction` are subclasses of both `Value` and `User`, while `BasicBlock` is a subclass of just `Value`. To understand this, let's analyze these two classes in depth:

- The `Value` class defines the `use_begin()` and `use_end()` methods to allow you to iterate through `User`s, offering an easy way to access its def-use chain. For every `Value` class, you can also access its name through the `getName()` method. This models the fact that any LLVM value can have a distinct identifier associated with it. For example, `%add1` can identify the result of an add instruction, `BB1` can identify a basic block, and `myfunc` can identify a function. `Value` also has a powerful method called `replaceAllUsesWith(Value *)`, which navigates through all of the users of this value and replaces it with some other value. This is a good example of how the SSA form allows you to easily substitute instructions and write fast optimizations. You can view the full interface at `http://llvm.org/docs/doxygen/html/classllvm_1_1Value.html`.

- The `User` class has the `op_begin()` and `op_end()` methods that allows you to quickly access all of the `Value` interfaces that it uses. Note that this represents the use-def chain. You can also use a helper method called `replaceUsesOfWith(Value *From, Value *To)` to replace any of its used values. You can view the full interface at `http://llvm.org/docs/doxygen/html/classllvm_1_1User.html`.

Writing a custom LLVM IR generator

It is possible to use the LLVM IR generator API to programmatically build the IR for `sum.ll` (created at the `-O0` optimization level, that is, without optimizations). In this section, you will see how to do it step by step. First, take a look at which header files are needed:

- `#include <llvm/ADT/SmallVector.h>`: This is used to make the `SmallVector<>` template available, a data structure to aid us in building efficient vectors when the number of elements is not large. Check `http://llvm.org/docs/ProgrammersManual.html` for help on LLVM data structures.

- `#include <llvm/Analysis/Verifier.h>`: The verifier pass is an important analysis that checks whether your LLVM module is well formed with respect to the IR rules.

- `#include <llvm/IR/BasicBlock.h>`: This is the header file that declares the `BasicBlock` class, an important IR entity that we already presented.

- `#include <llvm/IR/CallingConv.h>`: This header file defines the set of ABI rules used in function calls, such as where to store function arguments.

- `#include <llvm/IR/Function.h>`: This header file declares the `Function` class, which is an IR entity.

- `#include <llvm/IR/Instructions.h>`: This header file declares all of the subclasses of the `Instruction` class, a fundamental data structure of the IR.

- `#include <llvm/IR/LLVMContext.h>`: This header file stores the global scope data of the LLVM library, which allows multithread implementations to work using different contexts in each thread.

- `#include <llvm/IR/Module.h>`: This header file declares the `Module` class, the top-level entity in the IR hierarchy.

- `#include <llvm/Bitcode/ReaderWriter.h>`: This header file contains code to allow us to both read/write LLVM bitcode files.

- `#include <llvm/Support/ToolOutputFile.h>`: This header file declares a helper class used to write an output file.

In this example, we also import the symbols from the `llvm` namespace:

```
using namespace llvm;
```

Now, it is time to write the code in separate steps:

1. The first code we will write is to define a new helper function called `makeLLVMModule`, which returns a pointer to our `Module` instance, the top-level IR entity that contains all the other IR objects:

```
Module *makeLLVMModule() {
  Module *mod = new Module("sum.ll", getGlobalContext());
  mod->setDataLayout("e-p:64:64:64-i1:8:8-i8:8:8-i16:16:16-
    i32:32:32-i64:64:64-f32:32:32-f64:64:64-v64:64:64-
      v128:128:128-a0:0:64-s0:64:64-f80:128:128-
        n8:16:32:64-S128");
  mod->setTargetTriple("x86_64-apple-macosx10.7.0");
```

If we put the triple and data layout objects into our module, we enable optimizations that depend on this information, but it needs to match the data layout and triple strings used in the LLVM backend. However, you can leave these out of your module if you do not care about layout-dependent optimizations and intend to specify which target to use in the backend in an explicit way. To create a module, we get the current LLVM context from getGlobalContext() and define the name of the module. We chose to use the name of the file that we used as a model, sum.ll, but you can choose any other module name. The context is an instance of the LLVMContext class, which must be used in order to guarantee thread safety as multithreaded IR generation must be done with one context per thread. The setDataLayout() and setTargetTriple() functions allow us to set the strings that define the data layout and target triple of our module.

2. To declare our sum function, we first define the function signature:

```
SmallVector<Type*, 2> FuncTyArgs;
FuncTyArgs.push_back(IntegerType::get(mod->getContext(),
    32));
FuncTyArgs.push_back(IntegerType::get(mod->getContext(),
    32));
FunctionType *FuncTy = FunctionType::get(
    /*Result=*/ IntegerType::get(mod->getContext(), 32),
    /*Params=*/ FuncTyArgs, /*isVarArg=*/ false);
```

Our FunctionType object specifies a function that returns a 32-bit integer type, has no variable arguments, and has two 32-bit integer arguments.

3. We create a function using the Function::Create() static method — passing the function type FuncTy created previously, the linkage type, and the module instance. The GlobalValue::ExternalLinkage enumeration member means that the function can be referred from other modules (translation units):

```
Function *funcSum = Function::Create(
    /*Type=*/ FuncTy,
    /*Linkage=*/ GlobalValue::ExternalLinkage,
    /*Name=*/ "sum", mod);
funcSum->setCallingConv(CallingConv::C);
```

4. Next, we need to store the Value pointers of the arguments to be able to use them later. To do this, we use an iterator of function arguments. The int32_a and int32_b function arguments point to the first and second arguments, respectively. We also set the names of each argument, which is optional because LLVM can provide temporary names:

```
Function::arg_iterator args = funcSum->arg_begin();
Value *int32_a = args++;
int32_a->setName("a");
```

```
Value *int32_b = args++;
int32_b->setName("b");
```

5. To start the function body, we create the first basic block with the label (or value name) `entry` and store a pointer for it in `labelEntry`. We need to pass a reference to the function that this basic block will reside in:

```
BasicBlock *labelEntry = BasicBlock::Create(mod-
    >getContext(),  "entry", funcSum, 0);
```

6. The `entry` basic block is now ready to be filled with instructions. We add two `alloca` instructions to the basic block, creating 32-bit stack elements with a 4-byte alignment. In the constructor method for the instruction, we need to pass a reference to the basic block that it will reside in. By default, new instructions are inserted at the end of the basic block, as follows:

```
// Block entry (label_entry)
AllocaInst *ptrA = new AllocaInst(IntegerType::get(mod-
    >getContext(), 32), "a.addr", labelEntry);
ptrA->setAlignment(4);
AllocaInst *ptrB = new AllocaInst(IntegerType::get(mod-
    >getContext(), 32), "b.addr", labelEntry);
ptrB->setAlignment(4);
```

Alternatively, you can use a helper template class called `IRBuilder<>` to build IR instructions (see http://llvm.org/docs/doxygen/html/classllvm_1_1IRBuilder.html). However, we chose not to use it to be able to present you with the original interface. If you want to use it, you just need to include the `llvm/IR/IRBuilder.h` header file, instantiate it with an LLVM context object, and call the `SetInsertPoint()` method to define where you want to place your new instructions. Afterwards, just invoke any instruction-creating method such as `CreateAlloca()`.

7. We store the `int32_a` and `int32_b` function arguments into the stack locations using the pointers returned by the `alloca` instructions, `ptrA` and `ptrB`. Although the store instructions are referenced in the following code by `st0` and `st1`, these pointers are never used in this example since store instructions have no results. The third `StoreInst` argument specifies whether this is a volatile store, which is `false` in this example:

```
StoreInst *st0 = new StoreInst(int32_a, ptrA, false,
    labelEntry);
st0->setAlignment(4);
StoreInst *st1 = new StoreInst(int32_b, ptrB, false,
    labelEntry);
st1->setAlignment(4);
```

8. We also create nonvolatile load instructions, loading the values back from the stack location in `ld0` and `ld1`. These values are then placed as arguments for the `add` instruction, and the addition result, `addRes`, is set as the return value from the `sum` function. Next, the `makeLLVMModule` function returns the LLVM IR module with the `sum` function that we just created:

```
LoadInst *ld0 = new LoadInst(ptrA, "", false,
  labelEntry);
ld0->setAlignment(4);
LoadInst *ld1 = new LoadInst(ptrB, "", false,
  labelEntry);
ld1->setAlignment(4);
BinaryOperator *addRes =
  BinaryOperator::Create(Instruction::Add, ld0, ld1,
    "add", labelEntry);
ReturnInst::Create(mod->getContext(), addRes,
  labelEntry);

return mod;
}
```

There are plenty of variations for each instruction creation function. Consult the header files in `include/llvm/IR` or the doxygen documentation to check for all possible options.

9. For the IR generator program to be a standalone tool, it needs a `main()` function. In this `main()` function, we create a module by calling `makeLLVMModule` and validate the IR construction using `verifyModule()`. The `PrintMessageAction` enumeration member sets the error messages to `stderr` if the validation fails. Finally, the module bitcode is written to disk by the `WriteBitcodeToFile` function, as shown in the following code:

```
int main() {
  Module *Mod = makeLLVMModule();
  verifyModule(*Mod, PrintMessageAction);
  std::string ErrorInfo;
  OwningPtr<tool_output_file> Out(new tool_output_file(
"./sum.bc", ErrorInfo,
                                        sys:fs::F_None));
  if (!ErrorInfo.empty()) {
    errs() << ErrorInfo << '\n';
    return -1;
  }
  WriteBitcodeToFile(Mod, Out->os());
  Out->keep(); // Declare success
  return 0;
}
```

Building and running the IR generator

To build this tool, you can use the same Makefile from *Chapter 3, Tools and Design*. The most critical part of the Makefile is the `llvm-config --libs` call that defines which LLVM libraries your project will link with. In this project, you will use the `bitwriter` component instead of the `bitreader` component used in *Chapter 3, Tools and Design*. Therefore, change the `llvm-config` call to `llvm-config --libs bitwriter core support`. To build, run, and check the generated IR, use the following command:

```
$ make && ./sum && llvm-dis < sum.bc
...
define i32 @sum(i32 %a, i32 %b) {
entry:
  %a.addr = alloca i32, align 4
  %b.addr = alloca i32, align 4
  store i32 %a, i32* %a.addr, align 4
  store i32 %b, i32* %b.addr, align 4
  %0 = load i32* %a.addr, align 4
  %1 = load i32* %b.addr, align 4
  %add = add i32 %0, %1
  ret i32 %add
}
```

Learning how to write code to generate any IR construct with the C++ backend

The `llc` tool, detailed in *Chapter 6, The Backend*, has an interesting feature to assist developers with IR generation. The `llc` tool is capable of generating the C++ source code needed to generate the same IR file for a given LLVM IR file (bitcode or assembly). This makes the IR building API easier to use since it is possible to rely on other existing IR files to learn how to build even the trickiest IR expressions. LLVM implements this through the C++ backend, which is made available using the `llc` tool with the `-march=cpp` argument:

```
$ llc -march=cpp sum.bc -o sum.cpp
```

Open the `sum.cpp` file, and note that the generated C++ code is very similar to the one that we wrote in the previous section.

The C++ backend is included by default when you configure your LLVM build with all targets. However, if you specify targets during configuration, the C++ backend needs to be included as well. Use the cpp backend name to include the C++ backend, for example, `--enable-targets=x86,arm,mips,cpp`.

Optimizing at the IR level

Once translated to the LLVM IR, a program is subject to a variety of target-independent code optimizations. The optimizations can work, for example, on one function at a time or on one module at a time. The latter is used when the optimizations are interprocedural. To intensify the impact of the interprocedural optimizations, the user can use the `llvm-link` tool to link several LLVM modules together into a single one. This enables optimizations to work on a larger scope; these are sometimes called link-time optimizations because they are only possible in a compiler that optimizes beyond the translation-unit boundary. An LLVM user has access to all of these optimizations and can individually invoke them using the `opt` tool.

Compile-time and link-time optimizations

The `opt` tool uses the same set of optimization flags found in the Clang compiler driver: `-O0`, `-O1`, `-O2`, `-O3`, `-Os`, and `-Oz`. Clang also has support for `-O4`, but not `opt`. The `-O4` flag is a synonym of `-O3` with link-time optimizations (`-flto`), but as we discussed, enabling link-time optimizations in LLVM depends on how you organize the input files. Each flag activates a different optimization pipeline, which involves a set of optimizations that acts in a specific order. From the Clang man page file, we can read the following instructions:

–Ox flags: Specify which optimization level to use. -O0 means "no optimization": this level compiles the fastest and generates the most debuggable code. -O2 is a moderate level of optimization which enables most optimizations. -Os is like -O2 with extra optimizations to reduce code size. -Oz is like -Os (and thus -O2), but reduces code size further. -O3 is like -O2, except that it enables optimizations that take longer to perform or that may generate larger code (in an attempt to make the program run faster). On supported platforms, -O4 enables link-time optimization; object files are stored in the LLVM bitcode file format and whole program optimization is done at link time. -O1 is somewhere between -O0 and -O2.

To use any of these predefined sequences of optimizations, you can launch the `opt` tool, which works on bitcode files. For example, the following command optimizes the `sum.bc` bitcode:

```
$ opt -O3 sum.bc -o sum-O3.bc
```

You can also use a flag that activates standard, compile-time optimizations:

```
$ opt -std-compile-opts sum.bc -o sum-stdc.bc
```

Alternatively, you can use a set of standard, link-time optimizations:

```
$ llvm-link file1.bc file2.bc file3.bc -o=all.bc
$ opt -std-link-opts all.bc -o all-stdl.bc
```

It is also possible to apply individual passes using `opt`. A very important LLVM pass is `mem2reg`, which will promote `alloca`s to LLVM local values, possibly converting them to use the SSA form if they receive multiple assignments when converted into a local value. In this case, the conversion involves the use of *phi functions* (refer to `http://llvm.org/doxygen/classllvm_1_1PHINode.html`) — these are awkward to build for yourself when generating the LLVM IR, but are essential to enable SSA. For this reason, it is preferable to write suboptimal code that relies on `alloca`, `load`, and `store`, leaving the SSA version with long-lasting local values to the `mem2reg` pass. This is the pass that was responsible for optimizing our `sum.c` example in the previous section. For example, to run `mem2reg` and later count the number of each instruction in the module, in that order, we can use the following command (the order of the pass arguments matters):

```
$ opt sum.bc -mem2reg -instcount -o sum-tmp.bc -stats
===-------------------------------------------------------------------------===
---===
                     ... Statistics Collected ...
===-------------------------------------------------------------------------===
---===


1 instcount - Number of Add insts
1 instcount - Number of Ret insts
1 instcount - Number of basic blocks
2 instcount - Number of instructions (of all types)
1 instcount - Number of non-external functions
2 mem2reg   - Number of alloca's promoted
2 mem2reg   - Number of alloca's promoted with a single store
```

We use the `-stats` flag to force LLVM to print statistics about each pass. Otherwise, the instruction count pass will silently finish without reporting the number of instructions.

Using the `-time-passes` flag, we can also see how much execution time each optimization takes from the total execution time:

```
$ opt sum.bc -time-passes -domtree -instcount -o sum-tmp.bc
```

A complete list of LLVM analysis, transform, and utility passes can be found at http://llvm.org/docs/Passes.html.

> The phase-ordering problem states that the order used to apply optimizations to code greatly affects its performance gains and that each program has a different order that works best. Using a predefined sequence of optimizations with `-Ox` flags, you understand that this pipeline may not be the best for your program. If you want to run an experiment that exposes the complex interactions among optimizations, try to run opt `-O3` twice in your code and see how its performance can be different (not necessarily better) in comparison with running opt `-O3` only once.

Discovering which passes matter

Optimizations are usually composed of *analysis* and *transform* passes. The former recognizes proprieties and optimization opportunities while generating the necessary data structures that can later be consumed by the latter. Both are implemented as LLVM passes and can have dependency chains.

In our `sum.ll` example, we see that at the optimization level `-O0`, several `alloca`, `load`, and `store` instructions are used. However, when using `-O1`, all of these redundant instructions disappear because `-O1` includes the `mem2reg` pass. However, if you did not know that `mem2reg` is important, how would you discover which passes make a difference to your program? To understand this, let's call the unoptimized version, `sum-O0.ll`, and the optimized version, `sum-O1.ll`. To build the latter, you can use `-O1`:

```
$ opt -O1 sum-O0.ll -S -o sum-O1.ll
```

However, if you want more fine-grained information about which set of transformations actually had an influence on the outcome, you can pass the `-print-stats` option to the `clang` frontend (or pass `-stats` to `opt`):

```
$ clang -Xclang -print-stats -emit-llvm -O1 sum.c -c -o sum-O1.bc
===-------------------------------------------------------------------
---===
                        ... Statistics Collected ...
===-------------------------------------------------------------------
---===


1 cgscc-passmgr  - Maximum CGSCCPassMgr iterations on one SCC
1 functionattrs  - Number of functions marked readnone
2 mem2reg        - Number of alloca's promoted with a single store
1 reassociate    - Number of insts reassociated
1 sroa           - Maximum number of partitions per alloca
2 sroa           - Maximum number of uses of a partition
4 sroa           - Number of alloca partition uses rewritten
2 sroa           - Number of alloca partitions formed
2 sroa           - Number of allocas analyzed for replacement
2 sroa           - Number of allocas promoted to SSA values
4 sroa           - Number of instructions deleted
```

This output suggests that both `mem2reg` and `sroa` (the scalar replacement of aggregates) participated in the removal of redundant allocas. To see how each one acts, try to run just `sroa`:

```
$ opt sum-O0.ll -stats -sroa -o sum-O1.ll
===-------------------------------------------------------------------
---===
                        ... Statistics Collected ...
===-------------------------------------------------------------------
---===


1 cgscc-passmgr  - Maximum CGSCCPassMgr iterations on one SCC
1 functionattrs  - Number of functions marked readnone
2 mem2reg        - Number of alloca's promoted with a single store
1 reassociate    - Number of insts reassociated
1 sroa           - Maximum number of partitions per alloca
```

```
2 sroa          - Maximum number of uses of a partition
4 sroa          - Number of alloca partition uses rewritten
2 sroa          - Number of alloca partitions formed
2 sroa          - Number of allocas analyzed for replacement
2 sroa          - Number of allocas promoted to SSA values
4 sroa          - Number of instructions deleted
```

Note that `sroa` also employs `mem2reg`, even though you did not explicitly specify this at the command line. If you activate only the `mem2reg` pass, you will also see the same improvement:

```
$ opt sum-O0.ll -stats -mem2reg -o sum-O1.ll
==========================================================================
------===
                         ... Statistics Collected ...
==========================================================================
------===


2 mem2reg - Number of alloca's promoted
2 mem2reg - Number of alloca's promoted with a single store
```

Understanding pass dependencies

There are two main types of dependencies between transform passes and analyses:

- **Explicit dependency**: The transform pass requests an analysis, and the pass manager automatically schedules the analysis passes that it depends upon to run before it. If you try to run a single pass that depends on others, the pass manager will silently schedule all of the necessary passes to run before it. **Loop Info** and **Dominator Tree** are examples of analyses that provide information to other passes. Dominator trees are an essential data structure to allow the SSA construction algorithm to determine where to place the `phi` functions. In this way, the `mem2reg`, for instance, requests `domtree` in its implementation, establishing a dependency relation between these two passes:

  ```
  DominatorTree &DT = getAnalysis<DominatorTree>(Func);
  ```

- **Implicit dependency**: Some transform or analysis passes depend on the IR code to use specific idioms. In this way, it can easily identify patterns, even though the IR has a myriad of other ways of expressing the same computation. This implicit dependency can arise, for example, if a pass has specifically been engineered to work just after another transform pass. Thus, the pass may be biased to work with code that follows a particular idiom (from the previous pass). In this case, since this subtle dependence is on a transform pass rather than on an analysis, you need to manually add the passes to the pass queue in the correct order via the command-line tool (clang or opt) or using a *pass manager*. If the incoming IR does not use the idioms that the pass is expecting, the pass will silently skip its transformations because it is unable to match the code. The set of passes contained in a given optimization level are already self-contained, and no dependency problems emerge.

Using the opt tool, you can obtain information about how the pass manager schedules passes and which dependent passes are being used. For example, to discover the full list of passes used when you request just the mem2reg pass, you can issue the following command:

```
$ opt sum-O0.ll -debug-pass=Structure -mem2reg -S -o sum-O1.ll
Pass Arguments:  -targetlibinfo -datalayout -notti -basictti -x86tti
-domtree -mem2reg -preverify -verify -print-module
Target Library Information
Data Layout
No target information
Target independent code generator's TTI
X86 Target Transform Info
  ModulePass Manager
    FunctionPass Manager
      Dominator Tree Construction
      Promote Memory to Register
      Preliminary module verification
      Module Verifier
    Print module to stderr
```

In the `Pass Arguments` list, we can see that the pass manager considerably expanded the number of passes to enable the correct execution of `mem2reg`. The `domtree` pass, for instance, is requested by `mem2reg`, and thus, is included automatically by the pass manager. Next, the output details the structure used to run each pass; the passes in the hierarchy that are immediately after `ModulePass Manager` are applied on a per-module basis, while the passes in the hierarchy that are below `FunctionPass Manager` are applied on a per-function basis. We can also see the order of pass execution, in which the `Promote Memory to Register` pass runs after its dependency: the `Dominator Tree Construction` pass.

Understanding the pass API

The `Pass` class is the main resource to implement optimizations. However, it is never used directly, but only through well-known subclasses. When implementing a pass, you should pick the best subclass that suits the granularity that your pass will work best at, such as per function, per module, per loop, and per strongly connected component, among others. Common examples of such subclasses are as follows:

- `ModulePass`: This is the most general pass; it allows an entire module to be analyzed at once, without any specific function order. It also does not guarantee any proprieties for its users, allowing the deletion of functions and other changes. To use it, you need to write a class that inherits from `ModulePass` and overload the `runOnModule()` method.

- `FunctionPass`: This subclass allows the handling of one function at a time, without any particular order. It is the most popular type of pass. It forbids the change of external functions, the deletion of functions, and the deletion of globals. To use it, write a subclass that overloads the `runOnFunction()` method.

- `BasicBlockPass`: This uses basic blocks as its granularity. The same modifications forbidden in a `FunctionPass` class are also forbidden here. It is also forbidden to change or delete external basic blocks. Users need to write a class that inherits from `BasicBlockPass` and overload its `runOnBasicBlock()` method.

The overloaded entry points `runOnModule()`, `runOnFunction()`, and `runOnBasicBlock()` return a `bool` value of `false` if the analyzed unit (module, function, and basic block) remains unchanged, and they return a value of `true` otherwise. You can find the complete documentation on `Pass` subclasses at `http://llvm.org/docs/WritingAnLLVMPass.html`.

Writing a custom pass

Suppose that we want to count the number of arguments for each function in a program, outputting the function name as well. Let's write a pass to do this. First, we need to choose the right `Pass` subclass. `FunctionPass` seems appropriate since we require no particular function order and do not need to delete anything.

We name our pass `FnArgCnt` and place it under the LLVM source code tree:

```
$ cd <llvm_source_tree>
$ mkdir lib/Transforms/FnArgCnt
$ cd lib/Transforms/FnArgCnt
```

The `FnArgCnt.cpp` file, located at `lib/Transforms/FnArgCnt`, needs to contain the pass implementation, which is reproduced here:

```cpp
#include "llvm/IR/Function.h"
#include "llvm/Pass.h"
#include "llvm/Support/raw_ostream.h"

using namespace llvm;

namespace {
  class FnArgCnt : public FunctionPass {
  public:
    static char ID;
    FnArgCnt() : FunctionPass(ID) {}

    virtual bool runOnFunction(Function &F) {
      errs() << "FnArgCnt --- ";
      errs() << F.getName() << ": ";
      errs() << F.getArgumentList().size() << '\n';
      return false;
    }
  };
}

char FnArgCnt::ID = 0;
static RegisterPass<FnArgCnt> X("fnargcnt", "Function Argument
  Count Pass", false, false);
```

First, we include the necessary header files and gather symbols from the `llvm` namespace:

```cpp
#include "llvm/IR/Function.h"
#include "llvm/Pass.h"
#include "llvm/Support/raw_ostream.h"

using namespace llvm;
```

Next, we declare `FnArgCnt`—our `FunctionPass` subclass—and implement the main pass mechanism in the `runOnFunction()` method. From within each function context, we print the function name and the number of arguments it receives. The method returns `false` because no changes have been made to the analyzed function. The code of our subclass is as follows:

```
namespace {
  struct FnArgCnt : public FunctionPass {
    static char ID;
    FnArgCnt() : FunctionPass(ID) {}

    virtual bool runOnFunction(Function &F) {
      errs() << "FnArgCnt --- ";
      errs() << F.getName() << ": ";
      errs() << F.getArgumentList().size() << '\n';
      return false;
    }
  };
}
```

The ID is determined internally by LLVM to identify a pass, and it can be declared with any value:

```
char FnArgCnt::ID = 0;
```

Finally, we deal with the pass registration mechanism, which registers the pass with the current pass manager during the pass load time:

```
static RegisterPass<FnArgCnt> X("fnargcnt", "Function Argument
  Count Pass", false, false);
```

The first argument, `fnargcnt`, is the name used by the `opt` tool to identify the pass, whereas the second argument contains its extended name. The third argument tells us whether the pass changes the current CFG, and the last returns `true` only if it implements an analysis pass.

Building and running your new pass with the LLVM build system

To compile and install the pass, we need a Makefile within the same directory of the source code. Different from our previous projects, we are not building a standalone tool anymore, and this Makefile is integrated in the LLVM build system. Since it relies on the LLVM main Makefile, which implements a great deal of rules, its contents are considerably simpler than a standalone Makefile. Refer to the following code:

```
# Makefile for FnArgCnt pass

# Path to top level of LLVM hierarchy
```

```
LEVEL = ../../..

# Name of the library to build
LIBRARYNAME = LLVMFnArgCnt

# Make the shared library become a loadable module so the tools can
# dlopen/dlsym on the resulting library.
LOADABLE_MODULE = 1

# Include the makefile implementation stuff
include $(LEVEL)/Makefile.common
```

The comments in the `Makefile` are self-explanatory, and a shared library is created using the common LLVM Makefile. Using this infrastructure, our pass is installed together with other standard passes and can be loaded directly by `opt`, but it requires that you rebuild your LLVM installation.

We also want our pass to be compiled in the object directory, and we need to include our pass in the `Transforms` directory, `Makefile`. Thus, in `lib/Transforms/Makefile`, the `PARALLEL_DIRS` variable needs to be changed to include the `FnArgCnt` pass:

```
PARALLEL_DIRS = Utils Instrumentation Scalar InstCombine IPO
    Vectorize Hello ObjCARC FnArgCnt
```

With instructions from *Chapter 1, Build and Install LLVM*, the LLVM project needs to be reconfigured:

$ cd path-to-build-dir

$ /PATH_TO_SOURCE/configure --prefix=/your/installation/folder

Now, from within the object directory, go to the new pass directory and run `make`:

$ cd lib/Transforms/FnArgCnt

$ make

A shared library will be placed under the build tree in the directory `Debug+Asserts/lib`. `Debug+Asserts` should be replaced with your configuration mode, for example, Release if you configured a release build. Now, invoke `opt` with the custom pass (in Mac OS X):

$ opt -load <path_to_build_dir>/Debug+Asserts/lib/LLVMFnArgCnt.dylib
-fnargcnt < sum.bc >/dev/null

FnArgCnt --- sum: 2

The appropriate shared library extension needs to be used in Linux (`.so`). As expected, the `sum.bc` module has only one function with two integer arguments, as shown in the previous output.

Alternatively, you can rebuild the entire LLVM system and reinstall it. The build system will install a new opt binary that recognizes your pass without the `-load` command-line argument.

Building and running your new pass with your own Makefile

The dependence on the LLVM build system can be annoying, such as needing to reconfigure the entire project or rebuild all the LLVM tools with our new code. However, we can create a standalone Makefile that compiles our pass outside the LLVM source tree in the same way that we have been building our projects in previously. The comfort of being independent from the LLVM source tree is sometimes worth the extra effort of building your own Makefile.

We will base our standalone Makefile on the one used to build a tool in *Chapter 3, Tools and Design*. The challenge now is that we are not building a tool anymore, but a shared library that has the code of our pass and will be loaded on demand by the opt tool.

First, we create a separate folder for our project that does not live inside the LLVM source tree. We put the `FnArgCnt.cpp` file in this folder with the pass implementation. Second, we create the Makefile as follows:

```
LLVM_CONFIG?=llvm-config

ifndef VERBOSE
QUIET:=@
endif

SRC_DIR?=$(PWD)
LDFLAGS+=$(shell $(LLVM_CONFIG) --ldflags)
COMMON_FLAGS=-Wall -Wextra
CXXFLAGS+=$(COMMON_FLAGS) $(shell $(LLVM_CONFIG) --cxxflags)
CPPFLAGS+=$(shell $(LLVM_CONFIG) --cppflags) -I$(SRC_DIR)

ifeq ($(shell uname),Darwin)
LOADABLE_MODULE_OPTIONS=-bundle -undefined dynamic_lookup
else
LOADABLE_MODULE_OPTIONS=-shared -Wl,-O1
endif

FNARGPASS=fnarg.so
FNARGPASS_OBJECTS=FnArgCnt.o
```

```
default: $(FNARGPASS)

%.o : $(SRC_DIR)/%.cpp
    @echo Compiling $*.cpp
    $(QUIET)$(CXX) -c $(CPPFLAGS) $(CXXFLAGS) $<

$(FNARGPASS) : $(FNARGPASS_OBJECTS)
    @echo Linking $@
    $(QUIET)$(CXX) -o $@ $(LOADABLE_MODULE_OPTIONS) $(CXXFLAGS)
$(LDFLAGS) $^
clean::
    $(QUIET)rm -f $(FNARGPASS) $(FNARGPASS_OBJECTS)
```

The novelties (highlighted in the preceding code) in this Makefile, in comparison to the one from *Chapter 3, Tools and Design*, is the conditional definition of the LOADABLE_MODULE_OPTIONS variable, which is used in the command line that links our shared library. It defines the platform-dependent set of compiler flags that instructs it to generate a shared library instead of an executable. For Linux, for example, it uses the -shared flag to create a shared library as well as the -Wl,-O1 flag, which passes the -O1 flag to GNU ld. This flag asks the GNU linker to perform symbol table optimizations, reducing the library load time. If you do not use GNU linker, you can omit this flag.

We also removed the llvm-config --libs shell command from our linker command line. This command was used to supply the libraries that our project links to. Since we know that the opt executable already has all the necessary symbols that we use, we simply do not include any redundant libraries, allowing for faster link times.

To build your project, use the following command line:

```
$ make
```

To run your pass that was built in fnarg.so, use the following command lines:

```
$ opt -load=fnarg.so -fnargcnt < sum.bc > /dev/null
FnArgCnt --- sum: 2
```

Summary

The LLVM IR is the middle point between the frontend and backend. It is the place where target-independent optimizations take place. In this chapter, we explored the tools for the manipulation of the LLVM IR, the assembly syntax, and how to write a custom IR code generator. Moreover, we showed how the pass interface works, how to apply optimizations, and then provided examples on how to write our own IR transform or analysis passes.

In the next chapter, we will discuss how LLVM backends work and how we can build our own backend to translate LLVM IR code to a custom architecture.

6
The Backend

The backend is comprised of the set of code generation analysis and transform passes that converts the LLVM **intermediate representation** (**IR**) into object code (or assembly). LLVM supports a wide range of targets: ARM, AArch64, Hexagon, MSP430, MIPS, Nvidia PTX, PowerPC, R600, SPARC, SystemZ, X86, and XCore. All these backends share a common interface, which is part of the target-independent code generator, abstracting away the backend tasks by means of a generic API. Each target must specialize the code generator generic classes to implement target-specific behavior. In this chapter, we will cover many general aspects about an LLVM backend that are useful for readers interested in writing a new backend, maintaining an existing backend, or writing backend passes. We will cover the following topics:

- Overview of the LLVM backend organization
- How to interpret the various TableGen files that describe a backend
- What is and how does the instruction selection happen in LLVM
- What is the role of the instruction scheduling and register allocation phase
- How does code emission work
- How to write your own backend pass

Overview

There are several steps involved in transforming the LLVM IR into target assembly code. The IR is converted to a backend-friendly representation of instructions, functions, and globals. This representation changes as the program progresses through the backend phases and gets closer to the actual target instructions. The following diagram shows an overview of the necessary steps to go from LLVM IR to object code or assembly, while indicating, in white boxes, where extraneous optimization passes can act to further improve the translation quality.

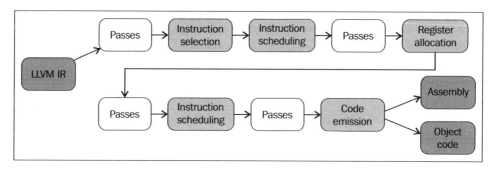

This translation pipeline is composed of different phases of the backend, which are shown in the light gray, intermediary boxes. They are also called *superpasses* because, internally, they are implemented with several smaller passes. The difference between these and white boxes is that, in general, the former represent a set of passes that are critical to the success of the backend, while the latter are more important for increasing the generated code efficiency. We give a brief description of the code generator phases illustrated in the preceding diagram in the following list:

- The **Instruction Selection** phase converts the in-memory IR representation into target-specific `SelectionDAG` nodes. Initially, this phase converts the three-address structure of the LLVM IR to a **Directed Acyclic Graph (DAG)** form, that is, one that uses a directed acyclic graph. Each DAG is capable of representing the computation of a single basic block, which means that each basic block is associated with a different DAG. While nodes typically represent instructions, the edges encode a dataflow dependence among them, but are not limited to it. The transformation to use DAGs is important to allow the LLVM code generator library to employ tree-based pattern-matching instruction selection algorithms that, with some adaptation, work on a DAG as well (not just trees). By the end of this phase, the DAG has all of its LLVM IR nodes converted to target-machine nodes, that is, nodes that represent machine instructions rather than LLVM instructions.

- After instruction selection, we already have a good idea about which target instructions will be used to perform the computation of each basic block. This is encoded in the `SelectionDAG` class. However, we need to return to a three-address representation to determine the order of instructions inside basic blocks, as a DAG does not imply ordering between instructions that do not depend on one other. The first instance of **Instruction Scheduling**, also called **Pre-register Allocation(RA) Scheduling**, orders the instructions while trying to explore instruction-level parallelism as much as possible. The instructions are then converted to the `MachineInstr` three-address representation.

- Recall that the LLVM IR has an infinite set of registers. This characteristic is preserved until we reach **Register Allocation**, which transforms an infinite set of virtual register references into a finite set of target-specific registers, generating spills whenever needed.

- The second instance of **Instruction Scheduling**, also called **Post-register Allocation(RA) Scheduling**, takes place. Since real register information is now available at this point, the presence of extra hazards and delays associated with certain types of registers can be used to improve the instruction order.

- The **Code Emission** phase converts instructions from the `MachineInstr` representation to `MCInst` instances. In this new representation, which is more suitable for assemblers and linkers, there are two options: to emit assembly code or emit binary blobs into a specific object code format.

Therefore, there are four distinct levels of instruction representation used throughout the backend pipeline: in-memory LLVM IR, `SelectionDAG` nodes, `MachineInstr`, and `MCInst`.

Using the backend tools

The `llc` is the main tool to use as a backend. If we continue our tour with the sum.bc bitcode from the previous chapter, we can generate its assembly code with the following command:

```
$ llc sum.bc -o sum.s
```

Alternatively, to generate object code, we use the following command:

```
$ llc sum.bc -filetype=obj -o sum.o
```

If you use the preceding commands, `llc` will try to select a backend that matches the target triple specified in the `sum.bc` bitcode. To override this and select specific backends, use the `-march` option. For example, use the following to generate MIPS object code:

```
$ llc -march=mips -filetype=obj sum.bc -o sum.o
```

If you issue the `llc -version` command, `llc` will show the complete list of supported `-march` options. Note that this list is compatible with the `--enable-targets` options used during LLVM configuration (see *Chapter 1, Build and Install LLVM*, for details).

Notice, however, that we just forced `llc` to use a different backend to generate code for a bitcode originally compiled for x86. In *Chapter 5, The LLVM Intermediate Representation*, we explained that the IR has target-dependent aspects despite being designed as a common language for all backends. Since C/C++ languages have target-dependent attributes, this dependence is reflected on the LLVM IR.

Thus, you must be careful when using `llc` with a bitcode target triple that does not match the `-march` target. This situation may lead to ABI mismatches, bad program behavior and, in some cases, failure in the code generator. In the majority of cases, however, the code generator does not fail and will generate code with subtle bugs, which is much worse.

To understand how the IR target dependency may appear in practice, let's see an example. Consider that your program allocates a vector of char pointers to store different strings, and you use the common C idiom `malloc(sizeof(char*)*n)` to allocate memory for your string vector. If you specify to the frontend that the target is, for instance, a 32-bit MIPS architecture, it will generate a bitcode that asks `malloc` to allocate *n times* 4 bytes of memory, since each pointer in the 32-bit MIPS is of 4 bytes. However, if you use this bitcode as input to `llc` and force it to compile on an x86_64 architecture, you will generate a broken program. At runtime, a potential segmentation fault will occur because x86_64 uses 8 bytes for each pointer, which makes our `malloc` call undersized. The correct `malloc` call for x86_64 would allocate *n times 8* bytes.

Learning the backend code structure

The backend implementation is scattered among different directories in the LLVM source tree. The main libraries behind code generation are found in the `lib` directory and its subfolders `CodeGen`, `MC`, `TableGen`, and `Target`:

- The `CodeGen` directory contains implementation files and headers for all generic code generation algorithms: instruction selection, scheduler, register allocation, and all analyses needed for them.

- The `MC` directory holds the implementation of low-level functionality for the assembler (assembly parser), relaxation algorithm (disassembler), and specific object file idioms such as `ELF`, `COFF`, `MachO`, and so on.

- The `TableGen` directory holds the complete implementation of the `TableGen` tool, which is used to generate C++ code based on high-level target descriptions found in `.td` files.

- Each target is implemented in a different subfolder under the `Target` folder (for example, `Target/Mips`) with several `.cpp`, `.h`, and `.td` files. Files implementing similar functionality in different targets tend to share similar names.

If you write a new backend, your code will live exclusively in a subfolder of the `Target` folder. As an example, let's use `Sparc` to illustrate the organization of the `Target/Sparc` subfolder:

Filenames	Description
`SparcInstrInfo.td`	Instruction and format definitions
`SparcInstrFormats.td`	
`SparcRegisterInfo.td`	Registers and register classes definitions
`SparcISelDAGToDAG.cpp`	Instruction selection
`SparcISelLowering.cpp`	`SelectionDAG` node lowering
`SparcTargetMachine.cpp`	Information about target-specific properties such as the data layout and the ABI
`Sparc.td`	Definition of machine features, CPU variations, and extension features
`SparcAsmPrinter.cpp`	Assembly code emission
`SparcCallingConv.td`	ABI-defined calling conventions

Since backends usually obey this code organization, developers can easily map how a specific issue of one backend is implemented in another target. For example, if you are writing the Sparc backend register information in `SparcRegisterInfo.td` and are wondering how the x86 backend implemented this, just take a look at the `X86RegisterInfo.td` file in the `Target/X86` folder.

Knowing the backend libraries

The `llc` non-shared code is quite small (see `tools/llc/llc.cpp`) and most of its functionality is implemented as reusable libraries, in the same way as other LLVM tools. In the case of `llc`, its functionality is provided by the code generator libraries. This set of libraries is composed of a target-dependent part and a target-independent one. The code generator target-dependent libraries are in different files from the target-independent ones, allowing you to link with a restricted set of desired target backends. For instance, by using `--enable-targets=x86,arm` during the LLVM configuration, only the x86 and the ARM backend libraries are linked into `llc`.

Recall that all LLVM libraries are prefixed with `libLLVM`. We omit this prefix here for clarity. The target-independent code generator libraries are the following:

- `AsmParser.a`: This library contains code to parse assembly text and implement an assembler

- `AsmPrinter.a`: This library contains code to print assembly language and implement a backend that generates assembly files

- `CodeGen.a`: This library contains the code generation algorithms

- `MC.a`: This library contains the `MCInst` class and related ones and is used to represent the program in the lowest level that LLVM allows

- `MCDisassembler.a`: This library contains the code to implement a disassembler that reads object code and decodes bytes to `MCInst` objects

- `MCJIT.a`: This library contains the implementation for the just-in-time code generator

- `MCParser.a`: This library contains the interface to the `MCAsmParser` class and is used to implement a component that parses assembly text and performs part of the work of an assembler

- `SelectionDAG.a`: This library contains `SelectionDAG` and related classes

- `Target.a`: This library contains the interfaces that allow the target-independent algorithms to solicit target-dependent functionality, although this functionality *per se* is implemented in other libraries (the target-dependent ones)

The target-specific libraries, on the other hand, are the following:

- `<Target>AsmParser.a`: This library contains the target-specific part of the `AsmParser` library, responsible for implementing an assembler for the target machine
- `<Target>AsmPrinter.a`: This library contains the functionality to print target instructions and allow the backend to generate assembly language files
- `<Target>CodeGen.a`: This library contains the majority of the target-dependent functionality of the backend, including specific register handling rules, instruction selection, and scheduling
- `<Target>Desc.a`: This library contains target-machine information regarding the low-level MC infrastructure and is responsible for registering target-specific MC objects such as `MCCodeEmitter`
- `<Target>Disassembler.a`: This library complements the `MCDisassembler` library with target-dependent functionality to build a system that is able to read bytes and decode them into `MCInst` target instructions
- `<Target>Info.a`: This library is responsible for registering the target in the LLVM code generator system and provides *façade* classes that allow the target-independent code generator libraries to access target-specific functionality

In these library names, `<Target>` must be replaced with the target name, for example, `X86AsmParser.a` is the name of the parser library of the `X86` backend. A complete LLVM installation contains these libraries in the `<LLVM_INSTALL_PATH>/lib` directory.

Learning how to use TableGen for LLVM backends

LLVM uses the record-oriented language TableGen to describe information used in several compiler stages. For example, in *Chapter 4, The Frontend*, we briefly discussed how TableGen files (with the `.td` extension) are used to describe different diagnostics of the frontend. TableGen was originally written by the LLVM team to help programmers write LLVM backends. Even though the code generator libraries' design emphasizes a clean separation of concerns between target characteristics, for example, using a different class to reflect register information and another for instructions, the backend programmer eventually ends up writing code that reflects the same machine aspect in several different files. The problem with this approach is that, despite the extra effort to write the backend code, it introduces information redundancy in the code that must be manually synchronized.

For example, if you want to change how the backend deals with a register, you would need to change several distinct parts of the code: the register allocator to show which types the register supports; the assembler printer to reflect how the register is printed; the assembler parser to reflect how it is parsed in assembly-language code; and the disassembler, which needs to know the register's encoding. Therefore, it becomes complex to maintain the code of a backend.

To mitigate this, TableGen was created as a declarative programming language to describe files that act as a central repository of information about the target. The idea was to declare machine aspects in a single location, for example, the machine instructions description in `<Target>InstrInfo.td`, and then use a TableGen backend that uses this repository with a specific goal, for example, generate the pattern-matching instruction selection algorithm, which is tediously long to write by yourself.

Nowadays, TableGen is used to describe all kinds of target-specific information, such as instruction formats, instructions, registers, pattern-matching DAGs, instruction selection matching order, calling conventions, and target CPU properties (supported **Instruction Set Architecture (ISA)** features and processor families).

Complete and automatic generation of the backend, a simulator, and the hardware-synthesis description file for a processor has been a long-sought goal in computer architecture research and is still an open problem. The typical approach involves putting all machine information in a declarative description language, similar to TableGen, and then use tools that try to derive all kinds of software (and hardware) that you need to evaluate and test the processor architecture. As expected, this is very challenging and the quality of the generated tools falls short when compared to hand-written ones. The approach of LLVM with TableGen is to aid the programmer in smaller code-writing tasks, still giving full control to the programmer to implement any custom logic with C++ code.

The language

The `TableGen` language is composed of definitions and classes that are used to form records. The definition `def` is used to instantiate records from the `class` and `multiclass` keywords. These records are further processed by TableGen backends to generate domain-specific information for the code generator, Clang diagnostics, Clang driver options, and static analyzer checkers. Therefore, the actual meaning of what records represent is given by the backend, while records solely hold up information.

Let's work out a simple example to illustrate how TableGen works. Suppose that you want to define ADD and SUB instructions for a hypothetical architecture, where ADD has the following two forms: all operands are all registers and operands are a register and an immediate.

The SUB instruction only has the first form. See the following sample code of our insns.td file:

```
class Insn<bits <4> MajOpc, bit MinOpc> {
  bits<32> insnEncoding;
  let insnEncoding{15-12} = MajOpc;
  let insnEncoding{11} = MinOpc;
}
multiclass RegAndImmInsn<bits <4> opcode> {
  def rr : Insn<opcode, 0>;
  def ri : Insn<opcode, 1>;
}
def SUB : Insn<0x00, 0>;
defm ADD : RegAndImmInsn<0x01>;
```

The Insn class represents a regular instruction and the RegAndImmInsn multiclass represents instructions with the forms mentioned above. The def SUB construct defines the SUB record whereas defm ADD defines two records: ADDrr and ADDri. By using the llvm-tblgen tool, you can process a .td file and check the resulting records:

```
$ llvm-tblgen -print-records insns.td
------------ Classes -----------------
class Insn<bits<4> Insn:MajOpc = { ?, ?, ?, ? }, bit Insn:MinOpc = ?> {
  bits<5> insnEncoding = { Insn:MinOpc, Insn:MajOpc{0},
  Insn:MajOpc{1}, Insn:MajOpc{2}, Insn:MajOpc{3} };
  string NAME = ?;
}
------------ Defs -----------------
def ADDri { // Insn ri
  bits<5> insnEncoding = { 1, 1, 0, 0, 0 };
  string NAME = "ADD";
}
def ADDrr { // Insn rr
  bits<5> insnEncoding = { 0, 1, 0, 0, 0 };
  string NAME = "ADD";
}
```

```
def SUB { // Insn
  bits<5> insnEncoding = { 0, 0, 0, 0, 0 };
  string NAME = ?;
}
```

The TableGen backends are also available to use in the `llvm-tblgen` tool; type `llvm-tblgen --help` to list all backend options. Note that our example uses no LLVM-specific domain and will not work with a backend. For more information on TableGen language aspects, refer to the page at `http://llvm.org/docs/TableGenFundamentals.html`.

Knowing the code generator .td files

As mentioned before, the code generator uses TableGen records extensively to express target-specific information. We present in this subsection a tour of the TableGen files used for code generation purposes.

Target properties

The `<Target>.td` file (for example, `X86.td`) defines the supported ISA features and processor families. For example, `X86.td` defines the AVX2 extension:

```
def FeatureAVX2 : SubtargetFeature<"avx2", "X86SSELevel", "AVX2",
                                   "Enable AVX2 instructions",
                                   [FeatureAVX]>;
```

The `def` keyword defines the record `FeatureAVX2` from the record class type `SubtargetFeature`. The last argument is a list of other features already included in the definition. Therefore, a processor with AVX2 contains all AVX instructions.

Moreover, we can also define a processor type and include which ISA extension or features it provides:

```
def : ProcessorModel<"corei7-avx", SandyBridgeModel,
                     [FeatureAVX, FeatureCMPXCHG16B, ...,
                     FeaturePCLMUL]>;
```

The `<Target>.td` file also includes all other `.td` files and is the main file for target-specific domain information. The `llvm-tblgen` tool must always use it to obtain any TableGen records for a target. For instance, to dump all possible records for x86, use the following commands:

```
$ cd <llvm_source>/lib/Target/X86
$ llvm-tblgen -print-records X86.td -I ../../../include
```

The `X86.td` file has part of the information that TableGen uses to generate the `X86GenSubtargetInfo.inc` file, but it is not limited to it and, in general, there is no direct mapping between a single `.td` file and a single `.inc` file. To understand this, consider that `<Target>.td` is an important top-level file that includes all others by means of TableGen's `include` directives. Therefore, when generating C++ code, TableGen always parses all backend `.td` files, which makes you free to put records wherever you think is most appropriate. Even though `X86.td` includes all other backend `.td` files, the contents of this file, excluding the `include` directives, are aligned with the definition of the `Subtarget` x86 subclass.

If you check the `X86Subtarget.cpp` file that implements the `x86Subtarget` class, you will find a C++ preprocessor directive called `#include "X86GenSubtargetInfo.inc"`, which is how we embed TableGen-generated C++ code into the regular code base. This particular `include` file contains processor feature constants, a vector of processor features that relates a feature with its string description, and other related resources.

Registers

Registers and register classes are defined in the `<Target>RegisterInfo.td` file. Register classes are used later in instruction definitions to tie an instruction operand to a particular set of registers. For instance, 16-bit registers are defined in `X86RegisterInfo.td` with the following idiom:

```
let SubRegIndices = [sub_8bit, sub_8bit_hi], ... in {
    def AX : X86Reg<"ax", 0, [AL,AH] >;
    def DX : X86Reg<"dx", 2, [DL,DH] >;
    def CX : X86Reg<"cx", 1, [CL,CH] >;
    def BX : X86Reg<"bx", 3, [BL,BH] >;
    ...
```

The `let` construct is used to define an extra field, `SubRegIndices` in this case, that is placed in all records inside the environment starting with { and ending with }. The 16-bit register definitions deriving from the `X86Reg` class hold, for each register, its name, number, and a list of 8-bit subregisters. The register class definition for 16-bit registers is reproduced as follows:

```
def GR16 : RegisterClass<"X86", [i16], 16,
                         (add AX, CX, DX, ..., BX, BP, SP,
                          R8W, R9W, ..., R15W, R12W, R13W) >;
```

The GR16 register class contains all 16-bit registers and their respective register allocation preferred order. Every register class name receives the suffix RegClass after TableGen processing, for example, GR16 becomes GR16RegClass. TableGen generates register and register classes definitions, method implementations to gather information about them, binary encoding for the assembler, and their DWARF (Linux debugging records format) information. You can check the TableGen-generated code using llvm-tblgen:

```
$ cd <llvm_source>/lib/Target/X86
$ llvm-tblgen -gen-register-info X86.td -I ../../../include
```

Alternatively, you can check the C++ file <LLVM_BUILD_DIR>/lib/Target/X86/X86GenRegisterInfo.inc that is generated during the LLVM build process. This file is included by X86RegisterInfo.cpp to help in the definition of the X86RegisterInfo class. It contains, among other things, the enumeration of processor registers, which makes this file a useful reference guide when you are debugging your backend and do not have a clue about what register is represented by the number 16 (which is the best guess your debugger can give you).

Instructions

Instruction formats are defined in <Target>InstrFormats.td and instructions are defined in <Target>InstrInfo.td. The instruction formats contain the instruction encoding fields necessary to write the instruction in binary form, while instruction records represent each one as a single instruction. You can create intermediary instruction classes, that is, TableGen classes used to derive instruction records, to factor out common characteristics, such as the common encoding of similar data processing instructions. However, every instruction or format must be a direct or indirect subclass of the Instruction TableGen class defined in include/llvm/Target/Target.td. Its fields show us what the TableGen backend expects to find in the instruction records:

```
class Instruction {
  dag OutOperandList;
  dag InOperandList;
  string AsmString = "";
  list<dag> Pattern;
  list<Register> Uses = [];
  list<Register> Defs = [];
  list<Predicate> Predicates = [];
  bit isReturn = 0;
  bit isBranch = 0;
  ...
```

A `dag` is a special TableGen type used to hold `SelectionDAG` nodes. These nodes represent opcodes, registers, or constants during the instruction selection phase. The fields present in the code play the following roles:

- The `OutOperandList` field stores resultant nodes, allowing the backend to identify the DAG nodes that represent the outcome of the instruction. For example, in the MIPS ADD instruction, this field is defined as `(outs GP32Opnd:$rd)`. In this example:
    - `outs` is a special DAG node to denote that its children are output operands
    - `GPR32Opnd` is a MIPS-specific DAG node to denote an instance of a MIPS 32-bit general purpose register
    - `$rd` is an arbitrary register name that is used to identify the node

- The `InOperandList` field holds the input nodes, for example, in the MIPS ADD instruction, `"(ins GPR32Opnd:$rs, GPR32Opnd:$rt)"`.

- The `AsmString` field represents the instruction assembly string, for example, in the MIPS ADD instruction, `"add $rd, $rs, $rt"`.

- `Pattern` is the list of `dag` objects that will be used to perform pattern matching during instruction selection. If a pattern is matched, the instruction selection phase replaces the matching nodes with this instruction. For example, in the `[(set GPR32Opnd:$rd, (add GPR32Opnd:$rs, GPR32Opns:$rt))]` pattern of the MIPS ADD instruction, `[` and `]` denote the contents of a list that has only one `dag` element, which is defined between parenthesis in a LISP-like notation.

- `Uses` and `Defs` record the lists of implicitly used and defined registers during the execution of this instruction. For example, the return instruction of a RISC processor implicitly uses the return address register, while the call instruction implicitly defines the return address register.

- The `Predicates` field stores a list of prerequisites that are checked before the instruction selection tries to match the instruction. If the check fails, there is no match. For example, a predicate may state that the instruction is only valid for a specific subtarget. If you run the code generator with a target triple that selects another subtarget, this predicate will evaluate to false and the instruction never matches.

- Other fields include `isReturn` and `isBranch`, among others, which augment the code generator with information about the behavior of the instructions. For example, if `isBranch = 1`, the code generator knows that the instruction is a branch and must live at the end of a basic block.

In the following code block, we can see the definition of the XNORrr instruction in SparcInstrInfo.td. It uses the F3_1 format (defined in SparcInstrFormats.td), which covers part of the F3 format from the SPARC V8 architecture manual:

```
def XNORrr : F3_1<2, 0b000111,
  (outs IntRegs:$dst), (ins IntRegs:$b, IntRegs:$c),
    "xnor $b, $c, $dst",
  [(set i32:$dst, (not (xor i32:$b, i32:$c)))]>;
```

The XNORrr instruction has two IntRegs (a target-specific DAG node representing the SPARC 32-bit integer register class) source operands and one IntRegs result, as seen in OutOperandList = (outs IntRegs:$dst) and InOperandList = (ins IntRegs:$b, IntRegs:$c).

The AsmString assembly refers to the operands specified by using the $ token: "xnor $b, $c, $dst". The Pattern list element (set i32:$dst, (not (xor i32:$b, i32:$c))) contains the SelectionDAG nodes that should be matched to the instruction. For instance, the XNORrr instruction is matched whenever the xor result has its bits inverted by a not and both xor operands are registers.

To check the XNORrr instruction record fields, you can use the following sequence of commands:

```
$ cd <llvm_sources>/lib/Target/Sparc
$ llvm-tblgen -print-records Sparc.td -I ../../../include | grep XNORrr
-A 10
```

Multiple TableGen backends utilize the information of instruction records to fulfill their role, generating different .inc files out of the same instruction records. This is aligned with the TableGen goal of creating a central repository that is used to generate code to several parts of the backend. Each one of the following files is generated by a different TableGen backend:

- <Target>GenDAGISel.inc: This file uses the information of the patterns field in the instruction records to emit the code that selects instructions of the SelectionDAG data structure. This file is included in the <Target>ISelDAGtoDAG.cpp file.

- <Target>GenInstrInfo.inc: This file contains an enumeration that lists all instructions in the target, among other instruction-describing tables. This file is included in <Target>InstrInfo.cpp, <Target>InstrInfo.h, <Target>MCTargetDesc.cpp, and <Target>MCTargetDesc.h. However, each file defines a specific set of macros before including the TableGen-generated file, changing how the file is parsed and used in each context.

- `<Target>GenAsmWriter.inc`: This file contains code that maps the strings that are used to print each instruction assembly. It is included in the `<Target>AsmPrinter.cpp` file.

- `<Target>GenCodeEmitter.inc`: This file contains functions that map the binary code to emit for each instruction, thus generating the machine code to fill an object file. It is included in the `<Target>CodeEmitter.cpp` file.

- `<Target>GenDisassemblerTables.inc`: This file implements tables and algorithms that are able to decode a sequence of bytes and identify which target instruction it represents. It is used to implement a disassembler tool and is included in the `<Target>Disassembler.cpp` file.

- `<Target>GenAsmMatcher.inc`: This file implements the parser of an assembler of target instructions. It is included two times in the `<Target>AsmParser.cpp` file, each one with a different set of preprocessor macros and, thus, changing how the file is parsed.

Understanding the instruction selection phase

Instruction selection is the process of transforming the LLVM IR into the `SelectionDAG` nodes (`SDNode`) representing target instructions. The first step is to build the DAG out of LLVM IR instructions, creating a `SelectionDAG` object whose nodes carry IR operations. Next, these nodes go through the lowering, DAG combiner, and legalization phases, making it easier to match against target instructions. The instruction selection then performs a DAG-to-DAG conversion using node pattern matching and transforms the `SelectionDAG` nodes into nodes representing target instructions.

> The instruction selection pass is one of the most expensive ones employed in the backend. A study compiling the functions of the SPEC CPU2006 benchmark reveals that, on average, the instruction selection pass alone uses almost half of the time spent in the `llc` tool with –O2, generating x86 code, in LLVM 3.0. If you are interested in knowing the average time spent in all –O2 target-independent and target-dependent passes, you can check out the appendix of the technical report of the LLVM JIT compilation cost analysis at `http://www.ic.unicamp.br/~reltech/2013/13-13.pdf`.

The SelectionDAG class

The `SelectionDAG` class employs a DAG to represent the computation of each basic block, and each `SDNode` corresponds to an instruction or operand. The following diagram was generated by LLVM and shows the DAG for `sum.bc`, which has only one function and one basic block:

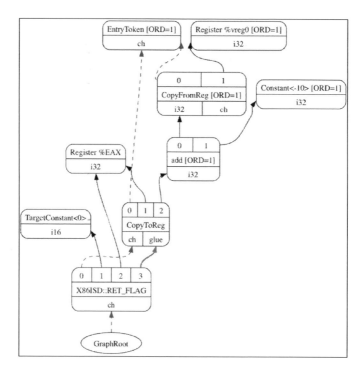

The edges of this DAG enforces ordering among its operations by means of a use-def relationship. If node B (for example, `add`) has an outgoing edge to node A (for example, `Constant<-10>`), this means that node A defines a value (the 32-bit integer `-10`) that node B uses (as an operand of an addition). Thus, the operation of A must execute before B. The black arrows represent regular edges showing a dataflow dependence, just as in our `add` example. The dashed blue arrows represent non-dataflow *chains* that exist to enforce order between two otherwise unrelated instructions, for example, load and store instructions must stick with their original program ordering if they access the same memory position. In the preceding diagram, we know that the `CopyToReg` operation must happen before `X86ISD::RET_FLAG` thanks to a dashed blue edge. The red edge guarantees that its adjacent nodes must be *glued* together, which means that they must be issued next to each other with no other instruction in between them. For example, we know that the same nodes `CopyToReg` and `X86ISD::RET_FLAG` must be scheduled right next to each other thanks to a red edge.

Each node can supply a different type of value depending on its relationship with its consumers. A value is not necessarily concrete, but may also be an abstract token. It may have any of the following types:

- The value supplied by the node can be a concrete value type representing either integer, floating, vector, or pointer. The result of a data processing node that calculates a new value out of its operands is an example of this category. The type can be i32, i64, f32, v2f32 (vector with two f32 elements), and iPTR, among others. When another node consumes this value, the producer-consumer relationship is depicted with a regular black edge in LLVM diagrams.

- The Other type is an abstract token used to represent chain values (**ch** in the diagram). When another node consumes an Other type value, the edge connecting the two is printed as a dashed blue line in LLVM diagrams.

- The Glue type represents glues. When another node consumes a Glue type value, the edge connecting the two receives the red color in LLVM diagrams.

The SelectionDAG objects have a special EntryToken to mark the basic block entry, which supplies a value of type Other to allow chained nodes to start by consuming this first token. The SelectionDAG object also has a reference to the graph root right next to the last instruction, whose relationship is also encoded as a chain of values of type Other.

In this stage, target-independent and target-specific nodes can co-exist as a result of the effort of preliminary steps, such as lowering and legalization, which is responsible for preparing the DAG for instruction selection. By the end of instruction selection, though, all nodes that are matched by target instructions will be target- specific. In the preceding diagram, we have the following target-independent nodes: CopyToReg, CopyFromReg, Register(%vreg0), add, and Constant. In addition, we have the following nodes that were already preprocessed and are target-specific (although they can still change after instruction selection): TargetConstant, Register(%EAX), and X86ISD::RET_FLAG.

We may also observe the following semantics from the example in the diagram:

- Register: This node may reference virtual or physical (target-specific) register(s).

- CopyFromReg: This node copies a register defined outside the current basic block's scope, allowing us to use it in the current context—in our example, it copies a function argument.

- `CopyToReg`: This node copies a value to a specific register without supplying any concrete value for other nodes to consume. However, this node produces a chain value (of type `Other`) to be chained with other nodes that do not generate a concrete value. For instance, to use a value written to `EAX`, the `X86ISD::RET_FLAG` node uses the `i32` result supplied by the `Register(%EAX)` node and consumes the chain produced by `CopyToReg` as well, guaranteeing that `%EAX` is updated with `CopyToReg`, because the chain enforces `CopyToReg` to be scheduled before `X86ISD::RET_FLAG`.

To go deeper into the details of the `SelectionDAG` class, refer to the `llvm/include/llvm/CodeGen/SelectionDAG.h` header file. For node result types, your reference should be the `llvm/include/llvm/CodeGen/ValueTypes.h` header file. The header file `llvm/include/llvm/CodeGen/ISDOpcodes.h` contains the definition of target-independent nodes and `lib/Target/<Target>/<Target>ISelLowering.h` defines the target-specific ones.

Lowering

In the previous subsection, we showed a diagram where target-specific and target-independent nodes co-existed. You may ask yourself, how come some target-specific nodes are already in the `SelectionDAG` class if this is an input to instruction selection? To understand this, we first show the big picture of all steps prior to instruction selection in the following diagram, starting with the LLVM IR step that is to the top-left:

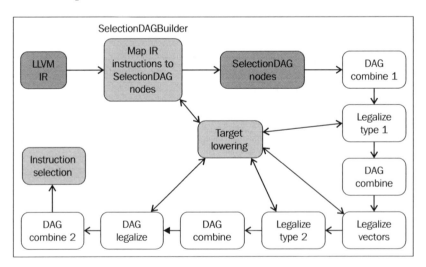

First, a `SelectionDAGBuilder` instance (see `SelectionDAGISel.cpp` for details) visits every function and creates a `SelectionDAG` object for each basic block. During this process, some special IR instructions such as `call` and `ret` already need target-specific idioms—for instance, how to pass call arguments and how to return from a function—to be transformed into `SelectionDAG` nodes. To solve this issue, the algorithms in the `TargetLowering` class are used for the first time. This class is an abstract interface that each target must implement, but also has plenty of common functionality used throughout all backends.

To implement this abstract interface, each target declares a `TargetLowering` subclass named `<Target>TargetLowering`. Each target also overloads methods that implement how a specific target-independent, *high-level* node should be *lowered* to a level closer to the one of this machine. As expected, only a small subset of nodes must be lowered in this way, while the majority of the others are matched and replaced at instruction selection. For instance, in `SelectionDAG` from `sum. bc`, the `X86TargetLowering::LowerReturn()` method (see `lib/Target/X86/X86ISelLowering.cpp`) is used to lower the IR `ret` instruction. While doing this, it generates the `X86ISD::RET_FLAG` node, which copies the function result to `EAX`—a target-specific way to handle the function return.

DAG combine and legalization

The `SelectionDAG` output from `SelectionDAGBuilder` is not yet ready for instruction selection and must pass through additional transformations—those shown in the preceding diagram. The sequence of passes applied prior to instruction selection is the following:

- The DAG combine pass optimizes suboptimal `SelectionDAG` constructions by matching a set of nodes and replacing them with a simpler construct whenever it is profitable. For example, the subgraph `(add (Register X), (constant 0))` can be *folded* to `(Register X)`. Similarly, target-specific combine methods can identify patterns of nodes and decide whether or not combining and folding them improves the quality of the instruction selection of this specific target. You can find the LLVM common DAG combine implementation in the `lib/CodeGen/SelectionDAG/DAGCombiner.cpp` file and target-specific combines in the `lib/Target/<Target_Name>/<Target>ISelLowering.cpp` file. The method `setTargetDAGCombine()` marks nodes that the target wants to combine. The MIPS backend, for instance, tries to combine additions—see `setTargetDAGCombine(ISD::ADD)` and `performADDCombine()` in `lib/Target/Mips/MipsISelLowering.cpp`.

The DAG combine runs after each legalization phase to minimize any `SelectionDAG` redundancy. Moreover, the DAG combine has knowledge of where in the pass chain it runs (for example, after type legalization or vector legalization) and can use that information to be more precise.

- The type legalization pass guarantees that instruction selection only needs to deal with *legal* types. Legal types are the ones natively supported by the target. For example, an addition with `i64` operands is *illegal* in a target that only supports `i32` types. In this case, the type legalizer action *integer expansion* breaks an `i64` operand into two `i32` operands while generating proper nodes to handle them. Targets define which register classes are associated with each type, explicitly declaring the supported types. Thus, illegal types must be detected and handled accordingly: scalar types can be promoted, expanded, or softened, and vector types can be split, scalarized, or widened — see `llvm/include/llvm/Target/TargetLowering.h` for explanations on each. Again, targets can also set up custom methods to legalize types. The type legalizer runs twice, after the first DAG combine and after vector legalization.

- There are cases when a vector type is directly supported by a backend, meaning that there is a register class for it, but a specific operation on a given vector type is not. For example, `x86` with `SSE2` supports the `v4i32` vector type. However, there is no `x86` instruction to support `ISD::OR` on `v4i32` types, but only on `v2i64`. Therefore, the vector legalizer handles those cases and promotes or expands the operations, using legal types for the instruction. The target can also handle the legalization in a custom manner. In the aforementioned `ISD::OR` case, the operation is promoted to use `v2i64` type. Have a look at the following code snippet of `lib/Target/X86/X86ISelLowering.cpp`:

```
setOperationAction(ISD::OR, v4i32, Promote);
AddPromotedToType (ISD::OR, v4i32, MVT::v2i64);
```

For certain types, expansion will remove the vector and use scalars instead. This may lead to unsupported scalar types for the target. However, the subsequent type legalizer instance will clean this up.

- The DAG legalizer has the same role as the vector legalizer, but handles any remaining operations with unsupported types (scalar or vectors). It supports the same actions: the promotion, expansion, and handling of custom nodes. For instance, x86 does not support any of the following three: signed integer to floating-point operation (`ISD::SINT_TO_FP`) for `i8` type and asks the legalizer to promote the operation; signed division (`ISD::SDIV`) on `i32` operands and issues an expansion request, issuing a *library call* to handle the division; and floating-point absolute (`ISD::FABS`) on `f32` operands and uses a custom handler to generate equivalent code with the same effect. x86 issues such actions (see `lib/Target/X86/X86ISelLowering.cpp`) in the following way:

```
setOperationAction(ISD::SINT_TO_FP, MVT::i8, Promote);
setOperationAction(ISD::SDIV, MVT::i32, Expand);
setOperationAction(ISD::FABS, MVT::f32, Custom);
```

DAG-to-DAG instruction selection

The purpose of the DAG-to-DAG instruction selection is to transform target-independent nodes into target-specific ones by using pattern matching. The instruction selection algorithm is local, working on `SelectionDAG` (basic block) instances at a time.

As an example, our final `SelectionDAG` structure after instruction selection is presented next. The `CopyToReg`, `CopyFromReg`, and `Register` nodes are untouched and remain until register allocation. In fact, the instruction selection phase may even generate additional ones. After instruction selection, our `ISD::ADD` node is transformed to the x86 instruction `ADD32ri8` and `X86ISD::RET_FLAG` to RET.

Note that there may be three types of instruction representations co-existing in the same DAG: generic LLVM `ISD` nodes such as `ISD::ADD`, target-specific `<Target>ISD` nodes such as `X86ISD::RET_FLAG`, and target physical instructions such as `X86::ADD32ri8`.

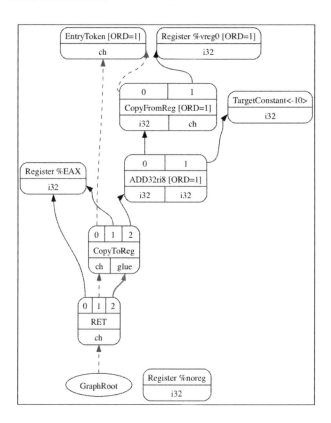

Pattern matching

Each target handles instruction selection by implementing the `Select` method from its `SelectionDAGISel` subclass named `<Target_Name>DAGToDAGISel`, for example, `SparcDAGToDAGISel::Select()` in SPARC (see the file `lib/Target/Sparc/SparcISelDAGToDAG.cpp`). This method receives an `SDNode` parameter to be matched and returns an `SDNode` value representing a physical instruction; otherwise an error occurs.

The `Select()` method allows two ways to match physical instructions. The most straightforward way is by calling the generated matching code from TableGen patterns, as shown in step 1 of the following list. However, patterns may not be expressive enough to cope with the odd behavior of some instructions. In such cases, custom C++ matching logic implementation must be written in this method, as shown in step 2 of the following list. We detail the approaches as follows:

1. The `Select()` method calls `SelectCode()`. TableGen generates the `SelectCode()` method for each target, and in this code, TableGen also generates the `MatcherTable`, mapping `ISD` and `<Target>ISD` nodes to physical-instruction nodes. The matcher table is generated from the instruction definitions in the `.td` files (usually, `<Target>InstrInfo.td`). The `SelectCode()` method ends by calling `SelectCodeCommon()`, a target-independent method to match the nodes by using the target matcher table. TableGen has a dedicated instruction selection backend to generate these methods and this table:

    ```
    $ cd <llvm_source>/lib/Target/Sparc
    $ llvm-tblgen -gen-dag-isel Sparc.td -I ../../../include
    ```

    The same output is present in the generated C++ files for each target in the file `<build_dir>/lib/Target/<Target>/<Target>GenDAGISel.inc`; for example, in SPARC, the methods and the table are available in the `<build_dir>/lib/Target/Sparc/SparcGenDAGISel.inc` file.

2. Provide custom matching code in `Select` prior to the `SelectCode` invocation. For instance, the `i32` node `ISD::MULHU` performs the multiplication of two `i32`, produces an `i64` result, and returns the high `i32` part. In 32-bit SPARC, the multiplication instruction `SP::UMULrr` returns the higher part in the special register `Y`, which requires the `SP::RDY` instruction to read it. TableGen is unable to represent this logic, but we solve this with the following code:

    ```
    case ISD::MULHU: {
      SDValue MulLHS = N->getOperand(0);
      SDValue MulRHS = N->getOperand(1);
      SDNode *Mul = CurDAG->getMachineNode(SP::UMULrr, dl,
        MVT::i32, MVT::Glue, MulLHS, MulRHS);
      return CurDAG->SelectNodeTo(N, SP::RDY, MVT::i32,
        SDValue(Mul, 1));
    }
    ```

Here, N is the SDNode argument to be matched and, in this context, N equals ISD::MULHU. Since sanity checks have already been performed before this case statement, we proceed to generate the SPARC-specific opcodes to replace ISD::MULHU. To do this, we create a node with the physical instruction SP::UMULrr by calling CurDAG->getMachineNode(). Next, by using CurDAG->SelectNodeTo(), we create an SP::RDY instruction node and change all the uses from the ISD::MULHU result to point to the SP::RDY result. The following diagram shows the SelectionDAG structure from this example before and after instruction selection. The preceding C++ code snippet is a simplified version of the code in lib/Target/Sparc/SparcISelDAGToDAG.cpp.

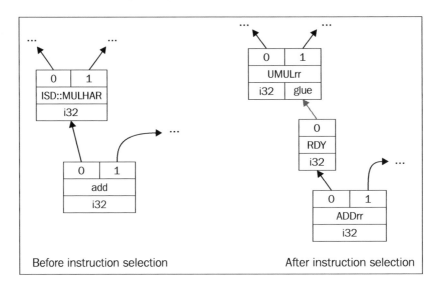

Before instruction selection   After instruction selection

Visualizing the instruction selection process

There are several llc options allowing the SelectionDAG visualization in different instruction-selection phases. If you use any of these options, llc will generate a .dot graph similar to the ones shown earlier in this chapter, but you will need to use the dot program to display it or dotty to edit it, which can both be found in the Graphviz package at www.graphviz.org. The following table shows each option sorted by execution order:

The llc option	Phase
-view-dag-combine1-dags	Before DAG combine 1
-view-legalize-types-dags	Before legalize type
-view-dag-combine-lt-dags	After legalize type 2 and before DAG combine

The llc option	Phase
`-view-legalize-dags`	Before legalization
`-view-dag-combine2-dags`	Before DAG combine 2
`-view-isel-dags`	Before instruction selection
`-view-sched-dags`	After instruction selection and before scheduling

Fast instruction selection

LLVM also supports an alternative instruction selection implementation called the fast instruction selection (in the `FastISel` class, which lives in the `<llvm_source>/lib/CodeGen/SelectionDAG/FastISel.cpp` file). The goal of fast instruction selection is to provide quick code generation at the expense of code quality, which suits the philosophy of the `-O0` optimization level pipeline. The speed gain occurs by avoiding complicated folding and lowering logic. TableGen descriptions are also used for simple operations, but more complicated matching of instructions require target-specific handling code.

 The `-O0` pipeline also uses a fast but suboptimal register allocator and scheduler, trading code quality for compilation speed. We will expose them in the next subsections.

Scheduler

After instruction selection, the `SelectionDAG` structure has nodes representing physical instructions—those directly supported by the processor. The next stage comprises a pre-register allocation scheduler working on `SelectionDAG` nodes (`SDNodes`). There are a few different schedulers to choose from and each one of them is a subclass of `ScheduleDAGSDNodes` (see the file `<llvm_source>/ lib/CodeGen/SelectionDAG/ScheduleDAGSDNodes.cpp`). The scheduler type can be selected in the `llc` tool by using the `-pre-RA-sched=<scheduler>` option. The possible values for `<scheduler>` are the following:

- `list-ilp`, `list-hybrid`, `source`, and `list-burr`: These options refer to list scheduling algorithms implemented by the `ScheduleDAGRRList` class (see the file `<llvm_source>/lib/CodeGen/SelectionDAG/ScheduleDAGRRList.cpp`)

- `fast`: The `ScheduleDAGFast` class (in `<llvm_source>/lib/CodeGen/SelectionDAG/ScheduleDAGFast.cpp`) implements a suboptimal but fast scheduler

- `vliw-td`: A VLIW-specific scheduler implemented by the `ScheduleDAGVLIW` class (see the file `<llvm_source>/lib/CodeGen/SelectionDAG/ScheduleDAGVLIW.cpp`)

The `default` option selects the best predefined scheduler for a target whereas the `linearize` option performs no scheduling. The available schedulers may use information from instruction itineraries and hazard recognizers to better schedule instructions.

There are three distinct scheduler executions in the code generator: two prior and one post register allocation. The first works on `SelectionDAG` nodes while the other two work on machine instructions, explained further in this chapter.

Instruction itineraries

Some targets provide instruction itineraries to represent instruction latency and hardware pipeline information. The scheduler uses these attributes during the scheduling decision to maximize throughput and avoid performance penalties. This information is described in TableGen files in each target directory, usually with the name `<Target>Schedule.td` (for example, `X86Schedule.td`).

LLVM provides the `ProcessorItineraries` TableGen class in `<llvm_source>/include/llvm/Target/TargetItinerary.td`, as follows:

```
class ProcessorItineraries<list<FuncUnit> fu, list<Bypass> bp,
                           list<InstrItinData> iid> {
  ...
}
```

Targets may define processor itineraries for a chip or family of processors. To describe them, targets must provide a list of functional units (`FuncUnit`), pipeline bypasses (`Bypass`), and instruction itinerary data (`InstrItinData`). For instance, the itinerary for ARM Cortex A8 instructions lives in `<llvm_source>/lib/Target/ARM/ARMScheduleA8.td`, as follows:

```
def CortexA8Itineraries : ProcessorItineraries<
  [A8_Pipe0, A8_Pipe1, A8_LSPipe, A8_NPipe, A8_NLSPipe],
  [], [
  ...
  InstrItinData<IIC_iALUi, [InstrStage<1, [A8_Pipe0, A8_Pipe1]>],
    [2, 2]>,
  ...
]>;
```

Here, we see that there are no bypasses. We also see the list of functional units (A8_ Pipe0, A8_Pipe1, and so on) of this processor and the itinerary data for instructions from the type IIC_iALUi. This type is a class of binary instructions of the form reg = reg + immediate, such as the ADDri and SUBri instructions. These instructions take one machine cycle to complete the stage involving the A8_Pipe0 and A8_Pipe1 functional units, as defined in InstrStage<1, [A8_Pipe0, A8_Pipe1]>.

Subsequently, the list [2, 2] represents the cycles after the issuing of the instruction that each operand takes to be read or defined. In this case, the destination register (index 0) and the source register (index 1) are both available after 2 cycles.

Hazard detection

A hazard recognizer computes hazards by using information from the processor itineraries. The ScheduleHazardRecognizer class provides an interface for hazard recognizer implementations and the ScoreboardHazardRecognizer subclass implements the scoreboard hazard recognizer (see the file <llvm_source>/lib/ CodeGen/ScoreboardHazardRecognizer.cpp), which is LLVM's default recognizer.

Targets are allowed to provide their own recognizer. This is necessary because TableGen may not be able to express specific constraints, in which case a custom implementation must be provided. For example, both ARM and PowerPC provide the ScoreboardHazardRecognizer subclasses.

Scheduling units

The scheduler runs before and after register allocation. However, the SDNode instruction representation is only available in the former while the latter uses the MachineInstr class. To cope with both SDNodes and MachineInstrs, the SUnit class (see the file <llvm_source>/include/llvm/CodeGen/ScheduleDAG.h) abstracts the underlying instruction representation as the unit used during instruction scheduling. The llc tool can dump scheduling units by using the option -view-sunit-dags.

Machine instructions

The register allocator works on an instruction representation given by the MachineInstr class (MI for short), defined in <llvm_source>/include/llvm/CodeGen/MachineInstr.h. The InstrEmitter pass, which runs after scheduling, transforms SDNode format into MachineInstr format. As the name implies, this representation is closer to the actual target instruction than an IR instruction. Differing from SDNode formats and their DAG form, the MI format is a three-address representation of the program, that is, a sequence of instructions rather than a DAG, which allows the compiler to efficiently represent a specific scheduling decision, that is, the order of each instruction. Each MI holds an opcode number, which is a number that has a meaning only for a specific backend, and a list of operands.

By using the llc option -print-machineinstrs, you can dump machine instructions after all registered passes or after a specific pass by using -print-machineinstrs=<pass-name>. The pass names have to be looked up in the LLVM source code. To do this, go to the LLVM source code folder and run a grep search for the macro that passes usually utilize to register their name:

```
$ grep -r INITIALIZE_PASS_BEGIN *
CodeGen/PHIElimination.cpp:INITIALIZE_PASS_BEGIN(PHIElimination, "phi-node-elimination"
(...)
```

For example, see the following SPARC machine instructions for sum.bc after all passes:

```
$ llc -march=sparc -print-machineinstrs sum.bc
Function Live Ins: %I0 in %vreg0, %I1 in %vreg1
BB#0: derived from LLVM BB %entry
    Live Ins: %I0 %I1
  %vreg1<def> = COPY %I1; IntRegs:%vreg1
  %vreg0<def> = COPY %I0; IntRegs:%vreg0
  %vreg2<def> = ADDrr %vreg1, %vreg0; IntRegs:%vreg2,%vreg1,%vreg0
  %I0<def> = COPY %vreg2; IntRegs:%vreg2
  RETL 8, %I0<imp-use>
```

MI contains significant meta-information about an instruction: it stores used and defined registers, it distinguishes between register and memory operands (among other types), stores the instruction type (branch, return, call, and terminator, among others), stores predicates such as whether it is commutable or not, and so on. It is important to preserve this information even at lower levels such as in MIs because passes running after InstrEmitter and prior to code emission rely on these fields to perform their analyses.

Register allocation

The basic task of the register allocation is to transform an endless number of virtual registers into physical (limited) ones. Since targets have a limited number of physical registers, some virtual registers are assigned to memory locations, the *spill slots*. Yet, some MI code fragments may already be using physical registers even before register allocation. This happens for machine instructions that need to use a specific register to write their result or because of an ABI requirement. For these cases, the register allocator respects this previous allocation and work to assign other physical registers to the remaining virtual registers.

Another important role of the LLVM register allocator is to deconstruct the SSA form of the IR. Up until this point, the machine instructions may also contain phi instructions that were copied from the original LLVM IR and are necessary to support the SSA form. In this way, you can implement machine-specific optimizations with the comfort of SSA. However, the traditional way to convert phi instructions to regular instruction is to replace them with copy instructions. Thus, SSA deconstruction must not be delayed beyond register allocation, which is the phase that will assign registers and eliminate redundant copy operations.

LLVM has four register allocation implementations that can be selected in `llc` by using the `-regalloc=<regalloc_name>` option. The `<regalloc_name>` options are the following: `pbqp`, `greedy`, `basic`, and `fast`.

- `pbqp`: This option maps the register allocation into a **Partitioned Boolean Quadratic Programming (PBQP)** problem. A PBQP solver is used to map the result of this problem back to registers.

- `greedy`: This option offers an efficient global (function-wide) register allocation implementation, supporting live-range splitting while minimizing spills. You can read a nice explanation about the algorithm at `http://blog. llvm.org/2011/09/greedy-register-allocation-in-llvm-30.html`.

- `basic`: This option uses a very simple allocator and provides an extension interface. Hence, it provides the basics for the development of new register allocators and is used as a baseline for register allocation efficiency. You can also read about its algorithm in the same blog post as of the greedy algorithm, shown in the preceding link.

- `fast`: This allocator option is local (operates on a per-BB fashion) and works by keeping values in registers and reusing them as much as possible.

The `default` allocator is mapped to one of the four options and is selected depending on the current optimization level (the `-o` option).

Although the register allocator, regardless of the chosen algorithm, is implemented in a single pass, it still depends on other analyses, composing the allocator framework. There are a few passes used in the allocator framework, and we expose here register coalescer and virtual register rewrite to illustrate their concept. The following figure illustrates how these passes interact with one other:

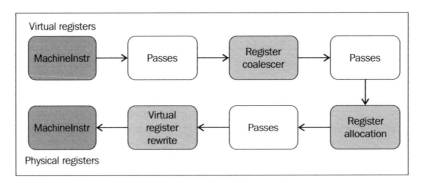

Register coalescer

The register coalescer removes redundant copy instructions (COPY) by joining intervals. The coalescing is implemented in the `RegisterCoalescer` class (see `lib/CodeGen/RegisterCoalescer.cpp`)—a machine function pass. A machine function pass is similar to an IR pass that operates on a per-function basis, but instead of working with IR instructions, it works with `MachineInstr` instructions. During coalescing, the method `joinAllIntervals()` iterates over a work list of copy instructions. The `joinCopy()` method creates `CoalescerPair` instances from copy machine instructions and coalesces copies away whenever possible.

An interval is a pair of program points, start and end, which starts when a value is produced and lasts while this value is held in a temporary location until it is finally used, that is, killed. Let's see what happens when the coalescer runs in our `sum.bc` bitcode example.

We check the debugging output from the coalescer by using the `regalloc` debug option in `llc`:

```
$ llc -march=sparc -debug-only=regalloc sum.bc 2>&1 | head -n30
Computing live-in reg-units in ABI blocks.
0B        BB#0 I0#0 I1#0
********* INTERVALS **********
```

```
I0 [0B,32r:0) [112r,128r:1)  0@0B-phi 1@112r

I1 [0B,16r:0)  0@0B-phi

%vreg0 [32r,48r:0)  0@32r

%vreg1 [16r,96r:0)  0@16r

%vreg2 [80r,96r:0)  0@80r

%vreg3 [96r,112r:0)  0@96r

RegMasks:

********** MACHINEINSTRS **********

# Machine code for function sum: Post SSA

Frame Objects:

  fi#0: size=4, align=4, at location[SP]

  fi#1: size=4, align=4, at location[SP]

Function Live Ins: $I0 in $vreg0, $I1 in %vreg1


0B BB#0: derived from LLVM BB %entry

      Live Ins: %I0 %I1

16B           %vreg1<def> = COPY %I1<kill>; IntRegs:%vreg1

32B           %vreg0<def> = COPY %I0<kill>; IntRegs:%vreg0

48B           STri <fi#0>, 0, %vreg0<kill>; mem:ST4[%a.addr]
IntRegs:%vreg0

64B           STri <fi#1>, 0, %vreg1; mem:ST4[%b.addr] IntRegs:$vreg1

80B           %vreg2<def> = LDri <fi#0>, 0; mem:LD4[%a.addr]
IntRegs:%vreg2

96B           %vreg3<def> = ADDrr %vreg2<kill>, %vreg1<kill>;
IntRegs:%vreg3,%vreg2,%vreg1

112B          %I0<def> = COPY %vreg3<kill>; IntRegs:%vreg3

128B          RETL 8, %I0<imp-use,kill>


# End machine code for function sum.
```

> You can enable internal debug messages for a specific LLVM pass or component with the -debug-only option. To find out components to debug, run grep -r "DEBUG_TYPE" * in the LLVM source folder. The DEBUG_TYPE macro defines the flag option that activates the debug messages of the current file, for example, #define DEBUG_TYPE "regalloc" is used in register allocation implementation files.

Notice that we redirected the standard error output where debug information is printed to the standard output with `2>&1`. Afterwards, we piped the standard output (and, with it, the debugging information) to `head -n30` to print only the first 30 lines of the output. In this way, we control the amount of information that is displayed in the terminal, because debug information can be quite verbose.

Let's first check the `** MACHINEINSTRS **` output. This is a dump of all machine instructions used as input to the register coalescer pass — the same that you would obtain if you used the `-print-machine-insts=phi-node-elimination` option that prints the machine instructions after the phi node elimination pass (which runs before the coalescer). The coalescer debugger output, however, augments the machine instructions with the index information for each MI: 0B, 16B, 32B, and so on. We need them to correctly interpret the intervals.

These indexes are also called *slot indexes*, assigning a different number to each live range slot. The letter B corresponds to block, used for live ranges entering/leaving a basic block boundary. In the case of our instructions, they are printed with an index followed by B because it is the default slot. A different slot, the letter r, found in the intervals, means register, which is used to signal a normal register use/def slot.

By reading the list of machine instructions, we already know important pieces for the register allocator superpass (the composition of smaller passes): `%vreg0`, `%vreg1`, `%vreg2`, and `%vreg3` are all virtual registers that need to be allocated to physical registers. Thus, at most four physical registers will be spent besides `%I0` and `%I1`, which are already in use. The reason is to obey the ABI calling convention that requires function parameters to be in these registers. Because the live variable analysis pass runs before coalescing, the code is also annotated with live variable information, showing at which points each register is defined and killed, which is very useful for us to see which registers interfere with one other, that is, are alive at the same time and need to live in distinct physical registers.

Independent of the result of the register allocator, the coalescer, on the other hand, is just looking for register copies. In a register-to-register copy, the coalescer will try to join the interval of the source register with the interval of the destination register, making them live in the same physical register and avoid the need for a copy instruction, just like the copies in the indexes 16 and 32.

The first messages after `*** INTERVALS ***` comes from another analysis that register coalescing depends on: the live interval analysis (different from live variable analysis) implemented in `lib/CodeGen/LiveIntervalAnalysis.cpp`. The coalescer needs to know the intervals where each virtual register is alive to be able to reason about which intervals to coalesce. For example, we can see from this output that the virtual register's `%vreg0` interval was determined to be `[32r:48r:0)`.

This means a half-open interval where `%vreg0` is defined at 32 and killed at 48. The number 0 after `48r` is a code to show where the first definition of this interval is, whose meaning is printed right after the interval: 0:32r. Thus, the definition 0 is at the index 32, which we already knew. However, this can be useful to help keep track of the original definition if intervals are split. Finally, the `RegMasks` show calls sites that clobber a large number of registers, which is a big source of interference. Since we do not have any calls in this function, there are no `RegMask` locations.

After reading the intervals, we can observe some very promising ones: The interval of the `%I0` register is `[0B,32r:0]`, the interval of the `%vreg0` register is `[32r,48r:0]`, and at 32, we have a copy instruction that copies `%I0` to `%vreg0`. Those are the prerequisites for a coalescing to happen: join the interval `[0B,32r:0]` with interval `[32r:48r:0]` and assign the same register to `%I0` and `%vreg0`.

Now, let's print the rest of the debug output to see what happens:

```
$ llc -march=sparc -debug-only=regalloc sum.bc
...
entry:
16B %vreg1<def> = COPY %I1; IntRegs:%vreg1
    Considering merging %vreg1 with %I1
    Can only merge into reserved registers.
32B %vreg0<def> = COPY %I0; IntRegs:%vreg0
    Considering merging %vreg0 with %I0
    Can only merge into reserved registers.
64B %I0<def> = COPY %vreg2; IntRegs:%vreg2
    Considering merging %vreg2 with %I0
    Can only merge into reserved registers.
....
```

We see that the coalescer considered joining `%vreg0` with `%I0`, as we wanted. However, it implements special rules when one of the registers is a physical register, such as `%I0`. The physical register must be *reserved* to have its interval joined. This means that the physical register must not be available to be allocated to other live ranges, which is *not* the case with `%I0`. The coalescer, then, discards this opportunity, fearing that prematurely assigning `%I0` to this whole range may not be beneficial in the long run and leaves this decision to the register allocator.

Therefore, the `sum.bc` program presented no opportunities for coalescing. Although it tries to merge virtual registers with the function argument registers, it fails because in this phase it can only merge virtual with reserved—not regularly allocable— physical registers.

Virtual register rewrite

The register allocation pass selects the physical registers to be used for each virtual one. Later on, `VirtRegMap` holds the result from register allocation, containing a map from virtual to physical registers. Next, the virtual register rewrite pass—represented by the `VirtRegRewriter` class implemented in `<llvm_source>/lib/CodeGen/VirtRegMap.cpp`—uses `VirtRegMap` and replaces virtual register references with physical ones. Spill code is generated accordingly. Moreover, the remaining identity copies of `reg = COPY reg` are deleted. For example, let's analyze how the allocator and rewriter deals with `sum.bc` using the `-debug-only=regalloc` option. First, the greedy allocator outputs the following text:

```
...
assigning %vreg1 to %I1: I1
...
assigning %vreg0 to %I0: I0
...
assigning %vreg2 to %I0: I0
```

Virtual registers 1, 0, and 2 are allocated to physical registers `%I1`, `%I0`, and `%I0`, respectively. The same output is present in the `VirtRegMap` dump as follows:

```
[%vreg0 -> %I0] IntRegs
[%vreg1 -> %I1] IntRegs
[%vreg2 -> %I0] IntRegs
```

The rewriter then replaces all virtual registers with physical registers and deletes identity copies:

```
> %I1<def> = COPY %I1
Deleting identity copy.
> %I0<def> = COPY %I0
Deleting identity copy.
...
```

We can see that, even though the coalescer was unable to remove this copy, the register allocator was able to assign the same register to both live ranges and delete the copy operation as we wanted. Finally, the resulting machine instructions for the sum function are significantly reduced:

```
0B BB#0: derived from LLVM BB %entry
    Live Ins: %I0 %I1
48B  %I0<def> = ADDrr %I1<kill>, %I0<kill>
```

```
80B   RETL 8, %IO<imp-use>
```

Note that copy instructions are removed and no virtual registers remain.

> The `llc` program options, `-debug` or `-debug-only=<name>`, are only available when LLVM is compiled in debug mode, by using `--disable-optimized` during configuration time. You can find more details about this in the *Building and installing LLVM* section of *Chapter 1, Build and Install LLVM*.
>
> The register allocator and the instruction scheduler are sworn enemies in any compiler. The job of the register allocator is to keep live ranges as short as possible, reducing the number of edges of the interference graph and thus reducing the number of necessary registers to avoid spills. To do this, the register allocator prefers to schedule instructions in a serial fashion (putting an instruction that depends on the other right next to it) because in this way the code uses less registers. The job of the scheduler is the opposite: to extract instruction-level parallelism, it needs to keep alive as much unrelated and parallel computations as possible, requiring a much larger number of registers to hold intermediary values and increasing the number of interferences among live ranges. Making an efficient algorithm to cope with scheduling and register allocation collaboratively is an open research problem.

Target hooks

During coalescing, virtual registers need to come from compatible register classes to be successfully coalesced. The code generator garners this type of information from target-specific descriptions obtained by abstract methods. The allocator can obtain all the information related to a register in subclasses of `TargetRegisterInfo` (for example, `X86GenRegisterInfo`); this information includes if it is reserved or not, its parent register classes, and whether it is physical or virtual.

The `<Target>InstrInfo` class is another data structure that provides target-specific information that is necessary for register allocation. Some of the examples are discussed here:

- The `isLoadFromStackSlot()` and `isStoreToStackSlot()` methods, from `<Target>InstrInfo`, are used during spill code generation to discover whether the machine instruction is a memory access to a stack slot.

- Additionally, the spiller generates target-specific memory access instructions to stack slots using the `storeRegToStackSlot()` and `loadRegFromStackSlot()` methods.

- The COPY instructions may remain after the rewriter because they were not coalesced away and are not identical copies. In such cases, the copyPhysReg() method is used to generate a target-specific register copy, even among different register classes when necessary. An example from SparcInstrInfo::copyPhysReg() is the following:

```
if (SP::IntRegsRegClass.contains(DestReg, SrcReg))
  BuildMI(MBB, I, DL, get(SP::ORrr), DestReg).addReg(SP::G0)
    .addReg(SrcReg, getKillRegState(KillSrc));
...
```

The BuildMI() method is used everywhere in the code generator to generate machine instructions. In this example, an SP::ORrr instruction is used to copy a CPU register to another CPU register.

Prologue and epilogue

Functions need a prologue and an epilogue to be complete. The former sets up the stack frame and callee-saved registers during the beginning of a function, whereas the latter cleans up the stack frame prior to function return. In our sum.bc example, when compiled for SPARC, this is how the machine instructions look like after prologue and epilogue insertion:

```
%O6<def> = SAVEri %O6, -96
%I0<def> = ADDrr %I1<kill>, %I0<kill>
%G0<def> = RESTORErr %G0, %G0
RETL 8, %I0<imp-use>
```

In this example, the SAVEri instruction is the prologue and RESTORErr is the epilogue, performing stack-frame-related setup and cleanup. Prologue and epilogue generation is target-specific and defined in the <Target>FrameLowering::emitPrologue() and <Target>FrameLowering::emitEpilogue() methods (see the file <llvm_source>/lib/Target/<Target>/<Target>FrameLowering.cpp).

Frame indexes

LLVM uses a virtual stack frame during the code generation, and stack elements are referred using frame indexes. The prologue insertion allocates the stack frame and gives enough target-specific information to the code generator to replace virtual frame indices with real (target-specific) stack references.

The method `eliminateFrameIndex()` in the `<Target>RegisterInfo` class implements this replacement by converting each frame index to a real stack offset for all machine instructions that contain stack references (usually loads and stores). Extra instructions are also generated whenever additional stack offset arithmetic is necessary. See the file `<llvm_source>/lib/Target/<Target>/<Target>RegisterInfo.cpp` for examples.

Understanding the machine code framework

The **machine code** (**MC** for short) classes comprise an entire framework for low-level manipulation of functions and instructions. In comparison with other backend components, this is a new framework that was designed to aid in the creation of LLVM-based assemblers and disassemblers. Previously, LLVM lacked an integrated assembler and was only able to proceed with the compilation until the assembly language emission step, which created an assembly text file as output and depended on external tools to carry on the rest of the compilation (assembler and linker).

MC instructions

In the MC framework, machine code instructions (`MCInst`) replace machine instructions (`MachineInstr`). The `MCInst` class, defined in the `<llvm_source>/include/llvm/MC/MCInst.h` file, defines a lightweight representation for instructions. Compared to MIs, `MCInst`s carry less information about the program. For instance, an `MCInst` instance can be created not only by a backend, but also by a disassembler right out of binary code, an environment with little information about the instruction context. In fact, it encodes the view of an assembler, that is, a tool whose purpose is not to apply rich optimizations but rather to organize instructions in the object file.

Each operand can be a register, immediate (integer or floating-point number), an expression (represented by `MCExpr`), or another `MCInstr` instance. Expressions are used to represent label computations and relocations. The `MI` instructions are converted to `MCInst` instances early in the code emission phase, which is the subject of our next subsection.

Code emission

The code emission phase takes place after all post-register allocation passes. Although the naming may seem confusing, the code emission starts at the assembly printer (AsmPrinter) pass. All the steps from an MI instruction to MCInst and then to an assembly or binary instruction are shown in the following diagram:

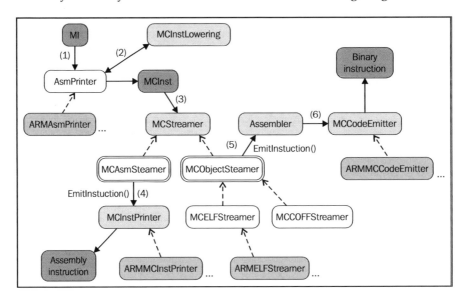

Let's have a walkthrough over the steps shown in the preceding diagram:

1. AsmPrinter is a machine function pass that first emits the function header and then iterates over all basic blocks, dispatching one MI instruction at a time to the EmitInstruction() method for further processing. Each target provides an AsmPrinter subclass that overloads this method.

2. The <Target>AsmPrinter::EmitInstruction() method receives an MI instruction as input and transforms it into an MCInst instance through the MCInstLowering interface—each target provides a subclass of this interface and has custom code to generate these MCInst instances.

3. At this point, there are two options to continue: emit assembly or binary instructions. The MCStreamer class processes a stream of MCInst instructions to emit them to the chosen output via two subclasses: MCAsmStreamer and MCObjectStreamer. The former converts MCInst to assembly language and the latter converts it to binary instructions.

4. If generating assembly instructions, MCAsmStreamer::EmitInstruction() is called and uses a target-specific MCInstPrinter subclass to print assembly instructions to a file.

5. If generating binary instructions, a specialized — target and object-specific — version of `MCObjectStreamer::EmitInstruction()` calls the LLVM object code assembler.

6. The assembler uses a specialized `MCCodeEmitter::EncodeInstruction()` method that is capable of — departing from a `MCInst` instance — encoding and dumping binary instruction blobs to a file in a target-specific manner.

You can also use the `llc` tool to dump `MCInst` fragments. For example, to encode `MCInst` into assembly comments, you can use the following command:

```
$ llc sum.bc -march=x86-64 -show-mc-inst -o -
...
pushq %rbp        ## <MCInst #2114 PUSH64r
                  ##   <MCOperand Reg:107>>
...
```

However, if you want to show each instruction binary encoding in the assembly comments, use the following command instead:

```
$ llc sum.bc -march=x86-64 -show-mc-encoding -o -
...
pushq %rbp        ## encoding: [0x55]
...
```

The `llvm-mc` tool also allows you to test and use the MC framework. For instance, to discover the assembler encoding for a specific instruction, use the `--show-encoding` option. The following is an example for an x86 instruction:

```
$ echo "movq 48879(,%riz), %rax" | llvm-mc -triple=x86_64 --show-encoding
    # encoding: [0x48,0x8b,0x04,0x25,0xef,0xbe,0x00,0x00]
```

The tool also provides disassembler functionality as follows:

```
$ echo "0x8d 0x4c 0x24 0x04" | llvm-mc --disassemble -triple=x86_64
    leal 4(%rsp), %ecx
```

Additionally, the `--show-inst` option shows the `MCInst` instance for the disassembled or assembled instruction:

```
$ echo "0x8d 0x4c 0x24 0x04" | llvm-mc --disassemble -show-inst
-triple=x86_64
    leal 4(%rsp), %ecx                # <MCInst #1105 LEA64_32r
                                      #   <MCOperand Reg:46>
                                      #   <MCOperand Reg:115>
```

```
#    <MCOperand Imm:1>
#    <MCOperand Reg:0>
#    <MCOperand Imm:4>
#    <MCOperand Reg:0>>
```

The MC framework allows LLVM to provide alternative tools to classic object file readers. For example, a default LLVM build currently installs the llvm-objdump and llvm-readobj tools. Both use the MC disassembler library and implement similar functionalities to the ones seen in the GNU Binutils package (objdump and readelf).

Writing your own machine pass

In this section, we will show how you can write a custom machine pass to count, just before code emission, how many machine instructions each function has. Differing from IR passes, you cannot run this pass with the opt tool, or load the pass and schedule it to happen via the command line. Machine passes are determined by the backend code. Therefore, we will modify an existing backend to run with our custom pass to see it in practice. We will choose SPARC for that end.

Recall from the *Demonstrating the pluggable pass interface* section in *Chapter 3, Tools and Design*, and from the white boxes in the first diagram of this chapter, that we have many options to decide where our pass should run. To use these methods, we should look for the TargetPassConfig subclass that our backend implements. If you use grep, you will find it at SparcTargetMachine.cpp:

```
$ cd <llvmsource>/lib/Target/Sparc
$ vim SparcTargetMachine.cpp  # use your preferred editor
```

Looking into the SparcPassConfig class that is derived from TargetPassConfig, we can see that it overrides addInstSelector() and addPreEmitPass(), but there are many more methods that we can override if we want to add a pass to other locations (see the link at http://llvm.org/doxygen/html/classllvm_1_1TargetPassConfig.html). We will run our pass before code emission; therefore, we will add our code in addPreEmitPass():

```
bool SparcPassConfig::addPreEmitPass() {
  addPass(createSparcDelaySlotFillerPass(getSparcTargetMachine()));
  addPass(createMyCustomMachinePass());
}
```

The extra line that we added is highlighted in the preceding code and adds our pass by calling the `createMyCustomMachinePass()` function. However, this function is not defined yet. We will add a new source file with the code of our pass and will take the opportunity to define this function as well. To do this, create a new file called `MachineCountPass.cpp` and fill it with the following content:

```cpp
#define DEBUG_TYPE "machinecount"
#include "Sparc.h"
#include "llvm/Pass.h"
#include "llvm/CodeGen/MachineBasicBlock.h"
#include "llvm/CodeGen/MachineFunction.h"
#include "llvm/CodeGen/MachineFunctionPass.h"
#include "llvm/Support/raw_ostream.h"
using namespace llvm;

namespace {
class MachineCountPass : public MachineFunctionPass {
public:
  static char ID;
  MachineCountPass() : MachineFunctionPass(ID) {}

  virtual bool runOnMachineFunction(MachineFunction &MF) {
    unsigned num_instr = 0;
    for (MachineFunction::const_iterator I = MF.begin(), E = MF.end();
        I != E; ++I) {
      for (MachineBasicBlock::const_iterator BBI = I->begin(),
          BBE = I->end(); BBI != BBE; ++BBI) {
        ++num_instr;
      }
    }
    errs() << "mcount --- " << MF.getName() << " has "
           << num_instr << " instructions.\n";
    return false;
  }
};
}

FunctionPass *llvm::createMyCustomMachinePass() {
  return new MachineCountPass();
}

char MachineCountPass::ID = 0;
static RegisterPass<MachineCountPass> X("machinecount", "Machine Count Pass");
```

In the first line, we define the macro DEBUG_TYPE to allow us to debug our pass later by using the -debug-only=machinecount flag; however, in this example, this code does not use the debug output. The rest of the code is very similar to the one we wrote in the previous chapter for the IR pass. The differences are in the following points:

- In the include files, we include the MachineBasicBlock.h, MachineFunction.h, and MachineFunctionPass.h headers, which define the classes that we use to extract information about MachineFunction and allow us to count the number of machine instructions in it. We also include the Sparc.h header file because we will declare createMyCustomMachinePass() there.

- We create a class that derives from MachineFunctionPass rather than FunctionPass.

- We override the runOnMachineFunction() method instead of the runOnFunction() one. Also, our method implementation is quite different. We iterate through all MachineBasicBlock instances of the current MachineFunction. Then, for each MachineBasicBlock, we count all of its machine instructions by also employing the begin()/end() idiom.

- We define the function createMyCustomMachinePass(), allowing this pass to be created and added as a pre-emit pass in the SPARC backend file that we changed.

Since we have defined the createMyCustomMachinePass() function, we must declare it in a header file. Let's edit the Sparc.h file to do this. Add our declaration next to the createSparcDelaySlotFillerPass() one:

```
FunctionPass *createSparcISelDag(SparcTargetMachine &TM);
FunctionPass *createSparcDelaySlotFillerPass(TargetMachiine &TM);
FunctionPass *createMyCustomMachinePass();
```

It is time to build the new SPARC backend with the LLVM build system. If you have not had the opportunity to configure your LLVM build yet, refer to *Chapter 1, Build and Install LLVM*. If you already have a build folder where you configured the project, go to this folder and run make to compile the new backend. Afterwards, you can install this new LLVM with the modified SPARC backend or, if you prefer, you can just run the new llc binary right out of your build folder without running make install:

```
$ cd <llvm-build>
$ make
$ Debug+Asserts/bin/llc -march=sparc sum.bc
mcount --- sum has 8 instructions.
```

If we want to see where our pass got inserted in the pass pipeline, we issue the following command:

```
$ Debug+Asserts/bin/llc -march=sparc sum.bc -debug-pass=Structure
(...)
        Branch Probability Basic Block Placement
        SPARC Delay Slot Filler
        Machine Count Pass
        MachineDominator Tree Construction
        Machine Natural Loop Construction
        Sparc Assembly Printer
mcount --- sum has 8 instructions.
```

We see that our pass was scheduled just after the SPARC Delay Slot Filler and before the Sparc Assembly Printer, where code emission takes place.

Summary

In this chapter, we presented a general overview of how the LLVM backend works. We saw the different code generator stages and internal instruction representations that change during compilation. We discussed instruction selection, scheduling, register allocation, code emission, and presenting ways for the reader to experiment with these stages by using the LLVM tools. At the end of this chapter, you should be able to read the llc -debug output, which prints a detailed log of the backend activities, and have a good idea about everything that is happening inside the backend. If you are interested in building your own backend, your next step is to refer to the official tutorial at http://llvm.org/docs/WritingAnLLVMBackend.html. If you are interested in reading more about the backend design, you should refer to http://llvm.org/docs/CodeGenerator.html.

In the next chapter, we will present the LLVM Just-in-Time compilation framework, which allows you to generate code on-demand.

7
The Just-in-Time Compiler

The **LLVM Just-in-Time (JIT)** compiler is a function-based dynamic translation engine. To understand what a JIT compiler is, let's go back to the original term. This term comes from Just-in-Time manufacturing, a business strategy where factories make or buy supplies on demand instead of working with inventories. In compilation, this analogy suits well because the JIT compiler does not store the program binaries on the disk (the inventory) but starts compiling program parts when you need them, during runtime. Despite the success of the business jargon, you might stumble upon other names as well, such as late or lazy compilation.

An advantage of the JIT strategy comes from knowing the precise machine and microarchitecture that the program will run on. This grants the JIT system the ability to tune code to your particular processor. Furthermore, there are compilers that will only know their input at runtime, in which case there is no other option besides implementing a JIT system. For example, the GPU driver compiles the shading language just in time and the same happens with an Internet browser with JavaScript. In this chapter, we will explore the LLVM JIT system and cover the following topics:

- The `llvm::JIT` class and its infrastructure
- How to use the `llvm::JIT` class for JIT compilation
- How to use `GenericValue` to simplify function calls
- The `llvm::MCJIT` class and its infrastructure
- How to use the `llvm::MCJIT` class for JIT compilation

Getting to know the LLVM JIT engine basics

The LLVM JIT compiler is function-based because it is able to compile a single function at a time. This defines the granularity at which the compiler works, which is an important decision of a JIT system. By compiling functions on demand, the system will only work on the functions that are actually used in this program invocation. For example, if your program has several functions but you supplied wrong command-line arguments while launching it, a function-based JIT system will only compile the function that prints the help message instead of the whole program.

In theory, we can push the granularity even further and compile only the traces, which are specific paths of the function. By doing this, you are already leveraging an important advantage of JIT systems: knowledge about which program paths deserve more compilation effort than others in a program invocation with a given input. However, the LLVM JIT system does not support trace-based compilation, which receives far more attention in research, in general. JIT compilation is the subject of endless discussions, with an-ample number of different tradeoffs that are worth a careful study, and it is not trivial to point out which strategy works best. Currently, the computer science community has roughly accumulated 20 years of research in JIT compilation and the area is still thriving with new papers each year, trying to address the open questions.

The JIT engine works by compiling and executing LLVM IR functions at runtime. During the compilation stage, the JIT engine will use the LLVM code generator to generate binary blobs with target-specific binary instructions. A pointer to the compiled function is returned, and the function can be executed.

You can read an interesting blog post that compares open source solutions for JIT compilation at http://eli.thegreenplace.net/2014/01/15/some-thoughts-on-llvm-vs-libjit, which analyzes LLVM and libjit, a smaller open source project aimed at JIT compilation. LLVM became more famous as a static compiler rather than as a JIT system because, for JIT compilation, the time spent in each pass is very important and it is tallied as the program execution overhead. The LLVM infrastructure places more emphasis on supporting slow but strong optimizations on par with GCC rather than fast but mediocre optimizations important to build a competitive JIT system. Nevertheless, LLVM has been successfully used in a JIT system to form the **Fourth Tier LLVM (FTL)** component of the Webkit JavaScript engine (see http://blog.llvm.org/2014/07/ftl-webkits-llvm-based-jit.html). Since the fourth tier is only used for long running JavaScript applications, the aggressive LLVM optimizations can help even if they are not as fast as the one in the lower tiers. The rationale is that if the application is running for long, we can afford to spend more time in expensive optimizations. To read more about this tradeoff, check *Modeling Virtual Machines Misprediction Overhead, by César et al.*, published in IISWC 2013, which is a study that exposes how much JIT systems lose by incorrectly using expensive code generation in code that is not worth the effort. This happens when your JIT system wasted a large amount of time optimizing a fragment that executes only a few times.

Introducing the execution engine

The LLVM JIT system employs an execution engine to support the execution of LLVM modules. The ExecutionEngine class declared in <llvm_source>/include/llvm/ExecutionEngine/ExecutionEngine.h is designed to support the execution by means of a JIT system or an interpreter (see the following information box). In general, an execution engine is responsible for managing the execution of an entire guest program, analyzing the next program fragment that needs to run, and taking appropriate actions to execute it. When performing JIT compilation, it is mandatory to have an execution manager to orchestrate the compilation decisions and run the guest program (a fragment at a time). In the case of LLVM's ExecutionEngine class, the ExecutionEngine class relinquishes the execution part to you, the client. It can run the compilation pipeline and produce code that lives in the memory, but it is up to you whether to execute this code or not.

Besides holding the LLVM module to be executed, the engine supports several scenarios as follows:

- **Lazy compilation**: The engine will only compile a function when it is called. With lazy compilation disabled, the engine compiles functions as soon as you request a pointer to them.

- **Compilation of external global variables**: This comprises the symbol resolution and memory allocation of entities outside the current LLVM module.

- **Lookup and symbol resolution for external symbols via dlsym**: This is the same process that is used at runtime in **dynamic shared object (DSO)** loading.

There are two JIT execution engine implementations in LLVM: the `llvm::JIT` class and the `llvm::MCJIT` class. An `ExecutionEngine` object is instantiated by using the `ExecutionEngine::EngineBuilder()` method with an IR `Module` argument. Next, the `ExecutionEngine::create()` method creates a `JIT` or an `MCJIT` engine instance, where each implementation significantly differs from the other—which will be made clear throughout this chapter.

Interpreters implement an alternative strategy for the execution of the guest code, that is, the code that is not natively supported by the hardware platform (the host platform). For example, the LLVM IR is considered the guest code in an x86 platform because the x86 processor cannot directly execute the LLVM IR. Different from JIT compilation, interpretation is the task of reading individual instructions, decoding them and executing their behavior, and mimicking the functionality of a physical processor in the software. Even though interpreters do not waste time by launching a compiler to translate the guest code, the interpreters are typically much slower, except when the time required to compile the guest code does not pay off the high overhead of interpreting the code.

Memory management

In general, the JIT engine works by writing binary blobs to the memory, which is accomplished by the `ExecutionManager` class. Afterwards, you can execute these instructions by jumping to the allocated memory area, which you do by calling the function pointer that `ExecutionManager` returns to you. In this context, memory management is essential to perform routine tasks such as allocation, deallocation, providing space for library loading, and memory permission handling.

The JIT and MCJIT classes each implement a custom memory management class that derives from the RTDyldMemoryManager base class. Any ExecutionEngine client may also provide a custom RTDyldMemoryManager subclass to specify where different JIT components should be placed in the memory. You can find this interface in the <llvm_source>/ include/llvm/ExecutionEngine/ RTDyldMemoryManager.h file.

For example, the RTDyldMemoryManager class declares the following methods:

- allocateCodeSection() and allocateDataSection(): These methods allocate memory to hold the executable code and data of a given size and alignment. The memory management client may track allocated sections by using an internal section identifier argument.

- getSymbolAddress(): This method returns the address of the symbols available in the currently-linked libraries. Note that this is not used to obtain JIT compilation generated symbols. You must provide an std::string instance holding the symbol name to use this method.

- finalizeMemory(): This method should be called once object loading is complete, and memory permissions can finally be set. For instance, you cannot run generated code prior to invoking this method. As explained further in this chapter, this method is directed towards MCJIT clients rather than JIT clients.

Although clients may provide custom memory management implementations, JITMemoryManager and SectionMemoryManager are the default subclasses for JIT and MCJIT, respectively.

Introducing the llvm::JIT framework

The JIT class and its framework represent the older engine and are implemented by using different parts of the LLVM code generator. It will be removed after LLVM 3.5. Even though the engine is mostly target-independent, each target must implement the binary instruction emission step for its specific instructions.

Writing blobs to memory

The JIT class emits binary instructions by using JITCodeEmitter, a MachineCodeEmitter subclass. The MachineCodeEmitter class is used for machine code emission that is not related to the new **Machine Code (MC)** framework—even though it is old, it is still present to support the functionality of the JIT class. The limitations are that only a few targets are supported, and for the supported targets, not all target features are available.

The `MachineCodeEmitter` class has methods that facilitate the following tasks:

- To allocate space (`allocateSpace()`) for the current function to be emitted

- To write binary blobs to memory buffers (`emitByte()`, `emitWordLE()`, `emitWordBE()`, `emitAlignment()`, and so on)

- To track the current buffer address (that is, the pointer to the address where the next instruction will be emitted)

- To add relocations relative to the instruction addresses in this buffer

The task of writing the bytes to the memory is performed by `JITCodeEmitter`, which is another class involved in the code emission process. It is a `JITCodeEmitter` subclass that implements specific JIT functionality and management. While `JITCodeEmitter` is quite simple and only writes bytes to buffers, the `JITEmitter` class has the following improvements:

- The specialized memory manager, `JITMemoryManager`, mentioned previously (also the subject of the next section).

- A resolver (`JITResolver`) instance to keep a track and resolve call sites to functions that are not yet compiled. It is essential for the lazy function compilation.

Using JITMemoryManager

The `JITMemoryManager` class (see `<llvm_source>/include/llvm/ExecutionEngine/JITMemoryManager.h`) implements low-level memory handling and provides buffers where the aforementioned classes can work. Besides the methods from `RTDyldMemoryManager`, it provides specific methods to help the JIT class such as `allocateGlobal()`, which allocates memory for a single global variable; and `startFunctionBody()`, which makes JIT calls when it needs to allocate memory marked as read/write executable to emit instructions to.

Internally, the `JITMemoryManager` class uses the `JITSlabAllocator` slab allocator (`<llvm_source>/lib/ExecutionEngine/JIT/JITMemoryManager.cpp`) and the `MemoryBlock` units (`<llvm_source>/include/llvm/Support/Memory.h`).

Target code emitters

Each target implements a machine function pass called `<Target>CodeEmitter` (see `<llvm_source>/lib/Target/<Target>/<Target>CodeEmitter.cpp`), which encodes instructions in blobs and uses `JITCodeEmitter` to write to the memory. `MipsCodeEmitter`, for instance, iterates over all the function basic blocks and calls `emitInstruction()` for each machine instruction (MI):

```
(...)
MCE.startFunction(MF);

for (MachineFunction::iterator MBB = MF.begin(), E = MF.end();
   MBB != E; ++MBB){
MCE.StartMachineBasicBlock(MBB);
for (MachineBasicBlock::instr_iterator I = MBB->instr_begin(),
    E = MBB->instr_end(); I != E;)
        emitInstruction(*I++, *MBB);
}
(...)
```

MIPS32 is a fixed-length, 4-byte ISA, which makes the `emitInstruction()` implementation straightforward:

```
void MipsCodeEmitter::emitInstruction(MachineBasicBlock::instr_
iterator
  MI, MachineBasicBlock &MBB) {
  ...
  MCE.processDebugLoc(MI->getDebugLoc(), true);
  emitWord(getBinaryCodeForInstr(*MI));
  ++NumEmitted;  // Keep track of the # of mi's emitted
  ...
}
```

The `emitWord()` method is a wrapper for `JITCodeEmitter`, and `getBinaryCodeForInstr()` is TableGen-generated for each target by reading the instruction encoding descriptions of the `.td` files. The `<Target>CodeEmitter` class must also implement custom methods to encode operands and other target-specific entities. For example, in MIPS, the `mem` operand must use the `getMemEncoding()` method to be properly encoded (see `<llvm_source>/lib/Target/Mips/MipsInstrInfo.td`):

```
def mem : Operand<iPTR> {
  (...)
  let MIOperandInfo = (ops ptr_rc, simm16);
  let EncoderMethod = "getMemEncoding";
  (...)
}
```

Therefore, `MipsCodeEmitter` must implement the `MipsCodeEmitter::getMemEncod ing()` method to match this TableGen description. The following diagram shows the relationship between the several code emitters and the JIT framework:

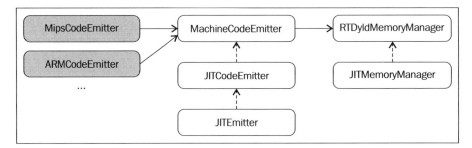

Target information

To support Just-in-Time compilation, each target must also provide a `TargetJITInfo` subclass (see `include/llvm/Target/TargetJITInfo.h`), such as `MipsJITInfo` or `X86JITInfo`. The `TargetJITInfo` class provides an interface for common JIT functionalities that each target needs to implement. Next, we show a list of the examples of such functionalities:

- To support situations where the execution engine needs to recompile a function—likely because it has been modified—each target implements the `TargetJITInfo::replaceMachineCodeForFunction()` method and patches the old function's location with instructions to jump or call the new version of the function. This is necessary for self-modifying code.

- The `TargetJITInfo::relocate()` method patches every symbol reference in the currently-emitted function to point to the correct memory addresses, similar to what dynamic linkers do.

- The `TargetJITInfo:: emitFunctionStub()` method emits a stub: a function to call another function at a given address. Each target also provides custom `TargetJITInfo::StubLayout` information, with the size in bytes and alignment for the emitted stub. This stub information is used by `JITEmitter` to allocate space for the new stub before emitting it.

Although the goal of the `TargetJITInfo` methods is not to emit regular instructions such as in a function body generation, they still need to emit specific instructions for stub generation and to call new memory locations. However, when the JIT framework was established, there was no interface to rely on in order to ease the task of emitting standalone instructions that live outside `MachineBasicBlock`. This is what `MCInsts` does for `MCJIT` nowadays. Without `MCInsts`, the old JIT framework forces the targets to manually encode the instructions.

To show how the `<Target>JITInfo` implementation needs to manually emit instructions, let's see the code of `MipsJITInfo::emitFunctionStub()` (see `<llvm_source>/lib/Target/Mips/MipsJITInfo.cpp`) which uses the following code to generate four instructions:

```
. . .
  // lui $9, %hi(EmittedAddr)
  // addiu $9, $9, %lo(EmittedAddr)
  // jalr $8, $9
  // nop
  if (IsLittleEndian) {
    JCE.emitWordLE(0xf << 26 | 25 << 16 | Hi);
    JCE.emitWordLE(9 << 26 | 25 << 21 | 25 << 16 | Lo);
    JCE.emitWordLE(25 << 21 | 24 << 11 | 9);
    JCE.emitWordLE(0);
. . .
```

Learning how to use the JIT class

`JIT` is an `ExecutionEngine` subclass declared in `<llvm_source>/lib/ExecutionEngine/JIT/JIT.h`. The `JIT` class is the entry point for compiling functions by means of the `JIT` infrastructure.

The `ExecutionEngine::create()` method calls `JIT::createJIT()`, with a default `JITMemoryManager`. Next, the `JIT` constructor executes the following tasks:

- Creates a `JITEmitter` instance
- Initializes the target information object
- Adds the passes for code generation
- Adds the `<Target>CodeEmitter` pass to be run in the end

The engine holds a `PassManager` object to invoke all code generation and JIT emission passes whenever it is asked to JIT compile a function.

To illustrate how everything takes place, we have described how to JIT compile a function of the `sum.bc` bitcode file used throughout *Chapter 5, The LLVM Intermediate Representation,* and *Chapter 6, The Backend.* Our goal is to retrieve the `Sum` function and use the JIT system to compute two different additions with runtime arguments. Perform the following steps:

1. First, create a new file called `sum-jit.cpp`. We need to include the JIT execution engine resources:

   ```
   #include "llvm/ExecutionEngine/JIT.h"
   ```

2. Include other header files for reading and writing LLVM bitcode, context interface, among others, and import the LLVM namespace:

```
#include "llvm/ADT/OwningPtr.h"
#include "llvm/Bitcode/ReaderWriter.h"
#include "llvm/IR/LLVMContext.h"
#include "llvm/IR/Module.h"
#include "llvm/Support/FileSystem.h"
#include "llvm/Support/MemoryBuffer.h"
#include "llvm/Support/ManagedStatic.h"
#include "llvm/Support/raw_ostream.h"
#include "llvm/Support/system_error.h"
#include "llvm/Support/TargetSelect.h"

using namespace llvm;
```

3. The `InitializeNativeTarget()` method sets up the host target and ensures that the target libraries to be used by the JIT are linked. As usual, we need a per-thread context `LLVMContext` object and a `MemoryBuffer` object to read the bitcode file from the disk, as shown in the following code:

```
int main() {
  InitializeNativeTarget();
  LLVMContext Context;
  std::string ErrorMessage;
  OwningPtr<MemoryBuffer> Buffer;
```

4. We read from the disk by using the `getFile()` method, as shown in the following code:

```
if (MemoryBuffer::getFile("./sum.bc", Buffer)) {
  errs() << "sum.bc not found\n";
  return -1;
}
```

5. The `ParseBitcodeFile` function reads data from `MemoryBuffer` and generates the corresponding LLVM `Module` class to represent it, as shown in the following code:

```
Module *M = ParseBitcodeFile(Buffer.get(), Context,
                             &ErrorMessage);
if (!M) {
  errs() << ErrorMessage << "\n";
  return -1;
}
```

6. Create an `ExecutionEngine` instance by using the `EngineBuilder` factory first and then by invoking its `create` method, as shown in the following code:

    ```
    OwningPtr<ExecutionEngine> EE(EngineBuilder(M).create());
    ```

    This method defaults to creating a `JIT` execution engine and is the `JIT` setup point; it calls the `JIT` constructor indirectly, which creates `JITEmitter`, `PassManager`, and initializes all code generation and target-specific emission passes. To this point, although the engine is aware of an LLVM `Module`, no function is compiled yet.

    To compile a function, you still need to call `getPointerToFunction()`, which gets a pointer to the native JIT-compiled function. If the function has not been JIT-compiled yet, the JIT compilation happens and the function pointer is returned. The following diagram illustrates the compilation process:

    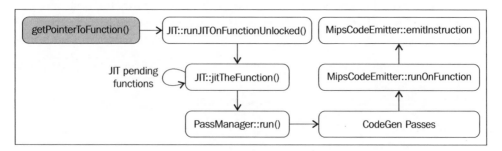

7. Retrieve the `Function` IR object that represents `sum` through the `getFunction()` method:

    ```
    Function *SumFn = M->getFunction("sum");
    ```

    Here, JIT compilation is triggered:

    ```
    int (*Sum)(int, int) = (int (*)(int, int))
        EE->getPointerToFunction(SumFn);
    ```

    You need to perform an appropriate cast to the function pointer type that matches this function. The `Sum` function has the `define i32 @sum(i32 %a, i32 %b)` LLVM prototype; hence, we use the `int (*)(int, int)` C prototype.

    Another option is to consider lazy compilation by using `getPointerToFunctionOrStub()` instead of `getPointerToFunction()`. This method will generate a stub function and return its pointer if the target function is not yet compiled and lazy compilation is enabled. Stub is a small function containing a placeholder that is later patched to jump/call the real function.

8. Next, we call the original Sum function via the JIT-compiled function pointed by Sum, as shown in the following code:

```
int res = Sum(4,5);
outs() << "Sum result: " << res << "\n";
```

When using lazy compilation, Sum calls the stub function, which then uses a compilation callback to JIT compile the real function. The stub is then patched to redirect the execution to the real function. Unless the original Sum function changes in Module, this function is never compiled again.

9. Call Sum again to compute the next result, as shown in the following code:

```
res = Sum(res, 6);
outs() << "Sum result: " << res << "\n";
```

In a lazy compilation environment, since the original function was already compiled in the first Sum invocation, the second call executes the native function directly.

10. We successfully computed two additions using the JIT-compiled Sum function. We now release the execution engine allocated memory that holds the function code, call the llvm_shutdown() function and return:

```
EE->freeMachineCodeForFunction(SumFn);
llvm_shutdown();
return 0;
}
```

To compile and link sum-jit.cpp, you can use the following command line:

```
$ clang++ sum-jit.cpp -g -O3 -rdynamic -fno-rtti $(llvm-config --cppflags
--ldflags --libs jit native irreader) -o sum-jit
```

Alternatively, you can use the Makefile from *Chapter 3, Tools and Design*, add the -rdynamic flag, and change your llvm-config invocation to use the libraries specified in the preceding command. Although this example makes no use of external functions, the -rdynamic flag is important to guarantee that external functions are resolved at runtime.

Run the example and check the output:

```
$ ./sum-jit
Sum result: 9
Sum result: 15
```

The generic value

In the previous example, we cast the returned function pointer to a proper prototype in order to call the function with a C-style function call. However, when dealing with multiple functions in a multitude of signatures and argument types, we need a more flexible way to execute functions.

The execution engine provides another way to call JIT-compiled functions. The runFunction() method compiles and runs a function with the arguments determined by a vector of GenericValue — it needs no prior invocation to getPointerToFunction().

The GenericValue struct is defined in <llvm_source>/include/llvm/ExecutionEngine/GenericValue.h and is capable of holding any common type. Let's change our last example to use runFunction() instead of getPointerToFunction() and castings.

First, create the sum-jit-gv.cpp file to hold this new version and add the GenericValue header file on top:

```
#include "llvm/ExecutionEngine/GenericValue.h"
```

Copy the rest from sum-jit.cpp, and let's focus on the modifications. After the SumFn Function pointer initialization, create FnArgs — a vector of GenericValue — and populate it with integer values by using the APInt interface (<llvm_source>/include/llvm/ADT/APInt.h). Use two 32-bit width integers to adhere to the original prototype, sum(i32 %a, i32 %b):

```
(...)
Function *SumFn = M->getFunction("sum");
std::vector<GenericValue> FnArgs(2);
FnArgs[0].IntVal = APInt(32,4);
FnArgs[1].IntVal = APInt(32,5);
```

Call runFunction() with the function parameter and the argument vector. Here, the function is JIT compiled and executed. The result is also GenericValue and can be accessed accordingly (the i32 type):

```
GenericValue Res = EE->runFunction(SumFn, FnArgs);
outs() << "Sum result: " << Res.IntVal << "\n";
```

We repeat the same process for the second addition:

```
FnArgs[0].IntVal = Res.IntVal;
FnArgs[1].IntVal = APInt(32,6);
Res = EE->runFunction(SumFn, FnArgs);
outs() << "Sum result: " << Res.IntVal << "\n";
(...)
```

Introducing the llvm::MCJIT framework

The MCJIT class is a novel JIT implementation for LLVM. It differs from the old JIT implementation by the MC framework, explored in *Chapter 6*, *The Backend*. MC provides a uniform representation for instructions and is a framework shared among the assembler, disassembler, assembly printer and MCJIT.

The first advantage of using the MC library is that targets need to specify their instruction encodings only once because this information is used by all the subsystems. Therefore, when writing an LLVM backend, if you implement the object code emission for your target, you have the JIT functionality as well.

The llvm::JIT framework is going to be removed after LLVM 3.5 and completely replaced by the llvm::MCJIT framework. So, why did we study the old JIT? Although they are different implementations, the ExecutionEngine class is generic and most concepts apply to both engines. Most importantly, as in the LLVM 3.4 release, the MCJIT design does not support some features such as lazy compilation and is still not a drop-in replacement for the old JIT.

The MCJIT engine

The MCJIT engine is created in the same way as the old JIT engine, by invoking ExecutionEngine::create(). This method calls MCJIT::createJIT(), which executes the MCJIT constructor. The MCJIT class is declared in `<llvm_source>/lib/ExecutionEngine/MCJIT/MCJIT.h`. The createJIT() method and the MCJIT constructor are implemented in `<llvm_source>/lib/ExecutionEngine/MCJIT/MCJIT.cpp`.

The MCJIT constructor creates a SectionMemoryManager instance; adds the LLVM module to its internal module container, OwningModuleContainer; and initializes the target information.

Learning the module's states

The MCJIT class designates states to the initial LLVM Module instances inserted during engine building. These states represent compilation stages of a module. They are the following:

- **Added**: These modules contain the set of modules that are not yet compiled but are already added to the execution engine. The existence of this state allows modules to expose function definitions for other modules and delay their compilation until necessary.

- **Loaded**: These modules are in a JIT-compiled state but are not ready for execution. Relocation remains unapplied and memory pages still need to be given appropriate permissions. Clients willing to remap JIT-compiled functions in the memory might avoid recompilation by using modules in the loaded state.

- **Finalized**: These modules contain functions ready for execution. In this state, functions cannot be remapped since relocations have been already applied.

One major distinction between `JIT` and `MCJIT` lies in the module states. In `MCJIT`, the entire module must be finalized prior to requests for symbol addresses (functions and other globals).

The `MCJIT::finalizeObject()` function transforms the added modules into loaded ones and then finalizes them. First, it generates loaded modules by calling `generateCodeForModule()`. Next, all the modules are finalized through the `finalizeLoadedModules()` method.

Unlike the old JIT, the `MCJIT::getPointerToFunction()` function requires the `Module` object to be finalized prior to its invocation. Therefore, `MCJIT::finalizeObject()` must be called before using it.

A new method added in LLVM 3.4 removes this restriction—the `getPointerToFunction()` method is deprecated in favor of `getFunctionAddress()` when MCJIT is used. This new method loads and finalizes the module prior to the symbol address request and no `finalizeObject()` invocation is necessary.

> Note that in the old JIT, individual functions are separately JIT compiled and executed by the execution engine. In MCJIT, the whole module (all the functions) must be JIT compiled prior to any function execution. Due to this increase in the granularity, we can no longer say that it is function-based, but it is a module-based translation engine.

Understanding how MCJIT compiles modules

The code generation takes place at a `Module` object loading stage and is triggered by the `MCJIT::generateCodeForModule()` method in `<llvm_source>/lib/ExecutionEngine/MCJIT/MCJIT.cpp`. This method performs the following tasks:

- Creates an `ObjectBuffer` instance to hold a `Module` object. If the `Module` object is already loaded (compiled), the `ObjectCache` interface is used to retrieve and avoid recompilation.

- Assuming that no previous cache exists, the MC code emission is performed by `MCJIT::emitObject()`. The result is an `ObjectBufferStream` object (an `ObjectBuffer` subclass with streaming support).

- The `RuntimeDyld` dynamic linker loads the resulting `ObjectBuffer` object and builds a symbol table via `RuntimeDyld::loadObject()`. This method returns an `ObjectImage` object.

- The module is marked as loaded.

The Object buffer, the cache, and the image

The `ObjectBuffer` class (`<llvm_source>/include/llvm/ExecutionEngine/ObjectBuffer.h`) implements a wrapper over the `MemoryBuffer` class (`<llvm_source>/include/llvm/Support/MemoryBuffer.h`).

The `MemoryBuffer` class is used by the `MCObjectStreamer` subclasses to emit instructions and data to the memory. Additionally, the `ObjectCache` class directly references the `MemoryBuffer` instances and is able to retrieve `ObjectBuffer` from them.

The `ObjectBufferStream` class is an `ObjectBuffer` subclass with additional standard C++ streaming operators (for example, `>>` and `<<`) and facilitates the memory buffer read/write operations from the point of view of implementation.

An `ObjectImage` object (`<llvm_source>/include/llvm/ExecutionEngine/ObjectImage.h`) is used to keep the loaded modules and has direct access to the `ObjectBuffer` and `ObjectFile` references. An `ObjectFile` object (`<llvm_source>/include/llvm/Object/ObjectFile.h`) is specialized by target-specific object file types such as ELF, COFF, and MachO. An `ObjectFile` object is capable of retrieving symbols, relocations, and sections directly from the `MemoryBuffer` objects.

The following diagram illustrates how each class relates to the other — solid arrows represent collaboration, and dashed arrows denote inheritance:

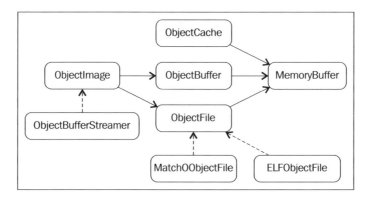

Dynamic linking

The MCJIT-loaded module objects are represented by the ObjectImage instances. As mentioned before, it has transparent access to memory buffers by a target-independent ObjectFile interface. Hence, it can handle symbols, sections, and relocations.

In order to generate the ObjectImage objects, MCJIT has dynamic linking facilities provided by the RuntimeDyld class. This class provides a public interface to access these facilities, whereas the RuntimeDyldImpl objects, which are specialized by each object's file type, provide the actual implementation.

Therefore, the RuntimeDyld::loadObject() method, which generates the ObjectImage objects out of ObjectBuffer, first creates a target-specific RuntimeDyldImpl object and then calls RuntimeDyldImpl::loadObject(). During this process, an ObjectFile object is also created and can be retrieved via the ObjectImage object. The following diagram illustrates the process:

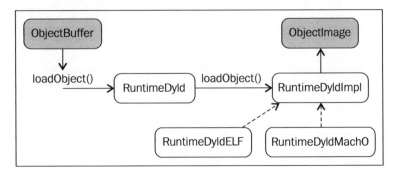

The runtime RuntimeDyld dynamic linker is used during Module finalization to resolve relocations and to register exception-handling frames for the Module object. Recall that the execution engine methods getFunctionAddress() and getPointerToFunction() require the engine to know symbol (function) addresses. To solve this, MCJIT also uses RuntimeDyld to ask for any symbol addresses via the RuntimeDyld::getSymbolLoadAddress() method.

The memory manager

The LinkingMemoryManager class, another RTDyldMemoryManager subclass, is the actual memory manager used by the MCJIT engine. It aggregates a SectionMemoryManager instance and sends proxy requests to it.

Whenever the `RuntimeDyld` dynamic linker requests for a symbol address through `LinkingMemoryManager::getSymbolAddress()`, it has two options: if the symbol is available in a compiled module, it retrieves the address from `MCJIT`; otherwise, it requests for the address from external libraries that are loaded and mapped by the `SectionMemoryManager` instance. The following diagram illustrates this mechanism. Refer to `LinkingMemoryManager::getSymbolAddress()` in `<llvm_source>/lib/ExecutionEngine/MCJIT/MCJIT.cpp` for details.

The `SectionMemoryManager` instance is a simple manager. As an `RTDyldMemoryManager` subclass, `SectionMemoryManager` inherits all its library lookup methods but implements the code and data section allocation by directly dealing with low-level `MemoryBlock` units (`<llvm_source>/include/llvm/Support/Memory.h`).

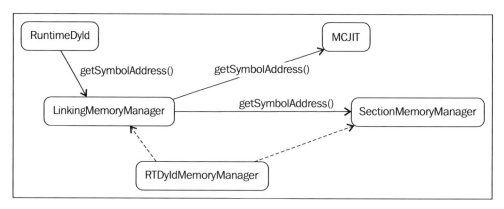

The MC code emission

MCJIT performs the MC code emission by calling `MCJIT::emitObject()`. This method performs the following tasks:

- Creates a `PassManager` object.
- Adds a target layout pass and calls `addPassesToEmitMC()` to add all the code generation passes and MC code emission.
- Runs all the passes by using the `PassManager::run()` method. The resulting code is stored in an `ObjectBufferStream` object.
- Adds the compiled object to the `ObjectCache` instance and returns it.

The code emission in `MCJIT` is more consistent than in the old JIT. Instead of providing the JIT with custom emitters and target information, MCJIT transparently uses all the information from the existing MC infrastructure.

Object finalization

Finally, the `Module` objects finalized in the `MCJIT::finalizeLoadedModules()`: relocations are resolved, loaded modules are moved to a finalized module group, and `LinkingMemoryManager::finalizeMemory()` is called to change memory page permissions. After object finalization, MCJIT-compiled functions are ready for execution.

Using the MCJIT engine

The following `sum-mcjit.cpp` source contains the necessary code to JIT compile the `Sum` function by using the MCJIT framework, instead of the old JIT. To illustrate how similar it is to the previous JIT example, we leave the old code around and use the `UseMCJIT` Boolean to determine whether the old JIT or MCJIT should be used. Since the code is quite similar to the code for `sum-jit.cpp`, we will avoid detailing the code fragments already exposed in the previous example.

1. First, include the `MCJIT` header, as shown in the following code:

   ```
   #include "llvm/ExecutionEngine/MCJIT.h"
   ```

2. Include all other necessary headers, and import the `llvm` namespace:

   ```
   #include "llvm/ADT/OwningPtr.h"
   #include "llvm/Bitcode/ReaderWriter.h"
   #include "llvm/ExecutionEngine/JIT.h"
   #include "llvm/IR/LLVMContext.h"
   #include "llvm/IR/Module.h"
   #include "llvm/Support/MemoryBuffer.h"
   #include "llvm/Support/ManagedStatic.h"
   #include "llvm/Support/TargetSelect.h"
   #include "llvm/Support/raw_ostream.h"
   #include "llvm/Support/system_error.h"
   #include "llvm/Support/FileSystem.h"
   using namespace llvm;
   ```

3. Set the `UseMCJIT` Boolean to `true` in order to test MCJIT. Set it to `false` in order to run this example using the old JIT, as shown in the following code:

   ```
   bool UseMCJIT = true;

   int main() {
     InitializeNativeTarget();
   ```

4. MCJIT requires the initialization of the assembly parser and the printer:

```
if (UseMCJIT) {
  InitializeNativeTargetAsmPrinter();
  InitializeNativeTargetAsmParser();
}


LLVMContext Context;
std::string ErrorMessage;
OwningPtr<MemoryBuffer> Buffer;

if (MemoryBuffer::getFile("./sum.bc", Buffer)) {
  errs() << "sum.bc not found\n";
  return -1;
}


Module *M = ParseBitcodeFile(Buffer.get(), Context,
  &ErrorMessage);
if (!M) {
  errs() << ErrorMessage << "\n";
  return -1;
}
```

5. Create the execution engine and call the `setUseMCJIT(true)` method to tell the engine to use MCJIT, as shown in the following code:

```
OwningPtr<ExecutionEngine> EE;
if (UseMCJIT)
  EE.reset(EngineBuilder(M).setUseMCJIT(true).create());
else
  EE.reset(EngineBuilder(M).create());
```

6. The old JIT requires the `Function` reference, which is used later to retrieve the function pointer and to destroy the allocated memory:

```
Function* SumFn = NULL;
if (!UseMCJIT)
  SumFn = cast<Function>(M->getFunction("sum"));
```

7. As mentioned before, using `getPointerToFunction()` is deprecated for MCJIT, while `getFunctionAddress()` is only available in MCJIT. Hence, we use the right method for each JIT type:

```
int (*Sum)(int, int) = NULL;
if (UseMCJIT)
   Sum = (int (*)(int, int)) EE->getFunctionAddress(std::string("
sum"));
   else
   Sum = (int (*)(int, int)) EE->getPointerToFunction(SumFn);
int res = Sum(4,5);
outs() << "Sum result: " << res << "\n";
res = Sum(res, 6);
outs() << "Sum result: " << res << "\n";
```

8. Since MCJIT compiles the whole module at once, releasing the machine code memory for the Sum function only makes sense in the old JIT:

```
if (!UseMCJIT)
   EE->freeMachineCodeForFunction(SumFn);

llvm_shutdown();
return 0;
}
```

To compile and link sum-mcjit.cpp, use the following command:

```
$ clang++ sum-mcjit.cpp -g -O3 -rdynamic -fno-rtti $(llvm-config
--cppflags --ldflags --libs jit mcjit native irreader) -o sum-mcjit
```

Alternatively, use your modified Makefile from *Chapter 3, Tools and Design*. Run the following example and check the output:

```
$ ./sum-mcjit
Sum result: 9
Sum result: 15
```

Using LLVM JIT compilation tools

LLVM provides a few tools to work with JIT engines. The examples of such tools are lli and llvm-rtdyld.

Using the lli tool

The interpreter tool (lli) implements an LLVM bitcode interpreter and JIT compiler as well by using the LLVM execution engines studied in this chapter. Let's consider the source file, sum-main.c:

```
#include <stdio.h>

int sum(int a, int b) {
  return a + b;
}

int main() {
  printf("sum: %d\n", sum(2, 3) + sum(3, 4));
  return 0;
}
```

The lli tool is capable of running bitcode files when a main function is provided. Generate the sum-main.bc bitcode file by using clang:

```
$ clang -emit-llvm -c sum-main.c -o sum-main.bc
```

Now, run the bitcode through lli by using the old JIT compilation engine:

```
$ lli sum-main.bc
sum: 12
```

Alternatively, use the MCJIT engine:

```
$ lli -use-mcjit sum-main.bc
sum: 12
```

There is also a flag to use the interpreter, which is usually much slower:

```
$ lli -force-interpreter sum-main.bc
sum:12
```

Using the llvm-rtdyld tool

The llvm-rtdyld tool (<llvm_source>/tools/llvm-rtdyld/llvm-rtdyld.cpp) is a very simple tool that tests the MCJIT object loading and linking framework. This tool is capable of reading binary object files from the disk and executing functions specified by the command line. It does not perform JIT compilation and execution, but allows you to test and run object files.

Consider the following three C source code files: `main.c`, `add.c`, and `sub.c`:

- `main.c`

```
int add(int a, int b);
int sub(int a, int b);

int main() {
    return sub(add(3,4), 2);
}
```

- `add.c`

```
int add(int a, int b) {
    return a+b;
}
```

- `sub.c`

```
int sub(int a, int b) {
    return a-b;
}
```

Compile these sources in object files:

```
$ clang -c main.c -o main.o
$ clang -c add.c -o add.o
$ clang -c sub.c -o sub.o
```

Execute the main function using the `llvm-rtdyld` tool with the `-entry` and `-execute` options:

```
$ llvm-rtdyld -execute -entry=_main main.o add.o sub.o; echo $?
loaded '_main' at: 0x104d98000
5
```

Another option is to print line information for the functions compiled with debug information using the `-printline` option. For example, let's look at the following code:

```
$ clang -g -c add.c -o add.o
$ llvm-rtdyld -printline add.o
Function: _add, Size = 20
  Line info @ 0: add.c, line:2
  Line info @ 10: add.c, line:3
  Line info @ 20: add.c, line:3
```

We can see the object abstractions from the MCJIT framework in practice in the llvm-rtdyld tool. The llvm-rtdyld tool works by reading a list of binary object files into the ObjectBuffer objects and generates the ObjectImage instances using RuntimeDyld::loadObject(). After loading all the object files, it resolves relocations using RuntimeDyld::resolveRelocations(). Next, the entry point is resolved via getSymbolAddress() and the function is called.

The llvm-rtdyld tool also uses a custom memory manager, TrivialMemoryManager. It is a simple RTDyldMemoryManager subclass implementation that is easy to understand.

This great proof-of-concept tool helps you to understand the basic concepts involved in the MCJIT framework.

Other resources

There are other resources to learn about the LLVM JIT through online documentation and examples. In the LLVM source tree, <llvm_source>/examples/HowToUseJIT and <llvm_source>/examples/ParallelJIT contain simple source code examples that are useful for learning the JIT basics.

The LLVM kaleidoscope tutorial at http://llvm.org/docs/tutorial contains a specific chapter on how to use JIT http://llvm.org/docs/tutorial/LangImpl4. html.

More information on MCJIT design and implementation can also be found at http://llvm.org/docs/MCJITDesignAndImplementation.html.

Summary

JIT compilation is a runtime compilation feature present in several virtual machine environments. In this chapter, we explored the LLVM JIT execution engine by showing the distinct implementations available, the old JIT and the MCJIT. Moreover, we examined implementation details from both approaches and provided real examples on how to build tools to use the JIT engines.

In the next chapter, we will cover cross-compilation, toolchains, and how to create an LLVM-based cross compiler.

8
Cross-platform Compilation

Traditional compilers transform the source code into native executables. In this context, native means that it runs on the same platform of the compiler, and a platform is a combination of hardware, operating system, **application binary interface (ABI)**, and system interface choices. These choices define a mechanism that the user-level program can use to communicate with the underlying system. Hence, if you use a compiler in your GNU/Linux x86 machine, it will generate executables that link with your system libraries and are tailored to run on this exact same platform.

Cross-platform compilation is the process of using a compiler to generate executables for different, non-native platforms. If you need to generate code that links with libraries different to the libraries of your own system, you can usually solve this by using specific compilation flags. However, if the target platform where you intend to deploy your executable is incompatible with your platform, such as when using a different processor architecture, operating system, ABI, or object file, you need to resort to cross compilation.

Cross-compilers are essential when developing applications for systems with limited resources; embedded systems, for instance, are typically composed of lower performance processors with constrained memory, and since the compilation process is CPU and memory intensive, running a compiler in such systems, if possible, is slow and delays the application development cycle. Therefore, cross-compilers are invaluable tools in such scenarios. In this chapter, we will cover the following topics:

- A comparison between the Clang and the GCC cross-compilation approaches
- What are toolchains?
- How to cross-compile with Clang command lines
- How to cross-compile by generating a custom Clang
- Popular simulators and hardware platforms to test target binaries

Comparing GCC and LLVM

Compilers such as GCC must be built with a special configuration to support cross compilation, requiring the installation of a different GCC for each target. A common practice, for example, is to prefix your `gcc` command with the target name, such as `arm-gcc` to denote a GCC cross-compiler for ARM. However, Clang/LLVM allows you to generate code for other targets by simply switching the command-line options of the same Clang driver between the desired target, paths to libraries, headers, the linker, and the assembler. One Clang driver, therefore, works for all targets. However, some LLVM distributions do not include all the targets owing to, for example, executable size concerns. On the other hand, if you build LLVM yourself, you get to choose which targets to support; see *Chapter 1, Build and Install LLVM*.

GCC is a much older, and subsequently, a more mature project than LLVM. It supports more than 50 backends and is widely utilized as a cross-compiler for these platforms. However, the design of GCC constrains its driver to deal with a single target library per installation. This is the reason why, in order to generate code for other targets, different GCC installations must be arranged.

In contrast, all target libraries are compiled and linked with the Clang driver in a default build. At runtime, even though Clang needs to know several target particularities, Clang/LLVM components can access whatever target information they need by using target-independent interfaces designed to supply information about any command-line-specified target. This approach gives the driver the flexibility to avoid the need for a target-specific Clang installation for each target.

The following diagram illustrates how a source code is compiled for different targets by both LLVM and GCC; the former dynamically generates the code for distinct processors, while the latter needs a different cross-compiler for each processor.

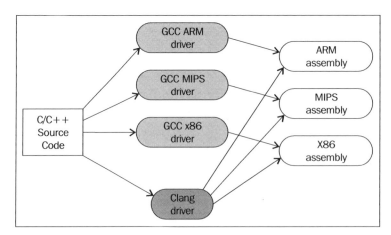

You can also build a specialized Clang cross-compiler driver just like GCC's. Although this choice demands more effort to build a separate Clang/LLVM installation, it leads to an easier to use command-line interface. During configuration time, the user can provide fixed paths to target libraries, headers, the assembler, and the linker, avoiding the necessity to pass a myriad of command-line options to the driver every time cross-compilation is needed.

In this chapter, we show you how to use Clang to generate code for multiple platforms by using driver command-line options, and how to generate a specific Clang cross-compiler driver.

Understanding target triples

We will start by presenting three important definitions as follows:

- Build is the platform where the cross-compiler is built
- Host designates the platform where the cross-compiler will run
- Target refers to the platform where executables or libraries generated by the cross-compiler run

In a standard cross-compiler, the build and host platforms are the same. You define the build, host, and target via target triples. These triples uniquely identify a target variation with information about the processor architecture, operating system flavor and version, C library kind, and object file type.

There is no strict format for triples. GNU tools, for instance, may accept triples composed of two, three, or even four fields in the `<arch>-<sys/vendor>-<other>-<other>` format, such as `arm-linux-eabi`, `mips-linux-gnu`, `x86_64-linux-gnu`, `x86_64-apple-darwin11`, and `sparc-elf`. Clang strives to maintain compatibility with GCC and thus recognizes this format, but it will internally canonicalize any triple into its own triple pattern, `<arch><sub>-<vendor>-<sys>-<abi>`.

The following table contains a list of possible options for each LLVM triple field; the `<sub>` field is not included, since it represents architecture variations, for example, `v7` in the `armv7` architecture. See `<llvm_source>/include/llvm/ADT/Triple.h` for the triple details:

Architecture (`<arch>`)	Vendor (`<vendor>`)	Operating system (`<sys>`)	Environment (`<abi>`)
`arm, aarch64, hexagon,` `mips, mipsel, mips64,` `mips64el, msp430,` `ppc, ppc64, ppc64le,` `r600, sparc, sparcv9,` `systemz, tce, thumb,` `x86, x86_64, xcore,` `nvptx, nvptx64, le32,` `amdil, spir,` and `spir64`	`unknown,` `apple, pc,` `scei, bgp,` `bgq, fsl,` `ibm,` and `nvidia`	`unknown, auroraux,` `cygwin, darwin,` `dragonfly, freebsd,` `ios, kfreebsd, linux,` `lv2, macosx, mingw32,` `netbsd, openbsd,` `solaris, win32, haiku,` `minix, rtems, nacl, cnk,` `bitrig, aix, cuda,` and `nvcl`	`unknown,` `gnu,` `gnueabihf,` `gnueabi,` `gnux32,` `eabi, macho,` `android,` and `elf`

Note that not all the combinations of `arch`, `vendor`, `sys`, and `abi` are valid. Each architecture supports a limited set of combinations.

The following diagram illustrates the concept of an ARM cross-compiler that is built on top of x86, runs on x86, and generates ARM executables. The curious reader may wonder what happens if the host and build are different. This combination results in a Canadian cross-compiler, a process which is a bit more complex and requires the darker compiler box in the following diagram to be another cross-compiler instead of a native compiler. The name Canadian cross was coined after the fact that Canada had three political parties at the time the name was created and the Canadian cross uses three different platforms. A Canadian cross is necessary, for example, if you are distributing cross-compilers for other users and wish to support platforms other than your own.

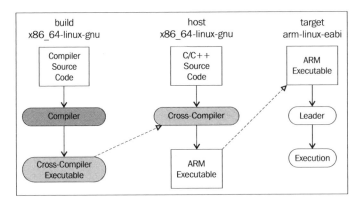

Preparing your toolchain

The term compiler implies a collection of compilation-related tasks performed by different components such as the frontend, backend, assembler, and linker. Some of them are implemented in separate tools, while others are integrated. However, while developing native applications or for any other target, a user needs more resources, such as platform-dependent libraries, a debugger, and tools to perform tasks, for example, to read the object file. Therefore, platform manufacturers usually distribute a bundle of tools for software development in their platform, thus providing the clients with a development toolchain.

In order to generate or use your cross-compiler, it is very important to know the toolchain components and how they interact with each other. The following diagram shows the main toolchain components necessary for successful cross-compilation, while the sections that follow describe each component:

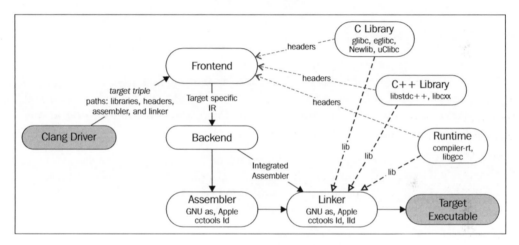

Standard C and C++ libraries

A C library is necessary to support standard C language functionalities such as memory allocation (`malloc()`/`free()`), string handling (`strcmp()`), and I/O (`printf()`/`scanf()`). The examples of popular C library header files include `stdio.h`, `stdlib.h`, and `string.h`. There are several C library implementations available. The GNU C library (`glibc`), `newlib`, and `uClibc` are widely known examples. These libraries are available for different targets and can be ported to new ones.

Likewise, the C++ standard library implements C++ functionalities such as input and output streams, containers, string handling, and thread support. GNU's `libstdc++` and LLVM's `libc++` (see `http://libcxx.llvm.org`) are implementation examples. In fact, the full GNU C++ library comprises of both `libstdc++` and `libsupc++`. The latter is a target-dependent layer to ease porting, which exclusively deals with exception handling and RTTI. LLVM's `libc++` implementation still depends on a third-party substitute for `libsupc++` for systems other than Mac OS X (see the *Introducing the libc++ standard library* section in *Chapter 2*, *External Projects*, for more details).

A cross-compiler needs to know the path of the target C/C++ libraries and headers in order to search for the right function prototypes and later do proper linking. It is important that the header files match the compiled libraries, both in version and in implementation. For example, a misconfigured cross-compiler may look into the native system headers instead, leading to compilation errors.

Runtime libraries

Each target needs to use special functions to emulate low-level operations that are not natively supported. For instance, 32-bit targets usually lack 64-bit registers and are unable to work directly with 64-bit types. Therefore, the target may use two 32-bit registers and invoke specific functions to perform simple arithmetic operations (addition, subtraction, multiplication, and division).

The code generator emits calls to these functions and expects them to be found at link time. The driver must provide the necessary libraries, not the user. In GCC, this functionality is implemented by the runtime library, `libgcc`. LLVM provides a drop-in replacement called `compiler-rt` (see *Chapter 2*, *External Projects*). Thus, the Clang driver invokes the linker using either `-lgcc` or `-lclang_rt` (to link with `compiler-rt`). Again, target-specific runtime libraries must be in the path in order to be correctly linked.

The assembler and the linker

The assembler and the linker are usually provided by separate tools and invoked by the compiler driver. For example, the assembler and the linker provided by GNU Binutils has support for several targets, and for the native target, they are usually found in the system path with the names `as` and `ld`, respectively. There is also an LLVM-based, but still experimental, linker called `lld` (`http://lld.llvm.org`).

To invoke such tools, the target triple is used in the assembler and linker name prefix and looked up in the PATH variable of the system. For example, when generating code for mips-linux-gnu, the driver may search for mips-linux-gnu-as and mips-linux-gnu-ld. Clang may perform this search differently depending on the target triple information.

Some targets need no external assembler invocation in Clang. Since LLVM provides direct object code emission through the MC layer, the driver can use the integrated MC assembler with the -integrated-as option, which is turned on by default for specific targets.

The Clang frontend

In *Chapter 5, The LLVM Intermediate Representation*, we explained that the LLVM IR emitted by Clang is not target-independent as the C/C++ language too is not independent. In addition to the backend, the frontend must also implement target-specific constraints. Hence, you must be aware that although support for a specific processor exists in Clang, if the target triple does not strictly match this processor, the frontend may generate imperfect LLVM IR that may lead to ABI mismatches and runtime errors.

Multilib

Multilib is a solution that allows users to run applications compiled for different ABIs on the same platform. This mechanism avoids multiple cross-compilers as long as one cross-compiler has access to the compiled versions of each ABI variation library and header. For example, multilib allows soft-float and hard-float libraries to coexist, that is, libraries that rely on the software emulation of floating-point arithmetic and libraries that rely on the processor FPU to handle floating-point numbers. GCC, for instance, has several versions of libc and libgcc for each version of multilib.

In MIPS GCC, for example, the multilib library folder structure is organized as follows:

- lib/n32: This folder holds n32 libraries, supporting the n32 MIPS ABI
- lib/n32/EL: This folder holds the little-endian versions of libgcc, libc, and libstdc++
- lib/n32/msoft-float: This folder holds n32 soft-float libraries
- lib/n64: This folder holds n64 libraries, supporting the n64 MIPS ABI
- lib/n64/EL: This folder holds the little-endian version of libgcc, libc, and libstdc++
- lib/n64/msoft-float: This folder holds n64 soft-float libraries.

Clang supports multilib environments as long as the right paths for libraries and headers are provided. However, since the frontend potentially generates different LLVM IR for different ABIs in some targets, it is good practice to double-check your paths and target triples to ensure that they match, avoiding runtime errors.

Cross-compiling with Clang command-line arguments

Now that you know each toolchain component, we will show you how to use Clang as a cross-compiler by using the appropriate driver arguments.

 All the examples in this section are tested in an x86_64 machine running Ubuntu 12.04. We use Ubuntu-specific tools to download some dependencies, but the Clang-related commands should work in any other OS environment without (or with minor) modifications.

Driver options for the target

Clang uses the `-target=<triple>` driver option to dynamically select the target triple for which code needs to be generated. Beyond the triple, other options can be used to make target selection more accurate:

- The `-march=<arch>` option selects the target base architecture. The examples of the `<arch>` values include `armv4t`, `armv6`, `armv7`, and `armv7f` for ARM and `mips32`, `mips32r2`, `mips64`, and `mips64r2` for MIPS. This option alone also selects a default base CPU to be used in the code generator.

- To select a specific CPU, use `-mcpu=<cpu>`. For example, `cortex-m3` and `cortex-a8` are ARM-specific CPUs and `pentium4`, `athlon64`, and `corei7-avx2` are x86 CPUs. Each CPU has a base `<arch>` value defined by the target and used by the driver.

- The `-mfloat-abi=<abi>` option determines which kind of registers are used to hold floating-point values: `soft` or `hard`. As mentioned previously, this determines whether to use software floating-point emulation. This also implies changes in calling conventions and other ABI specifications. The `-msoft-float` and `-mhard-float` aliases are also available. Note that if this is not specified, the ABI type conforms to the default type for the selected CPU.

To see other target-specific switches, use `clang --help-hidden`, which will reveal to you even the hidden options from the traditional help message.

Dependencies

We will use an ARM cross-compiler as a running example to demonstrate how to cross-compile with Clang. The first step is to install a complete ARM toolchain in your system and identify the provided components.

To install a GCC cross-compiler for ARM with a hard floating-point ABI, use the following command:

```
$ apt-get install g++-4.6-arm-linux-gnueabihf gcc-4.6-arm-linux-gnueabihf
```

To install a GCC cross-compiler for ARM with a soft floating-point ABI, use the following command:

```
$ apt-get install g++-4.6-arm-linux-gnueabi gcc-4.6-arm-linux-gnueabi
```

We just asked you to install a complete GCC toolchain, including the cross-compiler! Why would you need Clang/LLVM now? As explained in the toolchain section, during cross compilation, the compiler itself acts as a small piece that fits in an arrangement of several components that include the assembler, linker, and target libraries. You should seek the toolchain prepared by your target platform vendor because only this toolchain will have the correct headers and libraries used in your target platform. Typically, this toolchain is already distributed with a GCC compiler as well. What we want to do is to use Clang/LLVM instead, but we still depend on all other toolchain components to work.

If you want to build all the target libraries and prepare the entire toolchain yourself, you will also need to prepare an operating system image to boot the target platform. If you build the system image and the toolchain yourself, you guarantee that both agree with respect to the version of the libraries used in the target system. If you like to build everything from scratch, a good guide on how to do this is available in the Cross Linux from Scratch tutorials at `http://trac.cross-lfs.org`.

Although `apt-get` automatically installs the toolchain prerequisites, the basic packages needed and recommend for a Clang-based C/C++ ARM cross-compiler are the following:

- `libc6-dev-armhf-cross` and `libc6-dev-armel-cross`
- `gcc-4.6-arm-linux-gnueabi-base` and `gcc-4.6-arm-linux-gnueabihf-base`
- `binutils-arm-linux-gnueabi` and `binutils-arm-linux-gnueabihf`
- `libgcc1-armel-cross` and `libgcc1-armhf-cross`
- `libstdc++6-4.6-dev-armel-cross` and `libstdc++6-4.6-dev-armhf-cross`

Cross-compiling

Although we are not interested in the GCC cross-compilers themselves, the command in the preceding section installs the necessary prerequisites we will need for *our* cross-compiler: linker, assembler, libraries, and headers. You can compile the sum.c program (from *Chapter 7, The Just-in-Time Compiler*) for the arm-linux-gnueabihf platform using the following command:

```
$ clang --target=arm-linux-gnueabihf sum.c -o sum
$ file sum
sum: ELF 32-bit LSB executable, ARM, version 1 (SYSV), dynamically linked
(uses shared libs)...
```

Clang finds all the necessary components from GNU's arm-linux-gnueabihf toolchain and generates the final executable. In this example, the default architecture used is armv6, but we can be more specific in providing the --target value and use -mcpu to achieve more precise code generation:

```
$ clang --target=armv7a-linux-gnueabihf -mcpu=cortex-a15 sum.c -o sum
```

Installing GCC

The target triple in --target is used by Clang to search for a GCC installation with the same or similar prefix. If several candidates are found, Clang selects the one that it considers the closest match to the target:

```
$ clang --target=arm-linux-gnueabihf sum.c -o sum -v
clang version 3.4 (tags/RELEASE_34/final)
Target: arm--linux-gnueabihf
Thread model: posix
Found candidate GCC installation: /usr/lib/gcc/arm-linux-gnueabihf/4.6
Found candidate GCC installation: /usr/lib/gcc/arm-linux-gnueabihf/4.6.3
Selected GCC installation: /usr/lib/gcc/arm-linux-gnueabihf/4.6
(...)
```

Since a GCC installation usually comes with an assembler, a linker, libraries, and headers, it is used by Clang to reach the desired toolchain components. By providing a triple with the exact name of an existing toolchain in the system, it is usually straightforward to obtain such paths. However, if we provide a different or incomplete triple, the driver searches for and selects what it considers the best match:

```
$ clang --target=arm-linux sum.c -o sum -v
...
Selected GCC installation: /usr/lib/gcc/arm-linux-gnueabi/4.7
clang: warning: unknown platform, assuming -mfloat-abi=soft
```

Note that although we installed GCC toolchains for `arm-linux-gnueabi` and `arm-linux-gnueabihf`, the driver selects the former. In this example, since the selected platform is unknown, a *soft-float* ABI is assumed.

Potential problems

If we add the `-mfloat-abi=hard` option, the driver omits the warning but keeps selecting `arm-linux-gnueabi` instead of `arm-linux-gnueabihf`. This leads to a final executable that is likely to fail due to runtime errors, because a hard-float object is linked with a soft-float library:

```
$ clang --target=arm-linux -mfloat-abi=hard sum.c -o sum
```

The reason why `arm-linux-gnuebihf` was not selected even though `-float-abi=hard` was passed is because we did not specifically ask clang to use the `arm-linux-gnueabihf` toolchain. If you leave this decision to the driver, it will pick the first toolchain that it finds, which may not be adequate. This example is important to show you that the driver may not select the best option if you use a vague or incomplete target triple such as `arm-linux`.

It is very important to know the underlying toolchain components being used to confirm whether the right toolchain was selected, for example, by using the `-###` flag that prints which tool invocations were used by Clang to compile, assemble, and link your program.

Let's try to be even more vague about the target triple to see what happens. We will use just the `--target=arm` option:

```
$ clang --target=arm sum.c -o sum
/tmp/sum-3bbfbc.s: Assembler messages:
/tmp/sum-3bbfbc.s:1: Error: unknown pseudo-op: `.syntax'
/tmp/sum-3bbfbc.s:2: Error: unknown pseudo-op: `.cpu'
/tmp/sum-3bbfbc.s:3: Error: unknown pseudo-op: `.eabi_attribute'
(...)
```

By removing the OS from the triple, the driver gets confused and a compilation error occurs. What happened is that the driver tried to assemble the ARM assembly language by using the native (x86_64) assembler. Since the target triple was quite incomplete and the OS was missing, our `arm-linux` toolchains were not a satisfactory match for the driver, which resorted to using the system assembler.

Changing the system root

The driver is able to find toolchain support for the target by checking the presence of the GCC cross-compilers with the given triple in the system and by a list of the known prefixes it scans for in GCC installation directories (see `<llvm_source>/tools/clang/lib/Driver/ToolChains.cpp`).

In some other cases — malformed triples or absent GCC cross-compilers — special options must be passed to the driver in order to use the available toolchain components. For instance, the `--sysroot` option changes the base directory, where Clang searches for toolchain components and can be used whenever the target triple does not provide enough information. Similarly, you can also use `--gcc-toolchain=<value>` to specify the folder of a specific toolchain you want to use.

In the ARM toolchain installed in our system, the selected GCC installation path for the `arm-linux-gnueabi` triple is `/usr/lib/gcc/arm-linux-gnueabi/4.6.3`. From this directory, Clang is able to reach the other paths for libraries, headers, assembler, and linker. One path it reaches is `/usr/arm-linux-gnueabi`, which contains the following subdirectories:

```
$ ls /usr/arm-linux-gnueabi
bin   include   lib   usr
```

The toolchain components are organized in these folders in the same way as the native ones live in the filesystem's `/bin`, `/include`, `/lib`, and `/usr` root folders. Consider that we want to generate code for `armv7-linux` with a `cortex A9` CPU, without relying on the driver to find the components automatically for us. As long as we know where the `arm-linux-gnueabi` components are, we can provide a `--sysroot` flag to the driver:

```
$ PATH=/usr/arm-linux-gnueabi/bin:$PATH /p/cross/bin/clang
--target=armv7a-linux --sysroot=/usr/arm-linux-gnueabi -mcpu=cortex-a9
-mfloat-abi=soft sum.c -o sum
```

Again, this is very useful when there are toolchain components available, but there is no solid GCC installation. There are three main reasons why this approach works as follows:

- The `armv7a-linux: armv7a` triple activates code generation for ARM and `linux`. Among other things, it tells the driver to use the GNU assembler and linker invocation syntax. If no OS is specified, Clang defaults to the Darwin assembler syntax, yielding an assembler error.
- The `/usr`, `/lib`, and `/usr/include` folders are the default compiler search places for libraries and headers. The `--sysroot` option overrides the driver defaults to look into `/usr/arm-linux-gnueabi` for these directories instead of the system root.

- The PATH environment variable is changed, avoiding the default versions of as and ld from being used. We then force the driver to look at the /usr/arm-linux-gnueabi/bin path first, where the ARM versions of as and ld are found.

Generating a Clang cross-compiler

Clang dynamically supports the generation of code for any target, as seen in the previous sections. However, there are reasons to generate a target-dedicated Clang cross-compiler:

- If the user wishes to avoid using long command lines to invoke the driver
- If a manufacturer wishes to ship a platform-specific Clang-based toolchain to its clients

Configuration options

The LLVM configure system has the following options that assist in cross-compiler generation:

- --target: This option specifies the default target triple that the Clang cross-compiler generates code for. This relates to the target, host, and build concepts we defined earlier. The --host and --build options are also available, but these are guessed by the configure script—both refer to the native platform.

- --enable-targets: This option specifies which targets this installation will support. If omitted, all targets will be supported. Remember that you must use the command-line options previously explained to select targets different from the default one, which is specified with the --target flag.

- --with-c-include-dirs: This option specifies a list of directories that the cross-compiler should use to search for header files. Using this option avoids the excessive usage of -I to locate target-specific libraries, which may not be located in canonical paths. Additionally, these directories are searched prior to the system default ones.

- --with-gcc-toolchain: This option specifies a target GCC toolchain already present in the system. The toolchain components are located by this option and hardcoded in the cross-compiler as with a permanent --gcc-toolchain option.

- --with-default-sysroot: This option adds the --sysroot option to all the compiler invocations executed by the cross-compiler.

See `<llvm_source>/configure --help` for all the LLVM/Clang configuration options. Extra configuration options (hidden ones) can be used to explore target-specific features, such as `--with-cpu`, `--with-float`, `--with-abi`, and `--with-fpu`.

Building and installing your Clang-based cross-compiler

Instructions to configure, build, and install a cross-compiler are very similar to the traditional way of compiling LLVM and Clang explained in *Chapter 1, Build and Install LLVM*.

Therefore, assuming that the sources are in place, you can generate an LLVM ARM cross-compiler that targets Cortex-A9, by default, with the following command:

```
$ cd <llvm_build_dir>
$ <PATH_TO_SOURCE>/configure --enable-targets=arm --disable-optimized
--prefix=/usr/local/llvm-arm --target=armv7a-unknown-linux-gnueabi
$ make && sudo make install
$ export PATH=$PATH:/usr/local/llvm-arm
$ armv7a-unknown-linux-gnueabi-clang sum.c -o sum
$ file sum
sum: ELF 32-bit LSB executable, ARM, version 1 (SYSV), dynamically linked
(uses shared libs)...
```

Recall from the *Understanding target triples* section that our GCC-compatible target triple can have up to four elements, but some tools accept triples with less. In the case of the configure script used by LLVM, which is generated by GNU autotools, it expects the target triple to have all the four elements, with the vendor information in the second element. Since our platform does not have a specific vendor, we expand our triple to be `armv7a-unknown-linux-gnueabi`. If we insist on using a triple with three elements here, the configure script will fail.

No additional options are necessary to detect the toolchain because Clang performs the GCC installation lookup as usual.

Suppose that you compile and install extra ARM libraries and headers in the `/opt/arm-extra-libs/include` and `/opt/arm-extra-libs/lib` directories, respectively. By using `--with-c-include-dirs=/opt/arm-extra-libs/include`, you can permanently add this directory to the Clang header search path; it is still necessary to add `-L/opt/arm-extra-libs/lib` for proper linkage.

```
$ <PATH_TO_SOURCE>/configure --enable-targets=arm --disable-optimized
--prefix=/usr/local/llvm-arm --target=armv7a-unknown-linux-gnueabi
--with-c-include-dirs=/opt/arm-extra-libs/include
```

Similarly, we can add a sysroot (`--sysroot`) flag and also specify the GCC toolchain (`--with-gcc-toolchain`) to be always used by the driver. This is redundant for the chosen ARM triple, but it may be useful for other targets:

```
$ <PATH_TO_SOURCE>/configure --enable-targets=arm --disable-optimized
--prefix=/usr/local/llvm-arm --target=armv7a-unknown-linux-gnueabi
--with-gcc-toolchain=arm-linux-gnueabi --with-default-sysroot=/usr/arm-
linux-gnueabi
```

Alternative build methods

There are other tools available to generate LLVM/Clang-based toolchains, or we can use other build systems in LLVM. Another alternative way is to create a wrapper to facilitate the process.

Ninja

One alternative to generate cross-compilers is to use CMake and Ninja. The Ninja project is intended to be a small and fast build system.

Instead of the traditional configure and build steps to generate a cross-compiler, you can use special CMake options to generate suitable build instructions for Ninja, which then builds and installs the cross-compiler for the desired target.

The instructions and documentation on how to go about this approach are present at http://llvm.org/docs/HowToCrossCompileLLVM.html.

ELLCC

The ELLCC tool is an LLVM-based framework used to generate toolchains for embedded targets.

It aims at creating an easy resource for generating and using cross-compilers. It is extensible, supports new target configurations, and is easy to use for developers to multitarget their programs.

The ELLCC also compiles and installs several toolchain components, including a debugger and a QEMU for platform testing (if available).

The ecc tool is the final cross-compiler to use. It works by creating a layer over Clang cross-compilers and accepting GCC and Clang compatible command-line options to compile for any supported target. You can read more at http://ellcc.org/.

EmbToolkit

The embedded system toolkit is another framework for generating toolchains for embedded systems. It supports generating Clang or LLVM-based toolchains while compiling its components and providing a root filesystem at the same time.

It provides `ncurses` and GUI interfaces for component selection. You can find more details at `https://www.embtoolkit.org/`.

Testing

The most reasonable way to test a successful cross-compilation is to run the resulting executable on a real target platform. However, when real targets are not available or affordable, there are several simulators that can be used to test your programs.

Development boards

There are several development boards for a multitude of platforms. Nowadays, they are affordable and can be bought online. For instance, you can find ARM development boards ranging from simple Cortex-M series processors to multicore Cortex-A series.

The peripheral components vary, but it is very common to find Ethernet, Wi-Fi, USB, and memory cards on these boards. Hence, cross-compiled applications can be sent through the network, USB, or can be written to flash cards and can be executed on bare metal or on embedded Linux/FreeBSD instances.

The examples of such development boards include the following:

Name	Features	Architecture/ Processor	Link
Panda Board	Linux, Android, Ubuntu	ARM, Dual Core Cortex A9	`http://pandaboard.org/`
Beagle Board	Linux, Android, Ubuntu	ARM, Cortex A8	`http://beagleboard.org/`
SEAD-3	Linux	MIPS M14K	`http://www.timesys.com/ supported/processors/mips`
Carambola-2	Linux	MIPS 24K	`http://8devices.com/ carambola-2`

There are also plenty of mobile phones with ARM and MIPS processors running Android with development kits available. You can also try Clang on these.

Simulators

It is very common for manufacturers to develop simulators for their processors because a software development cycle starts even before a physical platform is ready. Toolchains with simulators are distributed to clients or used internally for testing products.

One way to test cross-compiled programs is through these manufacturer-provided environments. However, there are several open source emulators for a distinct number of architectures and processors also. QEMU is an open source emulator supporting user and system emulation.

In user emulation mode, QEMU is able to emulate standalone executables compiled for other targets in the current platform. For instance, an ARM-executable compiled and linked with Clang, as described in the previous sections, is likely to work out of the box in an ARM-QEMU user emulator.

The system emulator reproduces the behavior of an entire system, including peripherals and multiprocessors. Since the complete boot process is emulated, an operating system is needed. There are complete development boards emulated by QEMU. It is also ideal to test bare-metal targets or test programs that interface with peripherals.

QEMU supports architecture such as ARM, MIPS, OpenRISC, SPARC, Alpha, and MicroBlaze with different processor variations. You can read more at `http://qemu-project.org`.

Additional resources

The official Clang documentation contains very relevant information about using Clang as a cross-compiler. See `http://clang.llvm.org/docs/CrossCompilation.html`.

Summary

Cross-compilers are an important resource for developing an application for other platforms. Clang is designed in such a way that cross-compilation is a free feature and can be performed dynamically by the driver.

In this chapter, we present which elements compound a cross-compilation environment and how Clang interacts with them in order to produce target executables. We also see that a Clang cross-compiler may still be useful in some scenarios and provide instructions on how to build, install, and use a cross-compiler.

In the next chapter, we will present the Clang static compiler and show how you can search large code bases for common bugs.

9

The Clang Static Analyzer

Humans show difficulty in planning the construction of an abstract apparatus for which they cannot easily measure the size of and quantify effort. Not surprisingly, software projects show a remarkable history of failures owing to an unhandled increase in complexity. If building complex software requires an unusual amount of coordination and organization, maintaining it is perhaps an even tougher challenge.

Still, the older the software gets, the harder it becomes to maintain. It typically reflects the effort of different generations of programmers with contrasting views. When a new programmer is in charge of maintaining old software, it is common practice to simply tightly wrap unintelligible old code pieces, isolate the software, and turn it into an untouchable library.

Such complex code bases demand a new category of tools to aid programmers in taming obscure bugs. The purpose of the Clang Static Analyzer is to offer an automated way to analyze a large code base and lend a hand for humans to detect a wide range of common bugs in their C, C++, or Objective-C projects, before compilation. In this chapter, we will cover the following topics:

- What are the differences between warnings emitted by classic compiler tools versus the ones emitted by the Clang Static Analyzer
- How to use the Clang Static Analyzer in simple projects
- How to use the `scan-build` tool to cover large, real-world projects
- How to extend the Clang Static Analyzer with your own bug checkers

Understanding the role of a static analyzer

In the overall LLVM design, a project belongs to the Clang frontend if it operates on the original source-code level (C/C++) since recovering source-level information at the LLVM IR is challenging. One of the most interesting Clang-based tools is the Clang Static Analyzer, a project that leverages a set of **checkers** to build elaborate bug reports, similar to what *compiler warnings* traditionally do at a smaller scale. Each checker tests for a specific rule violation.

As with classic warnings, a static analyzer helps the programmer in finding bugs early in the development cycle without the need to postpone bug detection to runtime. The analysis is done after parsing, but before further compilation. On the other hand, the tool may require a lot of time to process a large code base, which is a good reason why it is not integrated in the typical compilation flow. For example, the static analyzer alone may spend hours to process the entire LLVM source code and run all of its checkers.

The Clang Static Analyzer has at least two known competitors: Fortify and Coverity. Hewlett Packard (HP) provides the former, while Synopsis provides the latter. Each tool has its own strengths and limitations, but only Clang is open source, allowing us to hack it and understand how it works, which is the goal of this chapter.

Comparing classic warnings versus the Clang Static Analyzer

The algorithm used in the Clang Static Analyzer has **exponential-time complexity**, which means that, as the program unit being analyzed grows, the required time to process it may get very large. As with many exponential-time algorithms that work in practice, it is *bounded*, which means that it is able to reduce the execution time and memory by using problem-specific tricks, albeit it is not enough to make it polynomial-time.

The exponential-time nature of the tool explains one of its biggest limitations: it is only able to analyze a single compilation unit at a time and does not perform inter-module analysis, or whole program processing. Nevertheless, it is a very capable tool because it relies on a **symbolic execution engine**.

To give an example of how a symbolic execution engine can help programmers find intricate bugs, let's first present a very simple bug that most compilers can easily detect and emit a warning. See the following code:

```
#include <stdio.h>
void main() {
    int i;
    printf ("%d", i);
}
```

In this code, we use a variable that was *uninitialized* and will cause the program output to depend on parameters that we cannot control or predict, such as the memory contents prior to program execution, leading to unexpected program behavior. Therefore, a simple automated check can save a huge headache in debugging.

If you are familiar with compiler analysis techniques, you may have noticed that we can implement this check by using a *forward dataflow analysis* that utilizes the *union confluence operator* to propagate the state of each variable, whether it is initialized or not. A forward dataflow analysis propagates state information about the variables in each basic block starting at the first basic block of the function and pushing this information to successor basic blocks. A confluence operator determines how to merge information coming from multiple preceding basic blocks. The *union confluence operator* will attribute to a basic block the result of the union of the sets of each preceding basic block.

In this analysis, if an uninitialized definition reaches a use, we should trigger a compiler warning. To this end, our dataflow framework will assign to each variable in the program the following states:

- The ⊥ symbol when we do not know anything about it (unknown state)
- The initialized label when we know that the variable was initialized
- The uninitialized label when we are sure that it was not initialized
- The ⊤ symbol when the variable can be either initialized or uninitialized (which means that we are not sure)

The following diagram shows our dataflow analysis for the simple C program that we just presented:

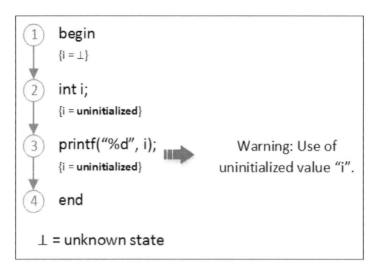

We see that this information gets easily propagated across lines of code. When it reaches the printf statement, which uses i, the framework checks what do we know about this variable and the answer is uninitialized, providing enough evidence to emit a warning.

Since this dataflow analysis relies on a polynomial-time algorithm, it is very fast.

To see how this simple analysis can lose precision, let's consider Joe, a programmer who is proficient at the art of making undetectable mistakes. Joe can very easily trick our detector and would cleverly obscure the actual variable state in separate program paths. Let's take a look at an example from Joe.

```
#include <stdio.h>
void my_function(int unknownvalue) {
    int schroedinger_integer;
    if (unknownvalue)
        schroedinger_integer = 5;
    printf("hi");
    if (!unknownvalue)
        printf("%d", schroedinger_integer);
}
```

Now let's take a look at how our dataflow framework computes the state of variables for this program:

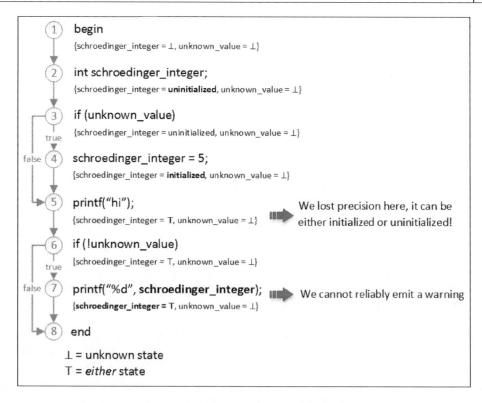

We see that, in node 4, the variable is initialized for the first time (shown in bold). However, two different paths reach node 5: the true and the false branches of the `if` statement from node 3. In one path, the variable `schroedinger_integer` is uninitialized while in the other it is initialized. The confluence operator determines how to sum the results of predecessors. Our union operator will try to keep both bits of data, declaring `schroedinger_integer` as T (either).

When the detector checks node 7, which uses `schroedinger_integer`, it is not sure about whether there is a bug or not in the code and that is because, according to this dataflow analysis, `schroedinger_integer` may or may not have been initialized. In other words, it is truly at a superposition of states, initialized and uninitialized. Our simple detector can try to warn people that a value may be used without initialization, and, in this case, it will correctly point to the bug. However, if the condition used in the last check of Joe's code is changed to `if (unknownvalue)`, emitting a warning would be a false positive, because now it is exercising the path where `schroedinger_integer` was indeed initialized.

This loss of precision in our detector happens because dataflow frameworks are not path-sensitive and cannot precisely model what happens in every possible execution path.

False positives are highly undesirable because they befuddle programmers with lists of warnings that blame code that do not contain actual bugs and it obscures the warnings that are actual bugs. In reality, if a detector generates even a small quantity of false positives warnings, programmers are likely to ignore all warnings.

The power of the symbolic execution engine

The symbolic execution engine helps when simple dataflow analyses are not enough to provide accurate information about the program. It builds a graph of reachable program states and is able to reason about all the possible code execution paths that may be taken when the program is running. Recall that when you run the program to debug, you are only exercising one path. When you debug your program with a powerful virtual machine such as valgrind to look for memory leaks, it is also only exercising one path.

Conversely, the symbolic execution engine is able to exercise them all without actually running your code. It is a very powerful feature, but demands large runtimes to process programs.

Just like classic dataflow frameworks, the engine will assign initial states to each variable that it finds when traversing the program in the order it would execute each statement. The difference comes when reaching a control-flow-changing construct: the engine splits the path in two and continues the analyses separately for each path. This graph is called the reachable program states graph and a simple example is shown in the following diagram, exposing how the engine would reason about Joe's code:

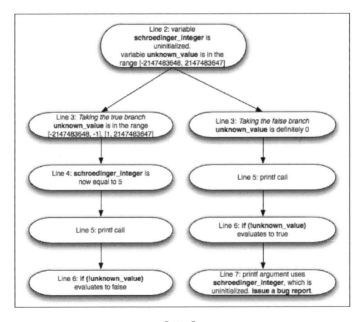

In this example, the first `if` statement in line 6 forks the reachable states graph in two different paths: in one path, `unknown_value` is not zero, while in the other, `unknown_value` is definitely zero. From this part, the engine operates with this important constraint on `unknown_value` and will use it to decide whether the next branches will be taken or not.

By using this strategy, the symbolic execution engine arrives at the conclusion that the left path in the figure will never evaluate `schroedinger_integer`, even though it has been defined in this path to be 5. On the other hand, it also concludes that the right path in the figure will evaluate `schroedinger_integer` to pass it as a `printf()` parameter. However, in this path, the value is not initialized. By using this graph, it reports the bug with precision.

Let's compare the reachable program states graph with a graph about the same code that shows control flow, a **control flow graph** (CFG) along with the typical reasoning that dataflow equations would provide us. See the following diagram:

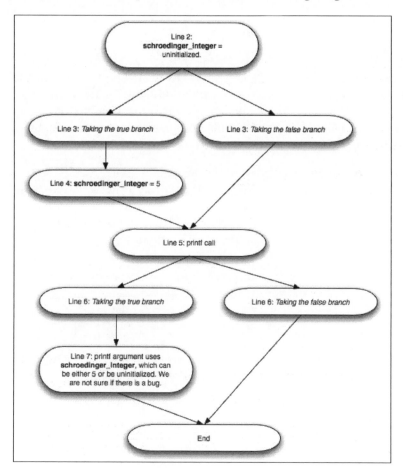

The first thing you will notice is that the CFG may fork to express control flow change, but it also merges nodes to avoid the combinatorial explosion seen in the reachable program states graph. When it merges, dataflow analyses can use a union or an intersection decision to merge the information coming from different paths (node for line 5). If it uses union, we conclude that `schroedinger_integer` is both uninitialized and equal to 5, as in our last example. If it uses intersection, we end up with no information about `schroedinger_integer` (the unknown state).

The necessity to merge data in typical dataflow analyses is a limitation that a symbolic execution engine does not have. This allows for much more precise results, on par with what you would get by testing your program with several inputs, but at the cost of increased runtime and memory consumption.

Testing the static analyzer

In this section, we will explore how to use the Clang Static Analyzer in practice.

Using the driver versus using the compiler

Before testing the static analyzer, you should always keep in mind that the command line `clang -cc1` refers directly to the compiler, while using the command line `clang` will trigger the compiler driver. The driver is responsible for orchestrating the execution of all other LLVM programs involved in a compilation, but it is also responsible for providing adequate parameters about your system.

While using the compiler directly is preferred among some developers, sometimes it may fail to locate system header files or other configuration parameters that only the Clang driver knows. On the other hand, the compiler may present exclusive developer options that allow us to debug it and see what is happening inside. Let's check how to use both to check a single source code file.

Compiler	`clang -cc1 -analyze -analyzer-checker=`**`<package>`** **`<file>`**
Driver	`clang --analyze -Xanalyzer -analyzer-checker=`**`<package>`** **`<file>`**

We used the tag `<file>` to denote the source code file that you want to analyze and the tag `<package>` to allow you to select a collection of specific headers.

When using the driver, notice that the `--analyze` flag triggers the static analyzer. The `-Xanalyzer` flag, however, routes the next flag directly to the compiler, allowing you to pass specific flags. Since the driver is an intermediary, throughout our examples we will directly use the compiler. Moreover, in our simple examples, using the compiler directly should suffice. If you feel that you need the driver to use the checkers in the official way, remember to use the driver and the `-Xanalyzer` option before each flag that we pass to the compiler.

Getting to know the available checkers

A checker is a single unit of analysis that the static analyzer can perform in your code. Each analysis looks for specific bug types. The static analyzer allows you to select any subset of checkers that suits your needs, or you can enable all of them.

If you do not have Clang installed, see *Chapter 1, Build and Install LLVM,* for installation instructions. To obtain the list of installed checkers, run the following command:

```
$ clang -cc1 -analyzer-checker-help
```

It will print a long list of installed checkers, showing all the analysis possibilities you get with Clang out of the box. Let's now check the output of the `-analyzer-checker-help` command:

```
OVERVIEW: Clang Static Analyzer Checkers List


USAGE: -analyzer-checker <CHECKER or PACKAGE,...>


CHECKERS:
   alpha.core.BoolAssignment        Warn about assigning non-{0,1} values
to Boolean variables
```

The name of the checkers obey the canonical form `<package>.<subpackage>.<checker>`, providing an easy way for the user to run only a specific set of related checkers.

In the following table, we show a list of the most important packages, as well as a list of checker examples that are part of each package.

Package Name	Content	Examples
`alpha`	Checkers that are currently in development	`alpha.core.BoolAssignment`, `alpha.security.MallocOverflow`, and `alpha.unix.cstring.NotNullTerminated`
`core`	Basic checkers that are applicable in a universal context	`core.NullDereference`, `core.DivideZero`, and `core.StackAddressEscape`
`cplusplus`	A single checker for C++ memory allocation (others are currently in alpha)	`cplusplus.NewDelete`
`debug`	Checkers that output debug information of the static analyzer	`debug.DumpCFG`, `debug.DumpDominators`, and `debug.ViewExplodedGraph`
`llvm`	A single checker that checks whether a code follows LLVM coding standards or not	`llvm.Conventions`
`osx`	Checkers that are specific for programs developed for Mac OS X	`osx.API`, `osx.cocoa.ClassRelease`, `osx.cocoa.NonNilReturnValue`, and `osx.coreFoundation.CFError`
`security`	Checkers for code that introduces security vulnerabilities	`security.FloatLoopCounter`, `security.insecureAPI.UncheckedReturn`, `security.insecureAPI.gets`, and `security.insecureAPI.strcpy`
`unix`	Checkers that are specific to programs developed for UNIX systems	`unix.API`, `unix.Malloc`, `unix.MallocSizeof`, and `unix.MismatchedDeallocator`

Let's run Joe's code, intended to fool the simple analysis that most compilers use. First, we try the classic warnings approach. In order to do this, we simply run the Clang driver and ask it to not proceed with the compilation, but only perform the syntactic checks:

```
$ clang -fsyntax-only joe.c
```

The `syntax-only` flag, intended to print warnings and check for syntax errors, fails to detect anything wrong with it. Now it is time to test how symbolic execution handles this:

```
$ clang -cc1 -analyze -analyzer-checker=core joe.c
```

Alternatively, if the preceding command line requires you to specify header locations, use the driver as follows:

```
$ clang --analyze -Xanalyzer -analyzer-checker=core joe.c

./joe.c:10:5: warning: Function call argument is an uninitialized value
    printf("%d", schroedinger_integer);
    ^~~~~~~~~~~~~~~~~~~~~~~~~~~~~~~~~~

1 warning generated.
```

Right on the spot! Remember that the `analyzer-checker` flag expects the fully qualified name of a checker, or the name of an entire package of checkers. We chose to use the entire package of core checkers, but we could have used only the specific checker `core.CallAndMessage` that checks parameters of functions calls.

Note that all static analyzer commands will always start with `clang -cc1 -analyzer`; thus, if you are looking to know all the commands that the analyzer offers, you can issue the following command:

```
$ clang -cc1 -help | grep analyzer
```

Using the static analyzer in the Xcode IDE

If you use the Apple Xcode IDE, you can use the static analyzer from within it. You need to first open a project and then select the menu item **Analyze** in the **Product** menu. You will see that the Clang Static Analyzer provides the exact path where this bug occurs, allowing the IDE to highlight it to the programmer as seen in the following screenshot:

The analyzer is able to export information using the `plist` format, which is then interpreted by Xcode and displayed in a user-friendly manner.

Generating graphical reports in HTML

The static analyzer is also able to export an HTML file that will graphically point out program paths in your code that exercises a dangerous behavior, in the same way as Xcode does. We also use the `-o` parameter along with a folder name that indicates where the report will be stored. For an example, check the following command line:

```
$ clang -cc1 -analyze -analyzer-checker=core joe.c -o report
```

Alternatively, you can use the driver as follows:

```
$ clang --analyze –Xanalyzer –analyzer-checker=core joe.c –o report
```

Using this command line, the analyzer will process `joe.c` and generate a similar report to the one seen in Xcode, putting the HTML file in the `report` folder. After the command completes, check the folder and open the HTML file to view the bug report. You should see a report that is similar to the one shown in the following screenshot:

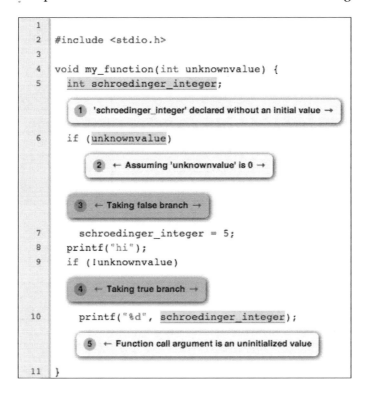

Handling large projects

If you want the static analyzer to check a large project, you will probably be unwilling to write a `Makefile` or a `bash` script to call the analyzer for each project source file. The static analyzer comes with a handy tool for this, called scan-build.

Scan-build works by replacing your cc or cxx environment variable, which defines your C/C++ compiler command, thus interfering in the regular build process of your project. It analyzes each compiled file before compilation and then finishes the compilation to allow the build process or script to continue working as expected. Finally, it generates HTML reports you can view in your browser. The basic command-line structure is pretty simple:

```
$ scan-build <your build command>
```

You are free to run any build command after `scan-build`, such as `make`. To build Joe's program, for example, we do not need a `Makefile`, but we can directly supply the compilation command:

```
$ scan-build gcc -c joe.c -o joe.o
```

After it finishes, you can run `scan-view` to check out the bug reports:

```
$ scan-view <output directory given by scan-build>
```

The last line printed by `scan-build` gives the parameter that is needed to run `scan-view`. It refers to a temporary folder that holds all the generated reports. You should see a nicely formatted website with error reports for each of your source files, as seen in the following screenshot:

Bug Summary

Bug Type	Quantity	Display?
All Bugs	1	☑
Logic error		
Uninitialized argument value	1	☑

Reports

Bug Group	Bug Type ▾	File	Line	Path Length			
Logic error	Uninitialized argument value	joe.c	10	5	View Report	Report Bug	Open File

A real-world example – finding bugs in Apache

In this example, we will explore how easy it is to check bugs in a big project. To exercise this, go to `http://httpd.apache.org/download.cgi` and fetch the source code tar ball of the most recent Apache HTTP Server. At the time of this writing, it was Version 2.4.9. In our example, we will download it via the console and decompress the file in the current folder:

```
$ wget http://archive.apache.org/dist/httpd/httpd-2.4.9.tar.bz2
$ tar -xjvf httpd-2.4.9.tar.bz2
```

To examine this source code base, we will rely on `scan-build`. In order to do this, we need to reproduce the steps to generate the build scripts. Notice that you do need all dependencies necessary to compile the Apache project. After checking that you do have all of the dependencies, use the following command sequence:

```
$ mkdir obj
$ cd obj
$ scan-build ../httpd-2.4.9/configure -prefix=$(pwd)/../install
```

We used the `prefix` parameter to denote a new installation path to this project and avoid the need to have administrative privileges on the machine. However, if you are not going to actually install Apache, you do not need to provide any extra parameter as long as you never run `make install`. In our case, we defined our installation path as a folder named `install` that will be created in the same directory where we downloaded the compressed source. Notice that we also prefixed this command with `scan-build`, which will override the `CC` and `CXX` environment variables.

After the `configure` script creates all the Makefiles, it is time to launch the actual build process. But instead of running just `make`, we intercept it with `scan-build`:

```
$ scan-build make
```

Since the Apache code is very large, it took us several minutes to finish the analysis and we found 82 bugs. This is an example `scan-view` report:

Bug Summary

Bug Type	Quantity	Display?
All Bugs	**82**	☑
Dead store		
Dead assignment	12	☑
Dead initialization	1	☑
Logic error		
Assigned value is garbage or undefined	5	☑
Branch condition evaluates to a garbage value	1	☑
Called function pointer is null (null dereference)	1	☑
Dereference of null pointer	20	☑
Dereference of undefined pointer value	18	☑
Division by zero	1	☑
Result of operation is garbage or undefined	3	☑
Uninitialized argument value	12	☑
Unix API	7	☑
Memory Error		
Memory leak	1	☑

After the infamous heartbleed bug hit all the OpenSSL implementations and all the attention this problem got, it is interesting to see that the static analyzer could still find six *possible bugs* in the Apache SSL implementation files `modules/ssl/ssl_util.c` and `modules/ssl/ssl_engine_config.c`. Please note that these occurrences may refer to paths that are never executed in practice and may not be real bugs, since the static analyzer works in a limited scope to finish the analysis in acceptable time frames. Thus, we do not claim that these are real bugs. We present here an example of an assigned value that is garbage or undefined:

```
996   const char *ssl_cmd_SSLVerifyClient(cmd_parms *cmd,
997                                       void *dcfg,
998                                       const char *arg)
999   {
1000      SSLDirConfigRec *dc = (SSLDirConfigRec *)dcfg;
1001      SSLSrvConfigRec *sc = mySrvConfig(cmd->server);
1002      ssl_verify_t mode;
```
    1 'mode' declared without an initial value →
```
1003      const char *err;
1004
1005      if ((err = ssl_cmd_verify_parse(cmd, arg, &mode))) {
```
        2 ← Calling 'ssl_cmd_verify_parse' →

        7 ← Returning from 'ssl_cmd_verify_parse' →

        8 ← Assuming 'err' is null →

        9 ← Taking false branch →
```
1006          return err;
1007      }
1008
1009      if (cmd->path) {
```
        10 ← Taking true branch →
```
1010          dc->nVerifyClient = mode;
```
            11 ← Assigned value is garbage or undefined

In this example, we see that the static analyzer showed us an execution path that finishes by assigning an undefined value to `dc->nVerifyClient`. Part of this path goes through the call to the `ssl_cmd_verify_parse()` function, showing the analyzer capability of checking complex inter-procedural paths within the same compilation module. In this helper function, the static analyzer shows a path where `mode` is not assigned to any value and, therefore, remains uninitialized.

The reason this may not be a real bug is because the code in `ssl_cmd_verify_parse()` may handle all cases of input `cmd_parms` *that actually happen in this program* (note the context dependence) correctly initializing `mode` in all of them. What `scan-build` did find is that this module, in isolation, may lead to this buggy path, but we have no evidence that the users of this module use the buggy inputs. The static analyzer is not powerful enough to analyze this module in the context of the entire project because such analysis would require an impractical time to finish (remember the exponential complexity of the algorithm).

While this path has 11 steps, the longest path that we found in Apache has 42 steps. This path happened in the `modules/generators/mod_cgid.c` module and violates a standard C API call: it calls the `strlen()` function with a null pointer argument.

If you are curious to see all these reports in detail, do not hesitate to run the commands yourself.

Extending the static analyzer with your own checkers

Thanks to its design, we can easily extend the static analyzer with custom checkers. Remember that a static analyzer is as good as its checkers, and if you want to analyze whether any code uses one of your APIs in an unintended way, you need to learn how to embed this domain-specific knowledge into the Clang Static Analyzer.

Getting familiar with the project architecture

The Clang Static Analyzer source code lives at `llvm/tools/clang`. The include files are at `include/clang/StaticAnalyzer`, and the source code can be found at `lib/StaticAnalyzer`. If you look at the folder content, you will observe that the project is split into three different subfolders: `Checkers`, `Core`, and `Frontend`.

The task of the core is to simulate program execution at the source-code level and, using a *visitor pattern*, to call registered checkers at each program point (prior or after an important statement) to enforce a given invariant. For example, if your checker ensures that the same allocated memory region is not freed twice, it would observe calls to `malloc()` and `free()`, generating a bug report when it detects a double free.

A symbolic engine cannot simulate the program with exact program values as those you see when a program is running. If you ask the user to input an integer value, you will definitely know, in a given run, that this value is 5, for example. The power of a symbolic engine is to reason about what happens in every possible outcome of the program and, to accomplish this noble goal, it works with symbols (SVals) rather than concrete values. A symbol may correspond to any number in the integer range, any floating-point, or even a completely unknown value. The more information it has about the value, the more powerful it is.

Three important data structures that are key in understanding the project implementation are ProgramState, ProgramPoint, and ExplodedGraph. The first represents the current execution context with respect to the current state. For example, when analyzing Joe's code, it would annotate that a given variable has the value 5. The second represents a specific point in the program flow, either before or after a statement, for example, the point after assigning 5 to an integer variable. The last represents the entire graph of reachable program states. Additionally, the nodes of this graph are represented by a tuple of ProgramState and ProgramPoint, which means that each program point has a specific state associated with it. For example, the point after assigning 5 to an integer variable has the state linking this variable to the number 5.

As already pointed out at the beginning of this chapter, ExplodedGraph, or in other words, the reachable states graph, represents a significant expansion over the classic CFG. Notice that a small CFG with two successive but non-nested ifs would explode, in the reachable state graphs representation, to four different paths — a combinatorial expansion. To save space, this graph is folded, which means that if you create a node that represents the same program point and state as the ones in another node, it does not allocate a new one, but reuses this existing node, possibly building cycles. To implement this behavior, ExplodedNode inherits from the LLVM library superclass llvm::FoldingSetNode. The LLVM library already includes a common class for these situations because folding is extensively used in the middle and backend of the compiler when representing programs.

The static analyzer's overall design can be divided into the following parts: the engine, which follows a simulation path and manages the other components; the state manager, taking care of ProgramState objects; the constraint manager, working on deducing constraints on ProgramState caused by following a given program path; and the store manager, taking care of the program storage model.

Another important aspect of the analyzer is how to model the memory behavior when simulating program execution along each path. This is quite challenging to do in languages such as C and C++ because they offer many ways for the programmer to access the same piece of memory, introducing aliases.

The analyzer implements a regional memory model described in a paper by Xu et al. (see references at the end of this chapter), which is even able to differentiate the state of each element of an array. Xu et al. propose a hierarchy of memory regions in which, for example, an array element is a subregion of the array, which is a subregion of the stack. Each `lvalue` in C, or, in other words, each variable or dereferenced reference, has a corresponding region that models the piece of memory they are working on. The content of each memory region, on the other hand, are modeled with bindings. Each binding associates a symbolic value with a region of memory. We know that this is too much information to absorb, so let's digest it in the best way possible — by writing code.

Writing your own checker

Let's consider that you are working on a specific embedded software that controls a nuclear reactor and that relies on an API with two basic calls: `turnReactorOn()` and `SCRAM()` (turn the reactor off). A nuclear reactor contains fuel, where the reaction happens, and control rods, which contain neutron absorbers to slow down the reaction and keep the reactor under the power plant category rather than the nuclear bomb one.

Your client advises you that calling `SCRAM()` twice may jam the control rods, and calling `turnReactorOn()` twice causes the reaction to go out of control. This is an API with strict usage rules, and your mission is to audit a large code base before it goes into production to ensure that it never violates these rules:

- No code path may call `SCRAM()` more than once without intervening `turnReactorOn()`

- No code path may call `turnReactorOn()` more than once without intervening `SCRAM()`

As an example, consider the following code:

```
int SCRAM();
int turnReactorOn();

void test_loop(int wrongTemperature, int restart) {
  turnReactorOn();
  if (wrongTemperature) {
    SCRAM();
  }
  if (restart) {
    SCRAM();
  }
```

```
   turnReactorOn();
   // code to keep the reactor working
   SCRAM();
}
```

This code violates the API if both `wrongTemperature` and `restart` are different than zero because that would result in calling `SCRAM()` two times without any intervening `turnReactorOn()` call. It also violates the API if both parameters are zero because then the code will call `turnReactorOn()` twice without any intervening `SCRAM()` call.

Solving the problem with a custom checker

You can either try to visually inspect the code, which is very tedious and error-prone, or use a tool such as the Clang Static Analyzer. The problem is, it does not understand the Nuclear Power Plant API. We will overcome this by implementing a special checker.

Our first step is to establish the concepts for our state model regarding the information we want to propagate across different program states. In this problem, we are concerned with whether the reactor is on or off. We may not know whether the reactor is on or off; thus, our state model contains three possible states: unknown, on, and off.

Now we have a decent idea on how our checker will work on states.

Writing the state class

Let's put this into practice. We will base our code on `SimpleStreamChecker.cpp`, a sample checker available in the Clang tree.

In `lib/StaticAnalyzer/Checkers`, we should create a new file, `ReactorChecker. cpp`, and start by coding our own class that represents the state that we are interested in tracking:

```cpp
#include "ClangSACheckers.h"
#include "clang/StaticAnalyzer/Core/BugReporter/BugType.h"
#include "clang/StaticAnalyzer/Core/Checker.h"
#include "clang/StaticAnalyzer/Core/PathSensitive/CallEvent.h"
#include "clang/StaticAnalyzer/Core/PathSensitive/CheckerContext.h"
using namespace clang;
using namespace ento;
class ReactorState {
private:
```

```
      enum Kind {On, Off} K;
  public:
    ReactorState(unsigned InK): K((Kind) InK) {}
    bool isOn() const { return K == On; }
    bool isOff() const { return K == Off; }
    static unsigned getOn() { return (unsigned) On; }
    static unsigned getOff() { return (unsigned) Off; }
    bool operator==(const ReactorState &X) const {
      return K == X.K;
    }
    void Profile(llvm::FoldingSetNodeID &ID) const {
      ID.AddInteger(K);
    }

  };
```

The data part of our class is restricted to a single instance of `Kind`. Notice that the `ProgramState` class will manage the state information that we are writing.

Understanding ProgramState immutability

An interesting observation about `ProgramState` is that it is designed to be immutable. Once built, it should never change: it represents the state calculated for a given program point in a given execution path. Differing from dataflow analyses that process a CFG, in this case, we deal with the reachable program states graph, which has a different node for every different pair of program point and state. In this way, if the program loops, the engine will create an entirely new path that records relevant information about this new iteration. Conversely, in a dataflow analysis, a loop causes the state of the loop body to be updated with new information until a fixed point is reached.

However, as stressed earlier, once the symbolic engine reaches a node that represents the same program point of a given loop body that has the same state, it concludes that there is no new information to process in this path and reuses the node instead of creating a new one. On the other hand, if your loop has a body that constantly updates the state with new information, you will soon reach a limitation of the symbolic engine: it will give up this path after simulating a predefined number of iterations, which is a configurable number when you launch the tool.

Dissecting the code

Since state is immutable once created, our `ReactorState` class does not need setters, or class member functions that can change its state, but we do need constructors. That is the purpose of the `ReactorState(unsigned InK)` constructor, which receives as input an integer encoding the current reactor state.

Finally, the `Profile` function is a consequence of the `ExplodedNode` being a subclass of `FoldingSetNode`. All subclasses must provide such methods to aid the LLVM folding to track the state of the node and determine if two nodes are equal (in which case they are folded). Therefore, our `Profile` function explains that K, a number, gives our state.

You can use any of the `FoldingSetNodeID` member functions starting with `Add` to inform unique bits that identify this object instance (see `llvm/ADT/FoldingSet.h`). In our case, we used `AddInteger()`.

Defining the Checker subclass

Now it is time to declare our `Checker` subclass:

```
class ReactorChecker : public Checker<check::PostCall> {
    mutable IdentifierInfo *IIturnReactorOn, *IISCRAM;
    OwningPtr<BugType> DoubleSCRAMBugType;
    OwningPtr<BugType> DoubleONBugType;
    void initIdentifierInfo(ASTContext &Ctx) const;
    void reportDoubleSCRAM(const CallEvent &Call,
                           CheckerContext &C) const;
    void reportDoubleON(const CallEvent &Call,
                        CheckerContext &C) const;
public:
    ReactorChecker();
    /// Process turnReactorOn and SCRAM
    void checkPostCall(const CallEvent &Call, CheckerContext &C) const;
};
```

 Clang version notice – Starting with Clang 3.5, the `OwningPtr<>` template was deprecated in favor of the standard C++ `std::unique_ptr<>` template. Both templates provide smart pointer implementations.

The first lines of our class specify that we are using a subclass of `Checker` with a template parameter. For this class, you can use multiple template parameters and they express the program points that your checker is interested in visiting. Technically, the template parameters are used to derive a custom `Checker` class that is a subclass of all of the classes specified as parameters. This means that, in our case, our checker will inherit `PostCall` from the base class. This inheritance is used to implement the visitor pattern that will call us only for the objects that we are interested and, as a consequence, our class must implement the member function `checkPostCall`.

You may be interested in registering your checker to visit a wide variety of types of program points (check `CheckerDocumentation.cpp`). In our case, we are interested in visiting the program points immediately after a call because we want to document a change of state after one of the nuclear power plant API functions gets called.

These member functions use the keyword `const`, respecting the design that relies on the checker being stateless. However, we do want to cache the results of retrieving `IdentifierInfo` objects that represent the symbol `turnReactorOn()` and `SCRAM()`. In this way, we use the `mutable` keyword, created to bypass `const` restrictions.

> Use the `mutable` keyword with care. We are not harming the checker design because we are only caching results to make a faster computation after the second call to our checker, but conceptually our checker is still stateless. The `mutable` keyword should only be used for mutexes or such caching scenarios.

We also want to inform the Clang infrastructure that we are handling a new type of bug. In order to do this, we must hold new instances of `BugType`, one for each new bug we are going to report: the bug that occurs when the programmer calls `SCRAM()` twice and the one that happens when the programmer calls `turnReactorOn()` twice. We also use the `OwningPtr` LLVM class to wrap our object, which is just an implementation of an automatic pointer, used to automatically de-allocate our object once our `ReactorChecker` object gets destroyed.

You should wrap the two classes that we just wrote, `ReactorState` and `ReactorChecker`, in an anonymous namespace. This saves our linker from exporting these two data structures that we know will be used only locally.

Writing the Register macro

Before we dive into the class implementation, we must call a macro to expand the `ProgramState` instance used by the analyzer engine with our custom state:

```
REGISTER_MAP_WITH_PROGRAMSTATE(RS, int, ReactorState)
```

Note that this macro does not use a semicolon at the end. This associates a new map with each `ProgramState` instance. The first parameter can be any name that you will use later to refer to this data, the second parameter is the type of map key, and the third parameter is the type of object that we will store (in our case, our `ReactorState` class).

Checkers typically use maps to store their state because it is common to associate a new state with a particular resource, for example, the state of each variable, initialized or uninitialized in our detector from the beginning of this chapter. In this case, the key of the map would be a variable name and the stored value would be a custom class that models the state uninitialized or initialized. For additional ways to register information into the program state, check out the macro definitions in `CheckerContext.h`.

Note that we do not really need a map because we will always store only one state per program point. Therefore, we will always use the key 1 to access our map.

Implementing the Checker subclass

Our checker class constructor is implemented as follows:

```
ReactorChecker::ReactorChecker() : IIturnReactorOn(0), IISCRAM(0) {
    // Initialize the bug types.
    DoubleSCRAMBugType.reset(
        new BugType("Double SCRAM",
            "Nuclear Reactor API Error"));
    DoubleONBugType.reset(new BugType("Double ON",
                                      "Nuclear Reactor API Error"));
}
```

 Clang version notice – Starting with Clang 3.5, our `BugType` constructor call needs to be changed to `BugType(this, "Double SCRAM", "Nuclear Reactor API Error")` and `BugType(this, "Double ON", "Nuclear Reactor API Error")`, adding the `this` keyword as the first parameter.

Our constructor instantiates new `BugType` objects by using the `reset()` member function of `OwningPtr`, and we give descriptions about our new kind of bug. We also initialize the `IdentifierInfo` pointers. Next, it is time to define our helper function to cache the results of these pointers:

```
void ReactorChecker::initIdentifierInfo(ASTContext &Ctx) const {
    if (IIturnReactorOn)
        return;
    IIturnReactorOn = &Ctx.Idents.get("turnReactorOn");
    IISCRAM = &Ctx.Idents.get("SCRAM");
}
```

The `ASTContext` object holds specific AST nodes that contain types and declarations used in the user program, and we can use it to find the exact identifier of the functions that we are interested in monitoring. Now, we implement the visitor pattern function, `checkPostCall`. Remember that it is a `const` function that should not modify the checker state:

```
void ReactorChecker::checkPostCall(const CallEvent &Call,
                                   CheckerContext &C) const {
  initIdentifierInfo(C.getASTContext());
  if (!Call.isGlobalCFunction())
    return;
  if (Call.getCalleeIdentifier() == IIturnReactorOn) {
    ProgramStateRef State = C.getState();
    const ReactorState *S = State->get<RS>(1);
    if (S && S->isOn()) {
      reportDoubleON(Call, C);
      return;
    }
    State = State->set<RS>(1, ReactorState::getOn());
    C.addTransition(State);
    return;
  }
  if (Call.getCalleeIdentifier() == IISCRAM) {
    ProgramStateRef State = C.getState();
    const ReactorState *S = State->get<RS>(1);
    if (S && S->isOff()) {
      reportDoubleSCRAM(Call, C);
      return;
    }
    State = State->set<RS>(1, ReactorState::getOff());
    C.addTransition(State);
    return;
  }

}
```

The first parameter, of type `CallEvent`, retains information about the exact function the program called just before this program point (see `CallEvent.h`), since we registered a post-call visitor. The second parameter, of type `CheckerContext`, is the only source of information about current state in this program point, since our checker is forced to be stateless. We used it to retrieve `ASTContext` and initialize our `IdentifierInfo` objects that are required to check the functions that we are monitoring. We enquire the `CallEvent` object to check if it is a call to the `turnReactorOn()` function. In case it is, we need to process the state transition to on status.

Before doing this, we first check the state to see whether it is already on, in which case we have a bug. Note that in the State->get<RS>(1) statement, RS is simply the name we gave when we registered the new trait in program state, and 1 is a fixed integer to always access the location of the map. Although we do not really need a map in this case, by using a map, you will be able to easily extend our checker to monitor more complex states if you want.

We recover our stored state as a const pointer because we are dealing with the information that reaches this program point, which is immutable. It is first necessary to check if it is a null reference, which represents the case when we do not know whether the reactor is on or off. If it is non-null, we check if it is on and in a positive case, we abandon further analysis to report a bug. In the other case, we create a new state by using the ProgramStateRef set member function and supply this new state to the addTransition() member function that will record information to create a new edge in ExplodedGraph. The edges are only created when a state actually changes. We employ similar logic to handle the SCRAM case.

We present the bug reporting member functions as follows:

```
void ReactorChecker::reportDoubleON(const CallEvent &Call,
                                    CheckerContext &C) const {
  ExplodedNode *ErrNode = C.generateSink();
  if (!ErrNode)
    return;
  BugReport *R = new BugReport(*DoubleONBugType,
      "Turned on the reactor two times", ErrNode);
  R->addRange(Call.getSourceRange());
  C.emitReport(R);
}
 void ReactorChecker::reportDoubleSCRAM(const CallEvent &Call,
                                        CheckerContext &C) const {
  ExplodedNode *ErrNode = C.generateSink();
  if (!ErrNode)
    return;
  BugReport *R = new BugReport(*DoubleSCRAMBugType,
      "Called a SCRAM procedure twice", ErrNode);
  R->addRange(Call.getSourceRange());
  C.emitReport(R);
}
```

Our first action is to generate a sink node, which, in the graph of reachable program states, means that we hit a critical bug in this path and that we do not want to continue analyzing this path. The next lines create a `BugReport` object, specifying that we have found a new bug of the specific type `DoubleOnBugType`, and we are free to add a description and supply the error node we just built. We also use the `addRange()` member function that will highlight where in the source code the bug has occurred and display it to the user.

Adding registration code

In order for the static analyzer tool to recognize our new checker, we need to define a registration function in our source code and later add a description of our checker in a `TableGen` file. The registration function appears as follows:

```
void ento::registerReactorChecker(CheckerManager &mgr) {
  mgr.registerChecker<ReactorChecker>();
}
```

The `TableGen` file has a table of checkers. It is located, relative to the Clang source folder, at `lib/StaticAnalyzer/Checkers/Checkers.td`. Before editing this file, we need to select a package for our checker to live in. We will put it into `alpha.powerplant`. Since this package does not exist yet, we will create it. Open `Checkers.td` and add a new definition after all existing package definitions:

```
def PowerPlantAlpha : Package<"powerplant">, InPackage<Alpha>;
```

Next, add our newly written checker:

```
let ParentPackage = PowerPlantAlpha in {

def ReactorChecker : Checker<"ReactorChecker">,
  HelpText<"Check for misuses of the nuclear power plant API">,
  DescFile<"ReactorChecker.cpp">;

} // end "alpha.powerplant"
```

If you use CMake to build Clang, you should add your new source file to `lib/StaticAnalyzer/Checkers/CMakeLists.txt`. If you use the GNU autotools configure script to build Clang, you do not need to modify any other file because the LLVM Makefile will scan for new source code files in the `Checkers` folder and link them in the static analyzer checkers library.

Building and testing

Go to the folder where you built LLVM and Clang and run `make`. The build system will now detect your new code, build it, and link it against the Clang Static Analyzer. After you finish building, the command `clang -cc1 -analyzer-checker-help` should list our new checker as a valid option.

A test case for our checker is `managereactor.c`, listed as follows (the same presented earlier):

```
int SCRAM();
int turnReactorOn();

void test_loop(int wrongTemperature, int restart) {
  turnReactorOn();
  if (wrongTemperature) {
    SCRAM();
  }
  if (restart) {
    SCRAM();
  }
  turnReactorOn();
  // code to keep the reactor working
  SCRAM();
}
```

To analyze it with our new checker, we use the following command:

```
$ clang --analyze -Xanalyzer -analyzer-checker=alpha.powerplant
managereactor.c
```

The checker will display the paths that it can find to be wrong and quit. If you ask for an HTML report, you will see a bug report similar to the one shown in the following screenshot:

```
1   int SCRAM();
2   int turnReactorOn();
3
4   void test_loop(int wrongTemperature, int restart) {
5     turnReactorOn();
6     if (wrongTemperature) {
```

> **1** Assuming 'wrongTemperature' is 0 →

> **2** ← Taking false branch →

```
7       SCRAM();
8     }
9     if (restart) {
```

> **3** ← Assuming 'restart' is 0 →

> **4** ← Taking false branch →

```
10      SCRAM();
11    }
12    turnReactorOn();
```

> **5** ← Turned on the reactor two times

```
13    // code to keep the reactor working
14    SCRAM();
15  }
16
```

Your mission is now complete: you have successfully developed a program to automatically check for violations of a specific API rule with path-sensitivity. If you want, you can check for the implementation of other checkers to learn more about working in more complex scenarios, or check the resources in the following section for more information.

More resources

You may check the following resources for more projects and other information:

- `http://clang-analyzer.llvm.org`: The Clang Static Analyzer project page.

- `http://clang-analyzer.llvm.org/checker_dev_manual.html`: A useful manual with more information for those who want to develop new checkers.

- `http://lcs.ios.ac.cn/~xzx/memmodel.pdf`: The paper *A Memory Model for Static Analysis of C* by Zhongxing Xu, Ted Kremenek, and Jian Zhang. It details theoretical aspects of the memory model that was implemented in the analyzer core.

- `http://clang.llvm.org/doxygen/annotated.html`: The Clang doxygen documentation.

- `http://llvm.org/devmtg/2012-11/videos/Zaks-Rose-Checker24Hours.mp4`: A talk explaining how to quickly build a checker, given by Anna Zaks and Jordan Rose, static analyzer developers, at the 2012 LLVM Developers' meeting.

Summary

In this chapter, we explored how the Clang Static Analyzer differs from simple bug detection tools that run on the compiler frontend. We provided examples where the static analyzer is more accurate and explained that there is trade-off between accuracy and computing time, and that the exponential-time static analyzer algorithm is unfeasible to be integrated into the regular compiler pipeline because of the time it needs to complete its analyses. We also presented how to use the command-line interface to run the static analyzer on simple projects and a helper tool called `scan-build` to analyze large projects. We finished this chapter by presenting how to extend the static analyzer with your own path-sensitive bug checker.

In the next chapter, we will present Clang tools that are built on top of the LibTooling infrastructure, which eases the process of building code-refactoring utilities.

10
Clang Tools with LibTooling

In this chapter, we will see how many tools use the Clang frontend as a library to manipulate C/C++ programs for different purposes. In particular, all of them rely on **LibTooling**, a Clang library that allows standalone tools to be written. In this case, instead of writing a plugin to fit into the Clang compilation pipeline, you design your very own tool that uses Clang parsing abilities, allowing your users to directly call your tool. The tools presented in this chapter are available in the Clang Extra Tools package; refer to *Chapter 2*, *External Projects*, for information on how to install them. We will finish this chapter with a working example of how to create your own code-refactoring tool. We will cover the following topics:

- Generating a compile command database
- Understanding and using several Clang tools that rely on LibTooling, such as Clang Tidy, Clang Modernizer, Clang Apply Replacements, ClangFormat, Modularize, PPTrace, and Clang Query
- Building your own LibTooling-based code-refactoring tool

Generating a compile command database

In general, a compiler is called from a build script, for example, Makefiles, with a series of parameters that configure it to adequately use project headers and definitions. These parameters allow the frontend to correctly lex and parse the input source code file. However, in this chapter, we will study standalone tools that will run on their own, and not as part of the Clang compilation pipeline. Thus, in theory, we would need a specific script to run our tool with the correct parameters for each source file.

For example, the following command shows the full command line used by Make to invoke a compiler to build a typical file from the LLVM library:

```
$ /usr/bin/c++   -DNDEBUG -D__STDC_CONSTANT_MACROS -D__STDC_FORMAT_MACROS
-D__STDC_LIMIT_MACROS  -fPIC -fvisibility-inlines-hidden -Wall -W -Wno-
unused-parameter -Wwrite-strings -Wmissing-field-initializers -pedantic
-Wno-long-long -Wcovered-switch-default -Wnon-virtual-dtor -fno-rtti
-I/Users/user/p/llvm/llvm-3.4/cmake-scripts/utils/TableGen -I/Users/
user/p/llvm/llvm-3.4/llvm/utils/TableGen -I/Users/user/p/llvm/llvm-3.4/
cmake-scripts/include -I/Users/user/p/llvm/llvm-3.4/llvm/include -fno-
exceptions -o CMakeFiles/llvm-tblgen.dir/DAGISelMatcher.cpp.o -c /Users/
user/p/llvm/llvm-3.4/llvm/utils/TableGen/DAGISelMatcher.cpp
```

In the case that you were working with this library, you would be quite unhappy if you had to issue commands that span 10 lines of your terminal to analyze each source file, and yet, you cannot discard a single character, since the frontend will use every bit of this information.

To allow a tool to easily process source code files, any project that uses LibTooling accepts a command database as the input. This command database has the correct compiler parameters for each source file of a specific project. To make it easier, CMake can generate this database file for you if it is called with the -DCMAKE_ EXPORT_COMPILE_COMMANDS flag. For example, suppose that you wish to run a LibTooling-based tool on a specific source code file from the Apache project. To obviate you from the need to pass the exact compiler flags needed to correctly parse this file, you can generate a command database with CMake as follows:

```
$ cd httpd-2.4.9

$ mkdir obj

$ cd obj

$ cmake -DCMAKE_EXPORT_COMPILE_COMMANDS=ON ../

$ ln -s $(pwd)/compile_commands.json ../
```

This is similar to the build commands you would issue to build Apache with CMake, but instead of actually building it, the -DCMAKE_EXPORT_COMPILE_COMMANDS=ON flag instructs it to generate a JSON file with the compiler parameters that it would use to compile each Apache source file. We need to create a link to this JSON file to appear at the root Apache source folder. Then, when we run any LibTooling program to parse a source file of Apache, it will look for parent directories until it finds compile_commands.json in it to find the appropriate parameters to parse this file.

Alternatively, if you don't want to build a compile commands database before running your tool, you can use double dash (--) to directly pass the compiler command you would use to process this file. This is useful if your project does not need many parameters for compilation. For example, look at the following command line:

```
$ my_libtooling_tool test.c -- -Iyour_include_dir -Dyour_define
```

The clang-tidy tool

In this section, we will present clang-tidy as an example of a LibTooling tool and explain how to use it. All other Clang tools will have a similar look and feel, thereby allowing you to comfortably explore them.

The clang-tidy tool is a linter, based on Clang. In general, a linter is a tool that analyzes code and denounces parts that do not follow best practices. It can check for specific characteristics, such as the following:

- Whether the code will be portable across different compilers
- If the code follows a specific idiom or code convention
- If the code may lead to a bug due to abuse of a dangerous language feature

In the specific case of clang-tidy, the tool is able to run two types of checkers: those from the original Clang Static Analyzer and those specially written for clang-tidy. Despite being able to run static analyzer checks, notice that clang-tidy and other LibTooling-based tools are based on source code analysis, and that this is quite different from the elaborated static analysis engine described in the previous chapter. Rather than simulating program execution, these checks merely traverse the Clang AST and are also much faster. Different from those of the Clang Static Analyzer, the checks written for clang-tidy are generally targeted at checking conformance with a particular coding convention. In particular, they check for the LLVM coding convention and for the Google coding convention as well as other general checks.

If you follow a particular code convention, you will find clang-tidy very useful to periodically check your code. With some effort, you can even configure it to run directly from some text editors. However, the tool is currently in its infancy and only implements a handful of tests.

Using clang-tidy to check your code

In this example, we will show how to use clang-tidy to check the code that we have written in *Chapter 9, The Clang Static Analyzer*. Since we wrote a plugin for the static analyzer, if we would like to submit this checker to the official Clang source tree, we would need to strictly follow LLVM coding conventions. It is time to check if we are really following it. The general command-line interface of clang-tidy is as follows.

```
$ clang-tidy [options] <source0> [... <sourceN>] [-- <compiler command>]
```

You can carefully activate each checker by name in the `-checks` argument, but you can also use the wildcard operator `*` to select many checkers that start with the same substring. When you need to disable a checker, just use the checker name preceded by a dash. For example, if you want to run all the checkers that belong to the LLVM coding conventions, you should use the following command:

```
$ clang-tidy -checks="llvm-*" file.cpp
```

> All the tools described in this chapter will only be available if you install Clang together with the Clang Extra Tools repository, which is separated from the Clang tree. If you do not have clang-tidy installed yet, read *Chapter 2, External Projects*, for instructions on how to build and install Clang Extra Tools.

Since our code is compiled together with Clang, we will need a compiler command database. We will start by generating it. Go to the folder where your LLVM source code is located, and create a separate sibling folder to hold the CMake files using the following commands:

```
$ mkdir cmake-scripts
$ cd cmake-scripts
$ cmake -DCMAKE_EXPORT_COMPILE_COMMANDS=ON ../llvm
```

> If you run into an unknown-source-file error that points to the code of the checker that you created in the previous chapter, you need to update the CMakeLists.txt file with the name of your checker source file. Use the following command line to edit this file and then run CMake again:
>
> ```
> $ vim ../llvm/tools/clang/lib/StaticAnalyzer/Checkers/
> CMakeLists.txt
> ```

Then, create a link in the LLVM root folder to point to the compiler-command database file.

```
$ ln -s $(pwd)/compile_commands.json ../llvm
```

Now, we can finally run clang-tidy:

```
$ cd ../llvm/tools/clang/lib/StaticAnalyzer/Checkers
$ clang-tidy -checks="llvm-*" ReactorChecker.cpp
```

You should see many complaints about header files included by our checker that does not strictly follow the LLVM rule that requires a comment after each closing curly brackets of namespaces (see `http://llvm.org/docs/CodingStandards.html#namespace-indentation`). The good news is that the code of our tool, excluding the headers, does not violate these rules.

Refactoring tools

In this section, we present many other tools that perform code analysis and source-to-source transformations by leveraging Clang's parsing abilities. You should feel comfortable to use them in a way that is similar to that of clang-tidy, relying on your commands' database to simplify their usage.

Clang Modernizer

The Clang Modernizer is a revolutionary standalone tool that aids the user in adapting old C++ code to use the newest standards, for example, C++11. It reaches this goal by performing the following transformations:

- **Loop convert transform**: This converts older C-style `for(;;)` loops to the newer range-based loop of the form `for(auto &...:..)`

- **Use-nullptr transform**: This converts older C-style usage of `NULL` or `0` constants to represent a null pointer to use the newer `nullptr` C++11 keyword

- **Use-auto transform**: This converts some type declarations to use the `auto` keyword in specific cases, which improves code readability

- **Add-override transform**: This adds the `override` specifier to virtual member function declarations that override a base class function

- **Pass-By-Value transform**: This uses the pass-by-value idiom in substitution for the `const` reference followed by a copy

- **Replace-auto_ptr transform**: This replaces uses of deprecated `std::auto_ptr` by `std::unique_ptr`

The Clang Modernizer is a compelling example of a source-to-source transformation tool that is made possible by the Clang LibTooling infrastructure. To use it, observe the following template:

```
$ clang-modernize [<options>] <source0> [... <sourceN>] [-- <compiler
command>]
```

Notice that if you do not provide any extra option besides the source file name, this tool will directly patch the source file with all transformations. Use the `-serialize-replacements` flag to force the suggestions to be written onto a disk, allowing you to read them before applying. There is a special tool to apply these on-disk patches, which we will present next.

Clang Apply Replacements

The development of Clang Modernizer (previously, C++ migrator) led to discussions on how to coordinate source-to-source transformations on a large code base. For instance, when analyzing different translation units, the same header files may be analyzed multiple times.

An option to handle this is to serialize the replacement suggestions and write them in a file. A second tool will be responsible for reading these suggestion files, discarding conflicting and duplicated suggestions, and applying the replacement suggestions to the source files. This is the purpose of Clang Apply Replacements, which was born to aid Clang Modernizer in the task of fixing large code bases.

Both Clang Modernizer, which produces replacement suggestions, and Clang Apply Replacements, which consumes these suggestions, work with a serialized version of the `clang::tooling::Replacement` class. This serialization uses the YAML format, which can be defined as a superset of JSON that is easier to read for humans.

Patch files, used by code revision tools, are precisely a form of serialization of suggestions, but Clang developers chose to use YAML to work directly with a serialization of the `Replacement` class and avoid parsing a patch file.

Therefore, the Clang Apply Replacements tool is not intended to be a general-purpose code-patching tool, but a rather specialized one, focusing on committing changes made by Clang tools that rely on the tooling API. Notice that if you are writing a source-to-source transformation tool, it is only necessary to use Clang Apply Replacements if you wish to coordinate multiple suggestions with de-duplication capabilities. Otherwise, you would simply patch the source files directly.

To see Clang Apply Replacements in action, we first need to use Clang Modernizer and force it to serialize its suggestions. Suppose we want to transform the following C++ source file `test.cpp` to use newer C++ standards:

```
int main() {
  const int size = 5;
  int arr[] = {1,2,3,4,5};
  for (int i = 0; i < size; ++i) {
    arr[i] += 5;
  }
  return 0;
}
```

According to the Clang Modernizer user's manual, it is safe to transform this loop to use the newer `auto` iterator. For that, we need to use the loop transformation of Clang Modernizer:

```
$ clang-modernize -loop-convert -serialize-replacements test.cpp
--serialize-dir=./
```

The last parameter is optional and specifies that the current folder will be used to store the replacement files. If we do not specify it, the tool will create a temporary folder to be later consumed by Clang Apply Replacements. Since we dumped all the replacements to the current folder, you are free to analyze the generated YAML files. To apply, simply run `clang-apply-replacements` with the current folder as its only parameter:

```
$ clang-apply-replacements ./
```

> After running this command, if you get the error message "trouble iterating over directory ./: too many levels of symbolic links", you can retry the last two commands by using /tmp as the folder to store the replacement files. Alternatively, you can create a new directory to hold these files, allowing you to easily analyze them.

Beyond this simple example, these tools are usually crafted to work in large code bases. Therefore, Clang Apply Replacements will not ask any questions, but will simply start parsing all YAML files that are available in the folder you specified, analyzing and applying the transformations.

You can even specify specific coding standards that the tool must follow when patching, that is, writing new code into the source files. This is the purpose of the `-style=<LLVM|Google|Chromium|Mozilla|Webkit>` flag. This functionality is a courtesy of the LibFormat library, which allows any refactoring tool to write new code in a specific format or coding convention. We will present more details about this notable feature in the next section.

ClangFormat

Imagine that you are the judge of a competition similar to the **International Obfuscated C Code Contest (IOCCC)**. To give you a feel of the competition, we will reproduce the code of one of the winners of the twenty-second edition, Michael Birken. Keep in mind that this code is licensed under Creative Commons Attribution-ShareAlike 3.0 license, which means that you can freely modify it as long as you maintain the license and the credits to the IOCCC.

```
char*_ = "'""/*";
#include <stdio.h>
#define m 21
#define o(l, k) for(l=0; l<k; l++)
#define n(k) o(T, k)


          int E,L,O,R,G[42][m],h[2][42][m],g[3][8],c
          [42][42][2],f[42]; char d[42]; void v( int
          b,int a,int j){ printf("\33[%d;%df\33[4%d"
          "m ",a,b,j); } void u(){ int T,e; n(42)o(
          e,m)if(h[0][T][e]-h[1][T][e]){ v(e+4+e,T+2
          ,h[0][T][e]+1?h[0][T][e]:0); h[1][T][e]=h[
          0][T][e]; } fflush(stdout); } void q(int l
                           ,int k,int p){
                           int T,e,a;  L=0
                           ; O=1; while(O
                           ){ n(4&&L){ e=
                           k+c[l] [T][0];
                           h[0][L-1+c[l][
                           T][1]][p?20-e:
e]=-1; } n(4){                                    e=k+c[l][T][0]; a=L+c[l][T][
1]+1; if(a==42                                    || h[0][a][p?20-e:e]+1){ O=0
; } } n(4){ e=                                    k+c[l][T][0]; h[0][L + c[l][
T][1]][p?20-e:                                    e]=g[1][f[p?19+l:l]]; } L++;
u(); } n(42) {                                    o(e,m)if(h[0][T][e]<0)break;
o(a, m&&e==m){                                    for(L=T; L; L--) { h[0][L][a]
]=h[0][L-1] [a                                    ]; } h[0][0][a]=-1; } } u();
}int main(){ int T,e,t,r,i,s              ,D,V,K; printf("\33[2J\33[?25l"); n(8)g[i=
1][T]=7-T; R--; n(42) o(e,m)              G[T][e]--; while(fgets(d,42,stdin)) { r=++
R; n(17){ e=d[T]-48; d[T]=0;              if ((e&7)==e) { g[0][e] ++; G[R][T+2]=e; }
} } n(8)if(g[0][7-T]){ t=g[i              ][0]; g[i][0++]=g[i][T]; g[i][T]=t; } n(8)
g[2][g[i][T]]=T; n(R+i)o(e,m              )if(G[T][e]+i) G[T][e]=g[2][G[T][e]]; n(19
)o(t,2){ f[T+t+T]=(T["+%#,4"              "5>GP9$5-,#C?NX"]-35)>>t*3&7; o(e,4){ c[T]
e][t]=("5'<$=$8)Ih$=h9i8'9"              "t=)83]l4(99{g9>##>4(" [T+t+T]-35)>>e*2&3;
} } n(15) { s=T>9?m:(T&3)-3?15:36;o(e,s)o(t,2)c[T+19][e][t]="6*6,8*6.608.6264826668\
865::(+;0(6+6-6/8,61638065678469.;88))()3(6,8*6.608.6264826668865:+;4)-*6-6/616365,\
-6715690.5;,89,81+,(023096/:40(8-7751)2)65;695(855(+*8)+;4**+4(((6.608.626482666886\
5:+;4+4)0(8)6/61638065678469.;88)-4,4*8+4(((60(/6264826668865:+;4-616365676993-9:54\
+-14).;./347.+18*):1;-*0-975/)936.+:4*,80987(8B7(0(*)4.*""/4,4*8+4(((6264826668865:\
+;4/4-4+8-4)0(8)6365678469.;88)1/(6*6,6.60626466686:8)8-8*818.8582/9863(+;/""*6,6.6\
0626466686:4(8)8-8*818.8582/9863(+;/,6.60626466686:8-818.8582/9864*4+4(0())+;/.6062\
6466686:8/8380/7844,4-4*4+4(0())69+;/0626466686:818582/9864.4/4,4-4*4+4(0())+;" [e+E
+e+t]-40; E+=s+s; } n(45){ if(T>i) { v(2,T,7); v(46,T,7); } v(2+T,44,7); } T=0; o(e,
42)o(t,m)h[T][e][t]--; while(R+i) { s = D=0; if (r-R) { n(19) if (G[R+i][T]+i) V=T/2
; else if(G[R][T]+i) s++; if(s) { if(V>4){ V=9-V; D++; } V+=29; n(20) q(c[V][T][0],c
[V][T][i],D); } } n(19) if((L=G[R][T])+i) { O=T-L; e=O>9; t=e?18-0 :0; o(K,((t&3)-3?
16:37)){ if(K){ L=c[t+19][K-i][0]; O=c[t+19][K-i][i] ; } q(L,O,K && e); } } if(s) q(
c[V][20][0], c[V][20][i], D); R--; } printf("\33[47;1f\33[?25h\33[40m"); return 0; }
```

In case you are wondering, yes, this is valid C code. Access `http://www.ioccc.`
`org/2013/birken` to download it. Now, let us demonstrate what ClangFormat
does for you in this example:

```
$ clang-format -style=llvm obf.c --
```

The following screenshot shows the result:

Better, right? In real life, you will fortunately not need to review obfuscated pieces of
code, but fixing formatting to respect particular coding conventions is also not a job
that humans particularly dream of. This is the purpose of the ClangFormat. It is not
only a tool, but also a library, LibFormat, which reformats code to match a coding
convention. In this way, if you create a tool that happens to generate C or C++ code,
you can leave formatting to ClangFormat while you concentrate on your project.

Besides expanding this obviously-contrived example and performing code indentation, ClangFormat is an ingenious tool that was carefully developed to seek the best way to break your code into an eighty-column format and improve its readability. If you ever stopped to think what the best way to break a long sentence is, you will appreciate how good ClangFormat is at this task. Give it a try by setting it up to work as an external tool of your favorite editor and configuring a hotkey to launch it. If you use a famous editor such as Vim or Emacs, be assured that another person already wrote custom scripts to integrate ClangFormat.

The topic of code formatting, organization, and clarity, also brings us to troublesome issues of C and C++ codes: the abuse of header files and how to coordinate them. We dedicate the next section to discuss a work-in-progress solution for this problem, and how a Clang tool can aid you in adopting this new approach.

Modularize

In order to understand the goals of the Modularize project, we first need to introduce you to the concept of modules in C and C++, which requires a digression from the main topic of this chapter. At the time of this writing, modules are not yet officially standardized. Readers who are not interested in how Clang is already implementing this new idea for C/C++ projects are encouraged to skip this section and proceed to the next tool.

Understanding C/C++ APIs' Definitions

Currently, C and C++ programs are divided into header files, for example, files with the `.h` extension, and implementation files, for example, files with the `.c` or `.cpp` extension. The compiler interprets each combination of the implementation file and includes headers as a separate translation unit.

When programming in C or C++, if you are working on a particular implementation file, you need to reason about which entities belong to a local scope and which entities belong to a global scope. For example, function or data declarations that will not be shared among different implementation files should be declared, in C, with the keyword `static`, or in C++, in an anonymous namespace. It signals the linker that this translation unit does not export these local entities, and thus, they are not available to be used by other units.

However, if you do want to share an entity across several translation units, the problems begin. For the sake of clarity, let us name the translation unit that exports an entity to be the exporters and the users of these entities to be the importers. We will also suppose that an exporter named `gamelogic.c` wants to export a simple integer variable called `num_lives` to the importer named `screen.c`.

The linker job

First, we will show how the linker handles symbol importing in our example.
After compiling and assembling `gamelogic.c`, we will have an object file called
`gamelogic.o` with a symbol table that says that the symbol `num_lives` is 4 bytes
in size and is available to be used by any other translation unit.

```
$ gcc -c gamelogic.c -o gamelogic.o
$ readelf -s gamelogic.o
```

Num	Value	Size	Type	Bind	Vis	Index	Name
7	00000000	4	OBJECT	GLOBAL	DEFAULT	3	num_lives

This table only presents the symbol of interest, omitting the rest. The `readelf` tool is
only available for Linux platforms that rely on ELF, the widely adopted **Executable
and Linkable Format**. If you use another platform, you can print the symbol table
using `objdump -t`. We read this table in the following way: our symbol `num_lives`
was assigned the seventh position in the table and occupies the first address (zero)
relative to the section of index 3 (the `.bss` section). The `.bss` section, in turn, holds
data entities that will be zero-initialized. To verify the correspondence between
section names and their indexes, print the section header with `readelf -S` or
`objdump -h`. We can also read from this table that our `num_lives` symbol is a
(data) `object` that has 4 bytes of size and is globally visible (`global` bind).

Similarly, the `screen.o` file will have a symbol table that says that this translation
unit depends on the symbol `num_lives`, which belongs to another translation unit.
To analyze `screen.o`, we will use the same commands we used for `gamelogic.o`:

```
$ gcc -c screen.c -o screen.o
$ readelf -s screen.o
```

Num	Value	Size	Type	Bind	Vis	Index	Name
10	00000000	0	NOTYPE	GLOBAL	DEFAULT	UND	num_lives

The entry is similar to the one seen in the exporter, but it has less information.
It has no size or type and the index that shows which ELF section contains this
symbol is marked as **UND (undefined)** which characterizes this translation unit as
an importer. If this translation unit gets selected to be included in the final program,
the link cannot succeed without resolving this dependency.

The linker receives both files as inputs and patches the importer with the address of its requested symbols, located in the exporter.

```
$ gcc screen.o gamelogic.o -o game
$ readelf -s game
```

Num	Value	Size	Type	Bind	Vis	Index	Name
60	0804a01c	4	OBJECT	GLOBAL	DEFAULT	25	num_lives

The value now reflects the complete virtual memory address of the variable when the program gets loaded, providing the symbol's location to the code segments of the importers, and completing the export-import agreement between two different translation units.

We conclude that, on the linker side, the sharing of entities between multiple translation units is simple and efficient.

The frontend counterpart

The simplicity seen in the handling of object files is not reflected in the language. In the importer implementation, which is different from the linker, the compiler cannot rely only on the name of the imported entities because it needs to verify that the semantics of this translation unit do not violate the language type system; it needs to know that num_lives is an integer. Therefore, the compiler also expects to have type information along with the names of the imported entities. Historically, C handled this problem by requiring header files.

Header files have type declarations along with the name of entities that will be used across different translation units. In this model, the importer uses an include directive to load type information about entities that it will import. However, header files can be way more flexible than necessary and can also carry, in fact, any piece of C or C++ code, not just declarations.

Problems of relying on the C/C++ preprocessor

Different from the import directive in a language such as Java, the semantics of the include directive are not restricted to provide the compiler with necessary information to import symbols, but, instead, to actually expand it with more C or C++ code that needs to be parsed. This mechanism is implemented by the preprocessor, which blindly copies and patches code before the actual compilation, and is no smarter than a text-processing tool.

This code size blowup is further complicated in C++ code where the usage of templates encourages a full-blown class implementation to be described in header files, which will then become a significant amount of extra C++ code injected into all importers, users of this header file.

This puts a heavy burden on the compilation of C or C++ projects that rely on many libraries (or externally-defined entities) because the compiler needs to parse many header files multiple times, once for each compilation unit that uses the headers.

In retrospect, entity importing and exporting, which could be solved by an extended symbol table, now requires careful parsing of thousands of lines of human-written header files.

Large compiler projects typically use a precompiled header scheme to avoid lexing each header again, for example, Clang with PCH files. However, this only mitigates the problem, since the compiler still needs to, for example, reinterpret the entire header in light of possible new macro definitions, and affects the way in which the current translation unit sees this header.

For example, suppose that our game implements `gamelogic.h` in the following way:

```
#ifdef PLATFORM_A
extern uint32_t num_lives;
#else
extern uint16_t num_lives;
#endif
```

When `screen.c` includes this file, the type of the imported entity `num_lives` depends on whether the macro `PLATFORM_A` is defined or not in the context of the translation unit `screen.c`. Further, this context is not necessarily the same for another translation unit. This forces the compiler to load the extra code in headers every time a different translation unit includes them.

To tame C/C++ importing and how library interfaces are written, modules propose a new method for describing this interface and are part of an on-going discussion for standardization. Furthermore, the Clang project is already implementing support for modules.

Understanding the working of modules

Instead of including header files, your translation unit can import a module, which defines a clear and unambiguous interface to use a specific library. An `import` directive would load the entities exported by a given library without injecting extra C or C++ code into your compilation unit.

However, there is no currently-defined syntax for imports, which is still an on-going discussion of the C++ standardization committee. Currently, Clang allows you to pass an extra flag called -fmodules, which will interpret include as a module's import directive when you are including a header file that belongs to a module-enabled library.

When parsing header files that belong to a module, Clang will spawn a new instance of itself with a clean state of the preprocessor to compile these headers, caching the results in a binary form to enable faster compilation of subsequent translation units that depend on the same set of header files that make a specific module. Therefore, the header files that aim at being part of a module should not depend on previously-defined macros or any other prior state of the preprocessor.

Using modules

To map a set of header files to a specific module, you can define a separate file called module.modulemap, which provides this information. This file should be placed in the same folder as that of the include files that define the API of a library. If this file is present and Clang is invoked with -fmodules, the compilation will use modules.

Let's extend our simple game example to use modules. Suppose that the game API is defined in two header files, gamelogic.h and screenlogic.h. The main file game.c imports entities from both files. The contents of our game API source code are the following:

- Contents of the gamelogic.h file:

  ```
  extern int num_lives;
  ```

- Contents of the screenlogic.h file:

  ```
  extern int num_lines;
  ```

- Contents of the gamelogic.c file:

  ```
  int num_lives = 3;
  ```

- Contents of the screenlogic.c file:

  ```
  int num_lines = 24;
  ```

Also, in our game API, whenever the user includes the gamelogic.h header file, it will also want to include screenlogic.h to print game data on the screen. Thus, we will structure our logical modules to express this dependency. The module.modulemap file for our project is, therefore, defined as follows:

```
module MyGameLib {
  explicit module ScreenLogic {
```

```
    header "screenlogic.h"
  }
  explicit module GameLogic {
    header "gamelogic.h"
    export ScreenLogic
  }
}
```

The `module` keyword is followed by the name you wish to use to identify it. In our case, we named it `MyGameLib`. Each module can have a list of enclosed submodules. The `explicit` keyword is used to tell Clang that this submodule is only imported if one of its header files is explicitly included. Afterwards, we use the `header` keyword to name which C header files make up this submodule. You can list many header files to represent a single submodule, but here, we use only one for each one of our submodules.

Since we are using modules, we can take advantage of them to make our life easier and our `include` directives simpler. Note that in the scope of the `GameLogic` submodule, by using the `export` keyword followed by the name of the `ScreenLogic` submodule, we are saying that whenever the user imports the `GameLogic` submodule, we also make visible the symbols of `ScreenLogic`.

To demonstrate this, we will write `game.c`, the user of this API, as follows:

```
// File: game.c
#include "gamelogic.h"
#include <stdio.h>
int main() {
  printf("lives= %d\nlines=%d\n", num_lives, num_lines);
  return 0;
}
```

Notice that we are using the symbols `num_lives`, defined in `gamelogic.h`, and `num_lines`, defined in `screenlogic.h`, which are not explicitly included. However, when `clang` with the `-fmodules` flag parses this file, it will convert the first `include` directive to have the effect of an `import` directive of the `GameLogic` submodule, which prompts for the symbols defined in `ScreenLogic` to be available. Therefore, the following command line should correctly compile this project:

```
$ clang -fmodules game.c gamelogic.c screenlogic.c -o game
```

On the other hand, invoking Clang without the modules system will cause it to report the missing symbol definition:

```
$ clang game.c gamelogic.c screenlogic.c -o game
screen.c:4:50: error: use of undeclared identifier 'num_lines'; did you
mean 'num_lives'?
    printf("lives= %d\nlines=%d\n", num_lives, num_lines);
                                               ^~~~~~~~~
                                               num_lives
```

However, keep in mind that you would like to make your projects to be as portable as possible, and therefore, it is interesting to avoid such scenarios that are correctly compiled with modules but not without them. The best scenarios for the adoption of modules are to simplify the utilization of a library API and to speed up the compilation of translation units that rely on many common headers.

Understanding Modularize

A good example would be to adapt an existing big project to use modules instead of including header files. In this way, remember that in the modules framework, the header files pertaining to each submodule are independently compiled. Many projects that rely on, for example, macros that are defined in other files prior to the inclusion, would fail to be ported to use modules.

The purpose of `modularize` is to help you in this task. It analyzes a set of header files, and reports if they provide duplicate variable definitions, duplicate macro definitions, or macro definitions that may evaluate to different results depending on the preprocessor's state. It helps you diagnose common impediments to create a module out of a set of header files. It also detects when your project uses `include` directives inside namespace blocks, which also forces the compiler to interpret `include` files in a different scope that is incompatible with the concept of modules. In this, the symbols defined in the header files must not depend on the context where the header was included.

Using Modularize

To use `modularize`, you must provide a list of header files that will be checked against each other. Continuing with our game project example, we would write a new text file called `list.txt` as follows:

```
gamelogic.h
screenlogic.h
```

Then, we simply run `modularize` with the list as a parameter:

```
$ modularize list.txt
```

If you change one of the header files to define the same symbol of the other, `modularize` will report that you are relying on unsafe behavior for modules and that you should fix your header files before trying to write a `module.modulemap` file for your project. When fixing your header files, keep in mind that each header file should be as independent as possible and that it should not change the symbols it defines, depending on which values were defined in the file that included this header. If you rely on this behavior, you should break this header file into two or more, each one defining the symbols that the compiler sees when using a specific set of macros.

Module Map Checker

The Module Map Checker Clang tool allows you to check a `module.modulemap` file to ensure that it covers all header files in a folder. You invoke it in our example from the previous section with the following command:

```
$ module-map-checker module.modulemap
```

The preprocessor was at the crux of our discussion about using `include` directives versus modules. In the next section, we present a tool that helps you in tracing the activity of this peculiar frontend component.

PPTrace

Look at the following quote from the Clang documentation on `clang::preprocessor` at `http://clang.llvm.org/doxygen/classclang_1_1Preprocessor.html`:

Engages in a tight little dance with the lexer to efficiently preprocess tokens.

As already pointed out in *Chapter 4*, *The Frontend*, the `lexer` class in Clang performs the first pass in analyzing the source files. It groups chunks of text into categories that will later be interpreted by the parser. The `lexer` class has no information on semantics, which is the responsibility of the parser, and about the included header files and macros expansions, which is the responsibility of the preprocessor.

The `pp-trace` Clang standalone tool outputs a trace of the preprocessor actions. It accomplishes this by implementing callbacks of the `clang::PPCallbacks` interface. It starts by registering itself as an observer of the preprocessor and then launches Clang to analyze the input files. For each preprocessor action, such as interpreting an `#if` directive, importing a module, and including a header file, among others, the tool will print a report in the screen.

Consider the following contrived "hello world" example in C:

```c
#if 0
#include <stdio.h>
#endif

#ifdef CAPITALIZE
#define WORLD "WORLD"
#else
#define WORLD "world"
#endif

extern int write(int, const char*, unsigned long);

int main() {
    write(1, "Hello, ", 7);
    write(1, WORLD, 5);
    write(1, "!\n", 2);
    return 0;
}
```

In the first lines of the preceding code, we use a preprocessor directive `#if` that always evaluates to false, forcing the compiler to ignore the contents of the source block until the next `#endif` directive. Next, we use the `#ifdef` directive to check if the CAPITALIZE macro has been defined. Depending on whether it is defined or not, the macro WORLD will be defined as an uppercase or lowercase string that contains world. Last, the code issues a series of calls to the `write` system call to output a message on the screen.

We run `pp-trace` as we would run other similar source analyzing Clang standalone tools:

$ pp-trace hello.c

The result is a series of preprocessor events regarding macro definitions that take place even before our actual source file is processed. The last events concern our specific file and appear as follows:

```
- Callback: If
  Loc: "hello.c:1:2"
  ConditionRange: ["hello.c:1:4", "hello.c:2:1"]
  ConditionValue: CVK_False
- Callback: Endif
  Loc: "hello.c:3:2"
```

```
        IfLoc: "hello.c:1:2"
  - Callback: SourceRangeSkipped
        Range: ["hello.c:1:2", "hello.c:3:2"]
  - Callback: Ifdef
        Loc: "hello.c:5:2"
        MacroNameTok: CAPITALIZE
        MacroDirective: (null)
  - Callback: Else
        Loc: "hello.c:7:2"
        IfLoc: "hello.c:5:2"
  - Callback: SourceRangeSkipped
        Range: ["hello.c:5:2", "hello.c:7:2"]
  - Callback: MacroDefined
        MacroNameTok: WORLD
        MacroDirective: MD_Define
  - Callback: Endif
        Loc: "hello.c:9:2"
        IfLoc: "hello.c:5:2"
  - Callback: MacroExpands
        MacroNameTok: WORLD
        MacroDirective: MD_Define
        Range: ["hello.c:13:14", "hello.c:13:14"]
        Args: (null)
  - Callback: EndOfMainFile
```

The first event refers to our first `#if` preprocessor directive. This region triggers three callbacks: `If`, `Endif`, and `SourceRangeSkipped`. Notice that the `#include` directive inside it was not processed, but skipped. Similarly, we see the events related to the definition of the WORLD macro: `IfDef`, `Else`, `MacroDefined`, and `EndIf`. Finally, `pp-trace` reports that we used the WORLD macro with the `MacroExpands` event and then reached the end of file and called the `EndOfMainFile` callback.

After preprocessing, the next steps in the frontend are to lex and to parse. In the next section, we present a tool that enables us to investigate the results of the parser, the AST nodes.

Clang Query

The Clang Query tool was introduced in LLVM 3.5 and allows you to read a source file and interactively query its associated Clang AST nodes. It's a great tool for inspecting and learning about how the frontend represents each piece of code. However, its main goal is not only to allow you to inspect the AST of a program, but also test AST matchers.

When writing a refactoring tool, you will be interested in using the AST matchers library, which contains several predicates that match segments of the Clang AST that you are interested in. Clang Query is the tool to help you in this part of the development because it allows you to inspect which AST nodes match a specific AST matcher. For a list of all available AST matchers, you can check the `ASTMatchers.h` Clang header, but a good guess is to use camel case for the name of the class that represents the AST node you are interested in. For example, `functionDecl` will match all `FunctionDecl` nodes, which represent function declarations. After you test which matchers exactly return the nodes you are interested in, you can use them in your refactoring tool to build an automated way of transforming these nodes for some specific purpose. We will explain how to use the AST matchers library later in this chapter.

As an example of AST inspection, we will run `clang-query` in our last "hello world" code used in PPTrace. Clang Query expects you to have a compile command database. If you are inspecting a file that lacks a compile command database, feel free to supply the compilation command after double dashes, or leave it empty if no special compiler flags are required, as shown in the following command line:

```
$ clang-query hello.c --
```

After issuing this command, `clang-query` will display an interactive prompt, waiting for your command. You can type the name of any AST matcher after the `match` command. For example, in the following command, we ask `clang-query` to display all nodes that are `CallExpr`:

```
clang-query> match callExpr()


Match #1:

hello.c:12:5: note: "root" node binds here
    write(1, "Hello, ", 7);
    ^~~~~~~~~~~~~~~~~~~~~~

...
```

The tool highlights the exact point in the program corresponding to the first token associated with the `CallExpr` AST node. The list of the commands that Clang Query understands is the following:

- `help`: Prints the list of commands.
- `match <matcher name>` or `m <matcher name>`: This command traverses the AST with the requested matcher.

- `set output <(diag | print | dump)>`: This command changes how to print the node information once it is successfully matched. The first option will print a Clang diagnostic message highlighting the node, and is the default option. The second option will simply print the corresponding source code excerpt that matched, while the last option will call the class `dump()` member function, which is quite sophisticated for debugging, and will also show all children nodes.

A great way to learn how a program is structured in the Clang AST is to change the output to `dump` and match a high-level node. Give it a try:

```
clang-query> set output dump
clang-query> match functionDecl()
```

It will show you all instances of classes that make up the statements and expressions of all function bodies in the C source code that you opened. On the other hand, keep in mind that this thorough AST dump is more easily obtained by using Clang Check, which we will present in the next section. Clang Query is more suited at crafting AST matcher expressions and checking their results. You will later witness how Clang Query can be an invaluable tool when helping us to craft our first code-refactoring tool, where we will cover how to build more complicated queries.

Clang Check

The Clang Check tool is a very basic one; it has less than a few hundreds of lines of code, which makes it easy to study. However, since it is linked against LibTooling, it features the entire Clang's parsing abilities.

Clang Check enables you to parse C/C++ source files and dump the Clang AST or perform basic checks. It can also apply "fix it" modifications suggested by Clang, leveraging the rewriter infrastructure built for Clang Modernizer.

For example, supposing that you want to dump the AST of `program.c`, you would issue the following command:

```
$ clang-check program.c -ast-dump --
```

Notice that Clang Check obeys the LibTooling way of reading source files and you should either use a command database file or supply adequate parameters after the double dash (`--`).

Since Clang Check is a small tool, consider it as a good example to study when writing your own tool. We will present another small tool in the next section to give you a feel of what small code-refactoring tools can do.

Remove c_str() calls

The `remove-cstr-calls` tool is a simple source-to-source transformation tool example, that is, a refactoring tool. It works by identifying redundant calls to `c_str()` on `std::string` objects and rewriting the code to avoid them in specific situations. Such redundant calls might arise when, first, building a new string object by using the result of `c_str()` on another string object, such as `std::string(myString.c_str())`. This could be simplified to use the string copy constructor directly, such as `std::string(myString)`. Secondly, when building new instances of the LLVM's specific classes `StringRef` and `Twine` out of a string object. In these cases, it is preferable to use the string object itself rather than the result of `c_str()`, using `StringRef(myString)` rather than `StringRef(myString.c_str())`.

The entire tool fits in a single C++ file, making it another excellent, easy-to-study example of how to use LibTooling to build a refactoring tool, which is the subject of our next topic.

Writing your own tool

The Clang project provides three interfaces that a user can rely on to utilize Clang features and its parsing capabilities, including syntactic and semantic analyses. First, there is `libclang`, the primary way of interfacing with Clang, which provides a stable C API and allows an external project to plug it in and have a high-level access to the entire framework. This stable interface seeks to preserve backwards compatibility with older versions, avoiding breaking your software when a newer `libclang` is released. It is also possible to use `libclang` from other languages, for example, using the Clang Python Bindings. Apple Xcode, for instance, interacts with Clang via `libclang`.

Secondly, there are Clang Plugins that allow you to add your own passes during compilation, as opposed to the offline analyses performed by tools such as Clang Static Analyzer. It is useful when you need to perform it every time you compile a translation unit. Therefore, you need to be concerned with the time required to perform such analyses in order to be feasible to run it frequently. On the other hand, integrating your analysis into a build system is as easy as adding flags to the compiler command.

The last alternative is the one we will explore, that is, using Clang via LibTooling. It is an exciting library that allows you to easily build standalone tools similar to the ones presented in this chapter, targeted at code refactoring or syntax checking. In comparison with LibClang, LibTooling has less compromise with backwards compatibility, but allows you to have full access to the Clang AST structure.

Problem definition – writing a C++ code refactoring tool

In the remainder of this chapter, we will work on an example. Suppose that you are launching a fictitious startup to promote a new C++ IDE called IzzyC++. Your business plan is based on capturing users that are tired of being unable to automatically refactor their code. You will use LibTooling to craft a simple yet compelling C++ code-refactoring tool; it will receive as parameters a C++ member function, a fully qualified name, and a replacement name. Its task is to find the definition of this member function, change it to use the replacement name, and change all invocations of such functions accordingly.

Configuring your source code location

The first step is to determine where the code of your tool will live. In the LLVM source folder, we will create a new folder called izzyrefactor inside tools/clang/ tools/extra to hold all the files for our project. Later, expand the Makefile in the extra folder to include your project. Simply look for the DIRS variable and add the name izzyrefactor alongside the other Clang tool projects. You may also want to edit the CMakeLists.txt file, in case you use CMake, and include a new line:

```
add_subdirectory(izzyrefactor)
```

Go to the izzyrefactor folder and create a new Makefile to flag the LLVM-build system that you are building a separate tool that will live independently of other binaries. Use the following contents:

```
CLANG_LEVEL := ../../..
TOOLNAME = izzyrefactor
TOOL_NO_EXPORTS = 1
include $(CLANG_LEVEL)/../../Makefile.config
LINK_COMPONENTS := $(TARGETS_TO_BUILD) asmparser bitreader support\
                   mc option
USEDLIBS = clangTooling.a clangFrontend.a clangSerialization.a \
           clangDriver.a clangRewriteFrontend.a clangRewriteCore.a \
           clangParse.a clangSema.a clangAnalysis.a clangAST.a \
           clangASTMatchers.a clangEdit.a clangLex.a clangBasic.a
include $(CLANG_LEVEL)/Makefile
```

This file is important for specifying all libraries that need to be linked together with your code to enable you to build this tool. You can optionally add the line NO_INSTALL = 1 right after the line that features TOOL_NO_EXPORTS if you do not want your new tool to be installed alongside other LLVM tools when you run `make install`.

We use TOOL_NO_EXPORTS = 1 because your tool will not use any plugins, and therefore, it does not need to export some symbols, reducing the size of the dynamic symbol table of the final binary, and with it, the time required to dynamically link and load the program. Notice that we finish by including the Clang master `Makefile` that defines all the necessary rules to compile our project.

If you use CMake instead of the auto tools configure script, create a new `CMakeLists.txt` file as well with the following contents:

```
add_clang_executable(izzyrefactor
  IzzyRefactor.cpp
  )
target_link_libraries(izzyrefactor
  clangEdit clangTooling clangBasic clangAST clangASTMatchers)
```

Alternatively, if you do not want to build this tool inside the Clang source tree, you can also build it as a standalone tool. Just use the same `Makefile` presented for the driver tool at the end of *Chapter 4, The Frontend*, making a small modification. Notice which libraries we used in the preceding `Makefile`, in the USEDLIBS variable, and which libraries we are using in the `Makefile` from *Chapter 4, The Frontend*, in the CLANGLIBS variable. They refer to the same libraries, except that USEDLIBS has clangTooling, which contains LibTooling. Therefore, add the line -lclangTooling\ after the line -lclang\ in the `Makefile` from *Chapter 4, The Frontend*, and you are done.

Dissecting tooling boilerplate code

All of your code will live in `IzzyRefactor.cpp`. Create this file and start adding the initial boilerplate code to it, as shown in the following code:

```
int main(int argc, char **argv) {
  cl::ParseCommandLineOptions(argc, argv);
  string ErrorMessage;
  OwningPtr<CompilationDatabase> Compilations (
    CompilationDatabase::loadFromDirectory(
      BuildPath, ErrorMessage));
  if (!Compilations)
    report_fatal_error(ErrorMessage);
  //...
}
```

Your main code starts with the `ParseCommandLineOptions` function from the `llvm::cl` namespace (command-line utilities). This function will do the dirty work of parsing each individual flag in `argv` for you.

> It is customary for LibTooling-based tools to use a `CommonOptionsParser` object to ease parsing common options shared between all refactoring tools (see `http://clang.llvm.org/doxygen/classclang_1_1tooling_1_1CommonOptionsParser.html` for a code example). In this example, we use the lower-level `ParseCommandLineOptions()` function to illustrate to you exactly which arguments we are going to parse and to train you to use it for other tools that do not use LibTooling. However, feel free to use `CommonOptionsParser` to ease your work (and as an exercise to write this tool in a different way).

You will verify that all LLVM tools use the utilities provided by the `cl` namespace (`http://llvm.org/docs/doxygen/html/namespacellvm_1_1cl.html`), and it is really simple to define which arguments our tool recognizes in the command line. For this, we declare new global variables of the template type `opt` and `list`:

```
cl::opt<string> BuildPath(
  cl::Positional,
  cl::desc("<build-path>"));
cl::list<string> SourcePaths(
  cl::Positional,
  cl::desc("<source0> [... <sourceN>]"),
  cl::OneOrMore);
cl::opt<string> OriginalMethodName("method",
  cl::desc("Method name to replace"),
  cl::ValueRequired);
cl::opt<string> ClassName("class",
  cl::desc("Name of the class that has this method"),
  cl::ValueRequired);
cl::opt<string> NewMethodName("newname",
  cl::desc("New method name"),
  cl::ValueRequired);
```

Declare these five global variables before the definition of your main function. We specialize the type `opt` according to what kind of data we expect to read as an argument. For example, if you need to read a number, you would declare a new `cl::opt<int>` global variable.

To read the values of these arguments, you first need to call `ParseCommandLineOptions`. Afterwards, you just need to refer to the name of the global variable associated with the argument in a code where you expect the associated datatype. For example, `NewMethodName` will evaluate the user-supplied string for this argument if your code expects a string, as in `std::out << NewMethodName`.

This works because the `opt_storage<>` template, a superclass of `opt<>`, defines a class that inherits from the datatype it manages (`string`, in this case). By inheritance, the `opt<string>` variable is also a string that can be used as such. If the `opt<>` class template cannot inherit from the wrapped datatype (for example, there is no `int` class) it will define a cast operator, for example, `operator int()` for the `int` datatype. This has the same effect in your code; when you refer to a `cl::opt<int>` variable, it can automatically cast to an integer and return the number it holds, as supplied by the user in the command line.

We can also specify different characteristics for an argument. In our example, we used a positional argument by specifying `cl::Positional`, which means that the user will not explicitly specify it by its name, but it will be inferred based on its relative position in the command line. We also pass a `desc` object to the `opt` constructor, which defines a description that is exhibited to the user when they print the help information by using the `-help` argument.

We also have an argument that uses the type `cl::list`, which differs from `opt` by allowing multiple arguments to be passed, in this case, a list of source files to process. These facilities require the inclusion of the following header:

```
#include "llvm/Support/CommandLine.h"
```

 As part of LLVM coding standards, you should organize your `include` statements by putting local headers first, followed by Clang and LLVM API headers. When two headers pertain to the same category, order them alphabetically. An interesting project is to write a new standalone tool to do this automatically for you.

The last three global variables allow the required options to use our refactoring tool. The first is an argument of name `-method`. The first string argument declares the argument name, without dashes, while the `cl::RequiredValues` signals the command-line parser, indicating that this value is required to run this program. This argument will supply the name of the method that our tool will look for and then change its name to the one provided in the `-newname` argument. The `-class` argument supplies the name of the class that has this method.

The next code excerpt from the boilerplate code manages a new
`CompilationDatabase` object. First, we need to include the header files that define
the `OwningPtr` class, which is a smart pointer used in LLVM libraries, that is, it
automatically de-allocates the contained pointer when it reaches the end of its scope.

```
#include "llvm/ADT/OwningPtr.h"
```

>
> **Clang version notice**
> Starting with Clang/LLVM Version 3.5, the `OwningPtr<>`
> template is deprecated in favor of the C++ standard
> `std::unique_ptr<>` template.

Second, we need to include the header file for the `CompilationDatabase` class,
which is the first one we use, that is officially a part of LibTooling:

```
#include "clang/Tooling/CompilationDatabase.h"
```

This class is responsible for managing the compilation database, whose configuration
was explained at the beginning of this chapter. It is a powerful list with the
compilation commands necessary to process each source file that the user is
interested in analyzing with your tool. To initialize this object, we use a factory
method called `loadFromDirectory`, which will load the compilation database file
from a specific build directory. This is the purpose of declaring the build path as an
argument to our tool; the user needs to specify where their sources, along with the
compilation database file, are located.

Notice that we pass two arguments to this factory member function: `BuildPath`,
our `cl::opt` object that represents a command-line object, and a recently-declared
`ErrorMessage` string. The `ErrorMessage` string will be filled with a message in
case the engine fails to load the compilation database, which we promptly display
if the factory member function did not return any `CompilationDatabase` object.
The `llvm::report_fatal_error()` function will trigger any installed LLVM
error-handling routines and quit our tool with an error code of `1`. It requires the
inclusion of the following header:

```
#include "llvm/Support/ErrorHandling.h"
```

In our example, since we are abbreviating the fully qualified names of many classes,
we will also need to add several `using` declarations at the global scope, but you are
free to use the fully qualified names if you want:

```
using namespace clang;
using namespace std;
```

```
using namespace llvm;
using clang::tooling::RefactoringTool;
using clang::tooling::Replacement;
using clang::tooling::CompilationDatabase;
using clang::tooling::newFrontendActionFactory;
```

Using AST matchers

AST matchers were briefly introduced in the *Clang Query* section of this chapter, but we will analyze them in greater detail here because they are very important for writing Clang-based code-refactoring tools.

The AST matcher library allows its users to easily match subtrees of the Clang AST that obey a specific predicate, for example, all AST nodes that represent a call to a function of name `calloc` with two arguments. Looking for specific Clang AST nodes and changing them is a fundamental task shared by every code-refactoring tool, and the utilization of this library greatly eases the task of writing such tools.

To help us in the task of finding the right matchers for our case, we will rely on Clang Query and on the AST matcher documentation available at `http://clang.llvm.org/docs/LibASTMatchersReference.html`.

We will begin by writing a test case named `wildlifesim.cpp` for your tool. This is a complex unidimensional animal life simulator where animals can walk in any direction along a line:

```
class Animal {
  int position;
public:
  Animal(int pos) : position(pos) {}
  // Return new position
  int walk(int quantity) {
    return position += quantity;
  }
};
class Cat : public Animal {
public:
  Cat(int pos) : Animal(pos) {}
  void meow() {}
  void destroySofa() {}
  bool wildMood() {return true;}
};
int main() {
  Cat c(50);
```

```
    c.meow();
    if (c.wildMood())
      c.destroySofa();
    c.walk(2);
    return 0;
}
```

We want your tool to be able to rename, for example, the `walk` member function to `run`. Let's start Clang Query and investigate what the AST looks like in this example. We will use the `recordDecl` matcher and dump the contents of all `RecordDecl` AST nodes, which are responsible for representing C structs and C++ classes:

```
$ clang-query wildanimal-sim.cpp --
clang-query> set output dump
clang-query> match recordDecl()
(...)
|-CXXMethodDecl 0x(...) <line:6:3, line 8:3> line 6:7 walk 'int (int)'
(...)
```

Inside the `RecordDecl` object that represents the `Animal` class, we observe that `walk` is represented as a `CXXMethodDecl` AST node. By looking at the AST matcher documentation, we discover that it is matched by the `methodDecl` AST matcher.

Composing matchers

The power of AST matchers comes from composition. If we want only `MethodDecl` nodes that declare a member function named `walk`, we can start by matching all named declarations with the name `walk` and later refine it to match only those that are also a method declaration. The `hasName("input")` matcher returns all named declarations with the name "input". You can test the composition of `methodDecl` and `hasName` in Clang Query:

```
clang-query> match methodDecl(hasName("walk"))
```

You will see that instead of returning all the eight different method declarations available in the code, it returns only one, the declaration of `walk`. Great!

Nonetheless, observe that it is not enough to change the definition of the `walk` method only on the `Animal` class because the derived classes may overload it. We do not want our refactoring tool to rewrite a method in a super class, but leave other overloaded methods in derived classes unchanged.

We need to find all classes that are named `Animal` or derived from it and that define a `walk` method. To find all classes that have the name `Animal` or are derived from it, we use the matcher `isSameOrDerivedFrom()`, which expects `NamedDecl` as a parameter. This parameter will be supplied by a composition with a matcher that selects all `NamedDecl` with a specific name, `hasName()`. Therefore, our query will look like this:

```
clang-query> match recordDecl(isSameOrDerivedFrom(hasName("Animal")))
```

We also need to select only those derived classes that overload the `walk` method. The `hasMethod()` predicate returns the class declarations that contain a specific method. We compose it with our first query to form the following:

```
clang-query> match recordDecl(hasMethod(methodDecl(hasName("walk"))))
```

To concatenate two predicates with the semantics of an `and` operator (all predicates must be valid), we use the `allOf()` matcher. It establishes that all matchers that are passed as its operands must be valid. We are now ready to build our final query to locate all declarations that we will rewrite:

```
clang-query> match recordDecl(allOf(hasMethod(methodDecl(hasName("wa
lk"))), isSameOrDerivedFrom(hasName("Animal"))))
```

With this query, we are able to precisely locate all method declarations of `walk` in classes that are named `Animal` or derived from it.

It will allow us to change all the declaration names, but we still need to change the method invocations. To do this, we will begin by focusing on the `CXXMemberCallExpr` nodes and its matcher `memberCallExpr`. Give it a try:

```
clang-query> match memberCallExpr()
```

Clang Query returns four matches because our code has exactly four method invocations: `meow`, `wildMood`, `destroySofa`, and `walk`. We are interested in locating only the last one. We already know how to select specific named declarations by using the `hasName()` matcher, but how to map named declarations to member call expressions? The answer is to use the `member()` matcher to select only named declarations that are linked with a method name, and then use the `callee()` matcher to link it with a call expression. The full expression is as follows:

```
clang-query> match memberCallExpr(callee(memberExpr(member(hasName("wa
lk")))))
```

However, by doing this, we are blindly selecting all method calls to walk().
We want to select only those walk calls that really map to Animal or derived classes.
The memberCallExpr() matcher accepts a second matcher as the argument. We will
use the thisPointerType() matcher to select only method calls whose called object
is a specific class. Using this principle, we build the full expression:

```
clang-query> match memberCallExpr(callee(memberExpr(member(hasName("wa
lk")))), thisPointerType(recordDecl(isSameOrDerivedFrom(hasName("Anim
al")))))
```

Putting the AST matcher predicates in the code

After we have decided which predicates to capture the right AST nodes in, it is time
to put this in the code of our tool. First, to use AST matchers, we will need to add
new include directives:

```
#include "clang/ASTMatchers/ASTMatchers.h"
#include "clang/ASTMatchers/ASTMatchFinder.h"
```

We also need to add a new using directive to make it easier to refer to these classes
(put it next to the other using directives):

```
using namespace clang::ast_matchers;
```

The second header file is necessary for using the actual finder mechanism, which
we will present shortly. Continuing to write the main function where we left off,
we start adding the remaining code:

```
RefactoringTool Tool(*Compilations, SourcePaths);
ast_matchers::MatchFinder Finder;
ChangeMemberDecl DeclCallback(&Tool.getReplacements());
ChangeMemberCall CallCallback(&Tool.getReplacements());
Finder.addMatcher(
  recordDecl(
    allOf(hasMethod(id("methodDecl",
                    methodDecl(hasName(OriginalMethodName)))),
          isSameOrDerivedFrom(hasName(ClassName)))),
  &DeclCallback);
Finder.addMatcher(
  memberCallExpr(
    callee(id("member",
             memberExpr(member(hasName(OriginalMethodName))))),
    thisPointerType(recordDecl(
```

```
            isSameOrDerivedFrom(hasName(ClassName))))),
        &CallCallback);
    return Tool.runAndSave(newFrontendActionFactory(&Finder));));
```

 Clang version notice: in Version 3.5, you need to change the last line of the preceding code to return Tool.runAndSave(newFrontendAct ionFactory(&Finder).get()); in order for it to work.

This completes the entire code of the `main` function. We will present the code for the callbacks later.

The first line of this code instantiates a new `RefactoringTool` object. This is the second class that we use from LibTooling, which needs an additional `include` statement:

```
#include "clang/Tooling/Refactoring.h"
```

The `RefactoringTool` class implements all the logic to coordinate basic tasks of your tool, such as opening source files, parsing them, running the AST matcher, calling your callbacks to perform an action when a match occurs and applying all source modifications suggested by your tool. This is the reason why after initializing all necessary objects, we end our `main` function with a call to `RefactoringTool::runAndSave()`. We transfer control to this class to allow it to perform all these tasks.

Next, we declare a `MatchFinder` object from the header that we already included. This class is responsible for performing the matches over the Clang AST, which you have already exercised with Clang Query. `MatchFinder` expects to be configured with AST matchers and a callback function, which will be called when an AST node matches with the provided AST matcher. In this callback, you will have the opportunity to change the source code. The callback is implemented as a subclass of `MatchCallback`, which we will explore later.

We then proceed to declare the callback objects and use the `MatchFinder::addFinder()` method to correlate a specific AST matcher with a callback. We declare two separate callbacks, one for rewriting method declarations and another for rewriting method invocations. We named these two callbacks as `DeclCallback` and `CallCallback`. We use the two compositions of AST matchers that we designed in the previous section, but we substituted the class name `Animal` with `ClassName`, which is the command-line argument that the user will utilize to supply their class name to be refactored. Also, we substituted the method name `walk` with `OriginalMethodName`, which is also a command-line argument.

We also strategically introduced new matchers called `id()`, which do not change which nodes the expression matches, but it does bind a name with a specific node. This is very important to allow the callbacks to generate replacements. The `id()` matcher takes two parameters, the first is the name of the node that you will use to retrieve it and the second is the matcher that will capture the named AST.

In the first AST composition that is in charge of locating member declarations, we named the `MethodDecl` node that identifies the method. In the second AST composition that is in charge of locating calls to member functions, we named the `CXXMemberExpr` node that is linked with the member function called.

Writing the callbacks

You need to define the action to perform when the AST nodes are matched. We perform this by creating two new classes that derive from `MatchCallback`, one for each match.

```
class ChangeMemberDecl : public
  ast_matchers::MatchFinder::MatchCallback{
  tooling::Replacements *Replace;
public:
  ChangeMemberDecl(tooling::Replacements *Replace) :
    Replace(Replace) {}
  virtual void run(const ast_matchers::MatchFinder::MatchResult
    &Result) {
    const CXXMethodDecl *method =
      Result.Nodes.getNodeAs<CXXMethodDecl>("methodDecl");
    Replace->insert(Replacement(
      *Result.SourceManager,
      CharSourceRange::getTokenRange(
        SourceRange(method->getLocation())), NewMethodName));
  }
};

class ChangeMemberCall : public
  ast_matchers::MatchFinder::MatchCallback{
  tooling::Replacements *Replace;
public:
  ChangeMemberCall(tooling::Replacements *Replace) :
    Replace(Replace) {}
  virtual void run(const ast_matchers::MatchFinder::MatchResult
    &Result) {
    const MemberExpr *member =
```

```
        Result.Nodes.getNodeAs<MemberExpr>("member");
      Replace->insert(Replacement(
        *Result.SourceManager,
        CharSourceRange::getTokenRange(
          SourceRange(member->getMemberLoc())), NewMethodName));
    }
  };
```

Both classes privately store a reference to a `Replacements` object, which is just a `typedef` for `std::set<Replacement>`. The `Replacement` class stores information about which lines need to be patched, in which file and with which text. Its serialization was discussed in our introduction to the Clang Apply Replacements tool. The `RefactoringTool` class internally manages the set of `Replacement` objects and that is the reason why we use the `RefactoringTool::getReplacements()` method to obtain this set and initialize our callbacks in the `main` function.

We define a basic constructor with a pointer to the `Replacements` objects that we will store for later use. We will implement the action of the callback by overriding the `run()` method, and its code is, again, surprisingly simple. Our function receives a `MatchResult` object as a parameter. The `MatchResult` class stores, for a given match, all the nodes that were bound by a name as solicited by our `id()` matcher.

These nodes are managed in the `BoundNodes` class, which are publicly visible in a `MatchResult` object with the name of `Nodes`. Thus, our first action in the `run()` function is to obtain our node of interest by calling the specialized method `BoundNodes::getNodeAs<CXXMethodDecl>`. As a result, we obtain a reference to a read-only version of the `CXXMethodDecl` AST node.

After having access to this node, to determine how to patch the code, we need a `SourceLocation` object that tells us the exact lines and columns that the associated token occupies in the source file. `CXXMethodDecl` inherits from the super class `Decl`, which represents generic declarations. This generic class makes available the `Decl::getLocation()` method, which returns exactly the `SourceLocation` object that we want. With this information, we are ready to create our first `Replacement` object and insert it into the list of source changes suggested by our tool.

The `Replacement` constructor that we use requires three parameters: a reference to a `SourceManager` object, a reference to a `CharSourceRange` object, and the string that contains the new text to be written at the location pointed by the first two parameters. The `SourceManager` class is a general Clang component that manages the source code loaded into memory. The `CharSourceRange` class contains useful code that analyzes a token and derives a source range (two points in the file) comprising this token, thereby determining the exact characters that need to be removed from the source code file to give place to the new text.

With this information, we create a new `Replacement` object and store it in the `set` managed by `RefactoringTool`, and we are done. `RefactoringTool` will take care of actually applying these patches, or removing conflicting ones. Do not forget to wrap all local declarations around an anonymous namespace; it is a good practice to avoid this translation unit to export local symbols.

Testing your new refactoring tool

We will use our wild life simulator code sample as a test case for your newly created tool. You should now run `make` and wait for LLVM to finish compiling and linking your new tool. After you have finished with it, feel free to play with the tool. Check how our arguments declared as `cl::opt` objects appear in the command-line interface:

```
$ izzyrefactor -help
```

To use the tool, we still need a compile commands database. To avoid the need to create a CMake configuration file and run it, we will manually create one. Name it `compile_commands.json` and type the following code. Substitute the tag `<FULLPATHTOFILE>` with the complete path to the folder where you put the source code of your wild life simulator:

```
[
{
  "directory": "<FULLPATHTOFILE>",
  "command": "/usr/bin/c++ -o wildlifesim.cpp.o -c <FULLPATHTOFILE>/
wildlifesim.cpp",
  "file": "<FULLPATHTOFILE>/wildlifesim.cpp"
}
]
```

After you saved the compile commands database, it is time to test the tool:

```
$ izzyrefactor -class=Animal -method=walk -newname=run ./ wildlifesim.cpp
```

You can now check the wild life simulator sources and see that the tool renamed all method definitions and invocations accordingly. This finishes our guide, but you can check more resources and further improve your knowledge in the next section.

More resources

You can find more resources at the following links:

- `http://clang.llvm.org/docs/HowToSetupToolingForLLVM.html`: This link contains more instructions on how to set up a commands database. Once you have this file, you can even configure your favorite text editor to run a tool to check the code on demand.

- `http://clang.llvm.org/docs/Modules.html`: This link presents more information on the Clang implementation of C/C++ modules.

- `http://clang.llvm.org/docs/LibASTMatchersTutorial`: This is another tutorial on using AST matchers and LibTooling.

- `http://clang.llvm.org/extra/clang-tidy.html`: This has the Clang Tidy user's manual along with the manual of other tools.

- `http://clang.llvm.org/docs/ClangFormat.html`: This contains the ClangFormat user's manual.

- `http://www.youtube.com/watch?v=yuIOGfcOH0k`: This contains Chandler Carruth's presentation for the C++Now, explaining how to build a refactoring tool.

Summary

In this chapter, we presented Clang tools built on top of the LibTooling infrastructure, which allows you to easily write tools that operate on the C/C++ source code level. We presented the following tools: Clang Tidy, which is the linter tool of Clang; Clang Modernizer, which automatically substitutes old C++ programming practices with newer ones; Clang Apply Replacements, which apply patches created by other refactoring tools; ClangFormat, which automatically indents and formats your C++ code; Modularize, which eases the task of using the yet-to-be standardized C++ modules framework; PPTrace, which documents the preprocessor activity; and Clang Query, which allows you to test AST matchers. Finally, we concluded this chapter by showing how to create your own tool.

This concludes this book, but this should be by no means an end to your studies. There is a lot of extra material about Clang and LLVM on the Internet, as either tutorials or formal documentation. Furthermore, Clang/LLVM is always evolving and introducing new features worth studying. To learn about these, visit the LLVM blog page at `http://blog.llvm.org`.

Happy hacking!

Index

W

Windows
  about 9
  LLVM, compiling on 21-25
Windows installers
  URL, for downloading 13

X

Xcode
  LLVM, compiling on 25-29
Xcode IDE
  static analyzer, using in 229

Thank you for buying
Getting Started with LLVM Core Libraries

About Packt Publishing

Packt, pronounced 'packed', published its first book "*Mastering phpMyAdmin for Effective MySQL Management*" in April 2004 and subsequently continued to specialize in publishing highly focused books on specific technologies and solutions.

Our books and publications share the experiences of your fellow IT professionals in adapting and customizing today's systems, applications, and frameworks. Our solution based books give you the knowledge and power to customize the software and technologies you're using to get the job done. Packt books are more specific and less general than the IT books you have seen in the past. Our unique business model allows us to bring you more focused information, giving you more of what you need to know, and less of what you don't.

Packt is a modern, yet unique publishing company, which focuses on producing quality, cutting-edge books for communities of developers, administrators, and newbies alike. For more information, please visit our website: www.packtpub.com.

About Packt Open Source

In 2010, Packt launched two new brands, Packt Open Source and Packt Enterprise, in order to continue its focus on specialization. This book is part of the Packt Open Source brand, home to books published on software built around Open Source licenses, and offering information to anybody from advanced developers to budding web designers. The Open Source brand also runs Packt's Open Source Royalty Scheme, by which Packt gives a royalty to each Open Source project about whose software a book is sold.

Writing for Packt

We welcome all inquiries from people who are interested in authoring. Book proposals should be sent to author@packtpub.com. If your book idea is still at an early stage and you would like to discuss it first before writing a formal book proposal, contact us; one of our commissioning editors will get in touch with you.

We're not just looking for published authors; if you have strong technical skills but no writing experience, our experienced editors can help you develop a writing career, or simply get some additional reward for your expertise.

OpenGL 4 Shading Language Cookbook

Second Edition

ISBN: 978-1-78216-702-0   Paperback: 394 pages

Over 70 recipes demonstrating simple and advanced techniques for producing high-quality, real-time 3D graphics using OpenGL and GLSL 4.x

1. Discover simple and advanced techniques for leveraging modern OpenGL and GLSL.

2. Learn how to use the newest features of GLSL including compute shaders, geometry, and tessellation shaders.

3. Get to grips with a wide range of techniques for implementing shadows using shadow maps, shadow volumes, and more.

Haskell Data Analysis Cookbook

ISBN: 978-1-78328-633-1   Paperback: 334 pages

Explore intuitive data analysis techniques and powerful machine learning methods using over 130 practical recipes

1. A practical and concise guide to using Haskell when getting to grips with data analysis.

2. Recipes for every stage of data analysis, from collection to visualization.

3. In-depth examples demonstrating various tools, solutions, and techniques.

Please check **www.PacktPub.com** for information on our titles

[PACKT] open source ✲
community experience distilled

PUBLISHING

C++ Multithreading Cookbook

ISBN: 978-1-78328-979-0   Paperback: 422 pages

Over 60 recipes to help you create ultra-fast multithreaded applications using C++ with rules, guidelines, and best practices

1. Create multithreaded applications using the power of C++.

2. Upgrade your applications with parallel execution in easy-to-understand steps.

3. Stay up to date with new Windows 8 concurrent tasks.

4. Avoid classical synchronization problems.

Advanced Quantitative Finance with C++

ISBN: 978-1-78216-722-8   Paperback: 124 pages

Create and implement mathematical models in C++ using Quantitative Finance

1. Describes the key mathematical models used for price equity, currency, interest rates, and credit derivatives.

2. The complex models are explained step-by-step along with a flow chart of every implementation.

3. Illustrates each asset class with fully solved C++ examples, both basic and advanced, that support and complement the text.

Please check **www.PacktPub.com** for information on our titles